The sun has never shone on a more bloodthirsty people than they [the Jews] are who imagine that they are God's people who have been commissioned and commanded to murder and to slay the Gentiles.

Martin Luther, "On the Jews and Their Lies"

—

Martin Luther's Anti-Semitism

Against His Better Judgment

Eric W. Gritsch

William B. Eerdmans Publishing Company
Grand Rapids, Michigan / Cambridge, U.K.

Published 2012 by
Wm. B. Eerdmans Publishing Co.
2140 Oak Industrial Drive N.E., Grand Rapids, Michigan 49505 /
P.O. Box 163, Cambridge CB3 9PU U.K.

Printed in the United States of America

18 17 16 15 14 13 12   7 6 5 4 3 2 1

Library of Congress Cataloging-in-Publication Data

Gritsch, Eric W.
Martin Luther's anti-Semitism: against his better judgment / Eric W. Gritsch.
p.   cm.
Includes bibliographical references (p.   ) and index.
ISBN 978-0-8028-6676-9 (pbk.: alk. paper)
1. Luther, Martin, 1483-1546. 2. Christianity and antisemitism. I. Title.

BR333.5.J4G75 2012
261.2′6092 — dc23

2011018128

www.eerdmans.com

In Memoriam

Viktor Frankl

(1905-1997)

Contents

Preface

In 1543, three years before his death, Luther wrote a treatise titled "On the Jews and Their Lies," urging secular rulers to execute a sevenfold program regarding Jews: (1) burning all synagogues and schools; (2) razing all private homes and properties; (3) confiscating religious writings; (4) prohibiting the teaching by rabbis on pain of loss of life; (5) no safe conduct on highways; (6) no money trading to avoid usury; and (7) labor camps for young Jews. "We are at fault in not slaying them," he fumed. He called on pastors to cooperate and, in addition, to prohibit Jews "on pain of death to praise God, to give thanks, to pray, and to teach publicly, [and] to utter the name of God within our hearing."[1]

Modern readers, aware of the Holocaust, cannot help but link such an attitude with twentieth-century National Socialists ("Nazis") who, led by Adolf Hitler, began their public anti-Semitic campaign in 1938 by the burning of synagogues, Jewish homes, and shops in all parts of Germany during the night before Luther's birthday (November 9-10); it is remembered as the infamous "Crystal Night" *(Kristallnacht)*.[2] Moreover, Hitler's "final solution" for the Jews through mass extermination, a holocaust, in labor camps, known as "concentration camps" *(Konzentrationslager)* echoes part of Luther's polemical outbursts. A best-selling American history of the Hitler regime cites the influence of Luther on "the behavior of most German Protestants in the first Nazi

---

1. WA 53, 523:1, 24, 30, 32; 524:16, 18; 525:31; 536:34-37. LW 47, 268-72, 286. Quotation 522:9-12. LW 47, 267.

2. Martin Gilbert, *Kristallnacht: Prelude to Destruction* (New York: HarperCollins, 2006).

years" because "the great founder of Protestantism was both a passionate anti-Semite and a ferocious believer in absolute obedience to political authority. . . . Luther employed a coarseness and brutality of language unequaled in German history until the Nazi time" (the German translation deleted the most offensive lines).[3] That is why Luther's portrait is often prominently displayed in Holocaust museums.

The topic "Luther and the Jews" has generated a flood of literature that discloses a wide variety of interpretations, stressing the difference between the history of the origins of his views *(Entstehungsgeschichte)* and the history of their after-effects *(Wirkungsgeschichte)*. Regarding the former, there is a collection of what Luther wrote and said about the Jews.[4] Concerning the latter, there are two helpful studies for the period from the Reformation through the twentieth century.[5] Faced with Luther's treatise of 1543, one can sympathize with the

---

3. William L. Shirer, *The Rise and Fall of the Third Reich: A History of Nazi Germany* (New York: Simon & Schuster, 1960), p. 236. The German translation *Aufstieg und Fall des dritten Reichs* (Frankfurt am Main: Buchgilde Gutenberg, 1962), p. 232, deleted this passage: "It is difficult to understand the behavior of most German Protestants in the first Nazi years unless one is aware of two things: their history and the influence of Martin Luther. The great founder of Protestantism was both a passionate anti-Semite and a ferocious believer in absolute obedience to political authority. He wanted Germany rid of the Jews and when they were sent away he advised that they be deprived of 'all their cash and jewels and silver and gold' and, furthermore, 'that their synagogues or schools be set on fire, that their houses be broken up and destroyed . . . and they be put under a roof or stable, like gypsies . . . in misery and captivity as they incessantly lament and complain to God about us.' . . . Luther employed a coarseness and brutality of language unequaled in German history until the Nazi time." Exposed by Heiko A. Oberman, "Luthers Beziehungen zu den Juden: Ahnen und Geahndete," in Helmar Junghans, ed., *Leben und Werk Martin Luthers von 1526-1546*. Festgabe zu seinem 500. Geburtstag, 2 vols. (Göttingen: Vandenhoeck & Ruprecht, 1983), vol. 1, pp. 519-30; vol. 2, pp. 894-904. Quotation in vol. 2, p. 894, n. 1. Reprinted with the title "Die Juden in Luthers Sicht" in Heinz Kremers, ed., *Die Juden und Martin Luther. Martin Luther und die Juden. Geschichte, Wirkungsgeschichte, Herausforderung,* 2nd ed. (Neukirchen-Vluyn: Neukirchener Verlag, 1987; first ed. 1985), pp. 136-62. Quotation on p. 136, n. 1. See the critique of Shirer in Uwe Siemon-Netto, *The Fabricated Luther: The Rise and Fall of William Shirer's Myth* (St. Louis: Concordia, 1995).

4. Walter Bienert, *Martin Luther und die Juden.* Ein Quellenbuch mit zeitgenössischen Illustrationen, mit Einführungen und Erläuterungen (Frankfurt am Main: Evangelisches Verlagswerk, 1982). Although the selection of sources is helpful, their evaluation is not. See below, pp. 129-33. See also C. Bernd Sucher, ed., *Luthers Stellung zu den Juden. Eine Interpretation aus germanistischer Sicht,* Bibliotheca humanistica et reformatoria 23 (Niewkoop: de Graaf, 1977). But the "interpretation" misconstrues Luther's theology.

5. By the Lutheran church historian Johannes Wallmann, "The Reception of Lu-

most respected sixteenth-century Jewish leader, Josel of Rosheim, who accompanied his request to the magistrate of Strasburg to prohibit the circulation of Luther's treatise with the observation that "never before has a *Gelehrter,* a scholar, advocated such tyrannical and outrageous treatment of our poor people."[6]

The International Congress for Luther Research, meeting every four or five years since its inception in 1956, has dealt with almost every topic in lectures and seminars except with the issue of "Luther and the Jews." As a long-term member of the Congress, I offer this study of Luther's anti-Semitism as one stimulus, among recent others, for an international discussion.[7] Its title is justified when viewed in the mirror of anti-Semitism, with its puzzling etymological plethora of definitions and its irrational historical trajectory as the "longest hatred."[8] Given Luther's consistent rejection of the Jews, ranging from theological polemics to political persecution, he is not just "anti-Judaic" (as some Luther research labeled him), but genuinely "anti-Semitic" in accordance with the broad, contemporary definition of anti-Semitism as "hostility to or prejudice against the Jews."[9] There is even a hint of racism in Luther when he commented on the unsubstantiated rumor that Jews killed Christian children. This crime *still shines forth from their eyes and their skin. We are at fault in not slaying them* [the Jews]." Such a declaration cannot be limited to a specific historical context. It is timeless and means "death to the Jews," whether it is uttered by Luther or Adolf Hitler.[10] Moreover, Luther himself was willing to kill "a blaspheming Jew": "I would slap his face and, if I could, fling him to the ground and,

---

ther's Writings on the Jews from the Reformation to the End of the 19th Century," in Harold H. Ditmanson, ed., *Stepping-Stones to Further Jewish-Lutheran Relationships: Key Lutheran Statements* (Minneapolis: Augsburg, 1990), pp. 120-36. Reprinted in *The Lutheran Quarterly* 1 (Spring 1987): 72-97. For the nineteenth and twentieth centuries by the Roman Catholic church historian Johannes Brosseder, *Luthers Stellung zu den Juden im Spiegel seiner Interpreten. Interpretation und Rezeption von Luthers Schriften und Äusserungen zum Judentum im 19. und 20. Jahrhundert vor allem im deutschsprachigen Raum,* Beiträge zur ökumenischen Theologie 8 (Munich: Hueber, 1972).

6. Quoted in LW 47, 135. See "Joselmann of Rosheim" in OER 2, 355-56.

7. See, for example, the collection of studies in the wake of the quincentenary of Luther's birthday (1483-1983), dealing with "history," "after-effects," and "challenge" in Kremer, ed., *Die Juden und Martin Luther.*

8. Robert S. Wistrich, *Anti-Semitism: The Longest Hatred* (London: Methuen, 1991).

9. NOAD.

10. Quotation in WA 53, 552:9-12. LW 47, 267.

in my anger, pierce him with my sword."[11] Luther's anger cannot be used as context for saying that he may not have meant to kill. His willingness to do so only reveals the dangerous irrationality of an anti-Semitism that hunted Jews to death for centuries.

I offer first a sketch of "anti-Semitism" (chapter 1). It demonstrates that, in the face of overwhelming etymological and historical evidence, hatred of the Jews includes all aspects of human hostility and is driven by irrationality and fantasy. Then I gather and interpret the anti-Semitic Luther texts in chronological order (chapter 2). Finally, I present a study of the after-effects of Luther's attitude, disclosing historical trajectories focusing on mission, German nationalism, and critical dialogue; I close the chapter with two radically different interpretations to illustrate an unbounded hermeneutics regarding the topic on "Luther and the Jews" — a "neuralgia," as it were, in the body of Luther research: "intense, typically intermittent pain along the course of a nerve, especially in the head and face"[12] (chapter 3). A "conclusion" summarizes my findings.

I let Luther speak through frequent quotations in order to convey the extraordinary ways of his work with one of the most enduring controversial issues in Christian history. He met the issue with the power of his fascinating personality: head-on, provoked, sarcastic, frustrated, annoyed, saddened, impatient, pastoral, fed up, and at times even serene. But when all is said and done about Luther's attitude to the Jews, embodied in his own particular anti-Semitism, the conclusion is warranted (and argued in this book) that in this matter he acted against his better judgment. I also include numerous quotations from interpreters of Luther's anti-Semitism to convey a sense and taste of its reception and interpretation during the half millennium since his first exposition of biblical texts in 1513.

Luther texts are quoted from WA and LW. When English versions are not available from publications, I use my own translation. Bible quotations are from the New Revised Standard Version.

The book is dedicated to the Jewish psychiatrist Viktor Frankl. He survived the Holocaust and was one of my first teachers and mentors when I began my theological education at the University of Vienna in 1950; he helped me to become a Christian theologian and historian af-

11. See below, p. 94.
12. NOAD.

ter my survival as a member of the Hitler Youth during the final days of World War II.[13] His experience in a Nazi *Konzentrationslager* made him a pioneer of a new school of psychology, "Logotherapy" — the search for the meaning of life as the basis for surviving described in his famous book, *Man's Search for Meaning.*[14]

I have learned much from others since 1983, when I participated with Rabbi Marc Tanenbaum, Director of International Relations for the American Jewish Committee in New York, at a Symposium, arranged by the Lutheran Council in the USA, on the occasion of Luther's 500th birthday. The presentations were published and televised for use by Lutheran and Jewish communities. Later, I continued my work on Luther's attitude with Martin Perry and Frederick M. Schweitzer in the volume *Jewish-Christian Encounters over the Centuries* — the "Bible," as it were, for any Jewish-Christian dialogue (see the entries in the bibliography). I am also grateful for the assistance of Norman A. Hjelm, my editor during my early years of teaching and writing. He is a good friend and now a consultant for Eerdmans publications. To them, embodied in the long career of William B. Eerdmans, I offer my final note of gratitude for their expedient process of publication.

On the threshold of the quincentenary   EWG
of Martin Luther's *Ninety-Five Theses* (1517-2017)

---

13. See Eric W. Gritsch, *The Boy from the Burgenland: From Hitler Youth to Seminary Professor.* Part I: Memoir. Part II: Literary Legacy (West Conshohocken, PA: Infinity, 2006), pp. 28-29. By the same author, *"Professor Heussi? I Thought You Were a Book!" A Memoir of Memorable Theological Educators, 1950-2009* (Eugene, OR: Wipf & Stock, 2009), pp. 6-9.

14. *Man's Search for Meaning: An Introduction to Logotherapy* (Boston: Beacon Press, 2006); first edition 1946 under the title, *Saying Yes to Life, Despite Everything: A Psychologist Experiences the Death Camp* (*Trotzdem Ja zum Leben sagen. Ein Psychologe erlebt das Konzentrationslager*) (Munich: Kösel-Verlag).

Abbreviations

BC   *The Book of Concord: The Confessions of the Evangelical Lutheran Church.* Edited by Robert Kolb and Timothy J. Wengert. Minneapolis: Fortress Press, 2000.

BSLK   *Die Bekenntnisschriften der evangelisch-lutherischen Kirche.* 3rd ed. Göttingen: Vandenhoeck & Ruprecht, 1930.

ET   English translation.

LW   *Luther's Works.* Edited by Jaroslav Pelikan and Helmut Lehmann. 55 vols. Philadelphia: Fortress Press; St. Louis: Concordia, 1955-1986.

NOAD   *The New Oxford American Dictionary.* 2nd ed. Edited by Erin McKean. Oxford: Oxford University Press, 2005.

OER   *The Oxford Dictionary of the Reformation.* Edited by Hans J. Hillerbrand. 4 vols. Oxford: Oxford University Press, 1997.

TRE   *Theologische Realenzyklopädie.* Edited by G. Krause and G. Müller. 31 vols. Berlin: De Gruyter, 1977-2004.

WA   *D. Martin Luthers Werke.* Kritische Gesamtausgabe. [Schriften] ("Writings"). 69 vols. plus. Weimar: Böhlaus, 1883-.

WA.BR   *Briefwechsel* ("Correspondence"). 16 vols. Weimar: Böhlaus, 1930-1948.

WA.DB   *Deutsche Bibel.* ("German Bible"). 15 vols. Weimar: Böhlaus Nachfolger, 1906-1961.

WA.TR   *Tischreden* ("Table Talks"). Weimar: Böhlaus Nachfolger, 1912-1921.

CHAPTER 1

The Riddle of Anti-Semitism

Efforts to define anti-Semitism have been so numerous and incon-clusive as to invite ridicule.[1]

An Etymological Plethora

"Semite" or "Semitic" refers to people who speak Semitic languages, such as Arabs and Assyrians, or to descendants of Shem, one of the three sons of Noah (Gen. 9:18). But "anti-Semitism" always refers to Jews.[2]

The word "anti-Semitic" (*antisemitisch* in German) appeared first in 1860 when the Austrian Jewish scholar Moritz Steinschneider spoke of "anti-Semitic prejudices" *(antisemitische Vorurteile)* in comments about the sensational *Life of Jesus* (*La Vie de Jésus*, 1863) from the pen of

---

1. Albert S. Lindemann, *Anti-Semitism before the Holocaust* (Harlow, UK: Pearson Education), p. 8. Some of the materials in this chapter are taken from Eric W. Gritsch, *Toxic Spirituality: Four Enduring Temptations of Christian Faith* (Minneapolis: Fortress Press, 2009), ch. 1: "Anti-Semitism." There is a flood of literature on anti-Semitism. See *Antisemitismus*, TRE 3, 113-68. Detailed history from classical antiquity to 1933 by Leon Poliakow, *The History of Anti-Semitism*, 4 vols. (Philadelphia: University of Pennsylvania Press, 2003; reprint of first ed. 1955-84). Marvin Lowenthal, *The Jews of Germany: The Story of Sixteen Centuries* (Philadelphia: Jewish Publication Society, 1936). For more recent sources see Robert Michael and Philip Rosen, eds., *Dictionary of Anti-Semitism* (Lanham, MD: Scarecrow Press, 2006). There are more than 700 entries in the bibliography of Olaf Roynesdal, *Martin Luther and the Jews* (Sioux Falls, SD: published by the author, 2009).

2. A consensus evidenced in dictionaries. See, for example, *Antisemitismus* in *Die Religion in Geschichte und Gegenwart*, 3rd ed., 7 vols. (Tübingen: Mohr, 1952-65), 1, 456. *Encyclopedia Britannica*, 2006. NOAD.

the French philosopher and historian Ernst Renan (1823-1892), who contended that "Semitic" races were inferior to "Aryan" races.[3] The designation "anti-Semitism" became popular in 1880 through a pamphlet by the German journalist Wilhelm Marr (1819-1904), "The Way to Victory of Germanicism over Judaism" (Der Weg zum Sieg des Germanentums über das Judentum).[4] He used the word "anti-Semitism" (Antisemitismus) to define the alleged threat to Germany posed by "Semitism" (Semitismus) embodied in Jewish commercialism. A "League of Anti-Semites" (Antisemiten-Liga) was to organize actions against Jews. In 1895, an international alliance of anti-Semites was organized in Bucharest, Alliance Anti-Semitique Universelle; it made agitation against Jews popular during and after World War I.

The well-known mayor of Vienna, Karl Lüger, increased the popularity of anti-Semitism as "Chairman of the Christian Social Union of the Parliament and of the Anti-Semitic Union of the Diet of Lower Austria." When he died in 1910, the obituary in The New York Times (March 11, 1910) mentioned his anti-Semitic leadership.[5] German Nazi propaganda under Hitler identified "German" with "anti-Semitic." As the Minister of Propaganda, Joseph Goebbels, put it: "The German people is anti-Semitic. It has no desire to have its rights restricted or to be provoked in the future by parasites of the Jewish race."[6] The Roman Catholic historian Edward H. Flannery identifies four aspects of anti-Semitism: (1) political and economic, exemplified by the Roman statesman, orator, and writer Marcus Tullius Cicero (106-43 B.C.E.) and the American aviator Charles Lindbergh (1902-1974); (2) theological or religious, also known as "anti-Judaism"; (3) nationalistic, exemplified by the French Enlightenment thinker Voltaire (1694-1778); and (4) racial, exemplified by the Nazi Holocaust.[7]

3. See Alex Bein, The Jewish Question: Biography of a World Problem (Madison, NJ: Fairleigh Dickinson University Press, 1990), p. 594.

4. Bern, 1879. See also Moshe Zimmermann, Wilhelm Marr: The Patriarch of Anti-Semitism (New York: Oxford University Press, 1986).

5. Richard Geehr, Karl Lueger: Mayor of Fin-de-Siècle Vienna (Detroit: Wayne State University Press, 1989), p. 3.

6. Daily Telegraph, November 12, 1938. Quoted in Martin Gilbert, Kristallnacht: Prelude to Destruction (New York: HarperCollins, 2006), p. 142.

7. Edward H. Flannery, The Anguish of the Jews: Twenty-Three Centuries of Anti-Semitism (Mahwah, NJ: Paulist Press, Stimulus Books, 2004; 1st ed. 1965). Roman Catholic anti-Semitism has been extensively and dramatically portrayed by James Carroll, Constantine's Sword: The Church and the Jews — A History (Boston: Houghton Mifflin,

The U.S. Department of State, in its 2005 Report on Global Anti-Semitism, defines it as a "hatred toward Jews — individually or as a group — that can be attributed to the Jewish religion and or ethnicity."[8] The European Monitoring Centre on Racism and Xenophobia (EUMC), a body of the European Union, offers an exhaustive description of anti-Semitism.[9]

> Anti-Semitism is a certain perception of Jews, which may be expressed as hatred toward Jews. Rhetorical and physical manifestations of anti-Semitism are directed toward Jewish or non-Jewish individuals and/or their property, toward Jewish community institutions and religious facilities. In addition, such manifestations could also target the state of Israel, conceived as a Jewish collectivity. Anti-Semitism frequently charges Jews with conspiring to harm humanity; it is often used to blame Jews for "why things go wrong."

The EUMC then lists "contemporary examples of anti-Semitism in public life, the media, schools, the workplace, and in the religious sphere." They include:

> Making mendacious, dehumanizing, demonizing, or stereotypical allegations about Jews; accusing Jews as a people of being responsible for real or imagined wrongdoing committed by a single Jewish person or group; denying the Holocaust; and accusing Jewish citizens of being more loyal to Israel, or to the alleged priorities of Jews worldwide, than to their own nations.

The EUMC also discussed ways in which attacking Israel could be anti-Semitic:

> Denying the Jewish people the right to self-determination, e.g. by claiming that the existence of a state of Israel is a racist endeavor; applying double standards by requiring of Israel a behavior not expected or demanded of any other democratic nation; using the symbols and images associated with classic anti-Semitism (for ex-

---

2001). See also the film version of *Constantine's Sword,* directed by Oren Jacobi (Vista, CA: Storyville Films, 2008).

8. "Report on Global Anti-Semitism," U.S. State Department, January 5, 2005.

9. "Working Definition of Anti-Semitism." Retrieved January 5, 2010, from EUMC. WebCite 5.

ample, claims of Jews killing Jesus or blood libel [killing children to use their blood in matzos at Passover]) to characterize Israel or Israelis; drawing comparisons of contemporary Israeli policy to that of the Nazis; holding Jews collectively responsible for actions of the state of Israel.

The EUMC added that criticism of Israel cannot be regarded as anti-Semitism so long as it is "similar to that leveled against any other country." Moreover, anti-Semitism also includes "anti-Zionism — rejection of Zionism, a political movement among Jews, which holds that the Jews are a nation and as such are entitled to a national homeland."[10]

In recent years, the term "new anti-Semitism" has been introduced. It focuses attention on opposition to the creation of a Jewish state.[11] In this sense, it broadens the attitude of anti-Semitism. Sometimes the "new anti-Semitism" includes bans on kosher slaughter, for example in Switzerland, Norway, and Sweden, even though the ban was motivated by cruelty to animals that should be stunned rather than slaughtered. The critical study of anti-Semitism has become part of academic curricula, such as the "Interdisciplinary Study of Anti-Semitism," part of Social and Policy Studies at Yale University. The Director of the study, Charles Small, said that the increase of anti-Semitism generated a "need to understand the current manifestation of this disease."[12]

The Racist Factor

The designation "anti-Semitism" becomes even more puzzling when linked to "race." The term "race" designates "people of common descent." It appeared first c. 1500, an English translation of the French *rasse* and the Italian *razza;* it may have been derived from the Arabic term *ra's,* meaning the head of someone or something. Beginning in 1774, the term was used to describe divisions of humankind with "phys-

10. The movement was founded by William Herzl in 1897. It was later led by Chaim Weizmann (1874-1952), who was the first president of the new state of Israel (1949-52).

11. Phyllis Chesler, *The New Anti-Semitism: The Current Crisis and What We Must Do about It* (San Francisco: Jossey-Bass, 2003).

12. "Yale Creates Center to Study Anti-Semitism." Associated Press, September 19, 2006.

ical peculiarities." This definition has been rejected by anthropologists.[13] It is one of the ironies of history that the leading minds of the European Enlightenment spread the myth of a hierarchy of biological races, with the white race at the top. The German philosopher Immanuel Kant (1724-1804), the "English Kant" David Hume (1711-1776), and the American statesman Thomas Jefferson (1743-1826) believed in the superiority of the white race. Kant called Jews "vile," "immoral," and a "nation of swindlers," climaxing in the amazing statement that "the euthanasia of Judaism is the pure moral religion."[14] "There never was a civilized nation of any other complexion than white," declared Hume.[15] Jefferson viewed slaves as inferior and slavery as a necessary evil for the time being.[16] Such views were linked to nationalism, or a "folk spirit" *(Volksgeist)* in the eighteenth and nineteenth centuries, especially in Germany. The renowned philosopher and churchman Johann Gottfried von Herder (1744-1803) urged care for the purity of the "volksgeist" in every nation by resisting foreign elements.[17] European and American colonialists quickly combined racism with slavery, especially in Africa. It took a long period of "demythologizing" the issue of race. "Pure races do not exist in the human species today, nor is there any evidence that they ever existed in the past."[18]

Anti-Semitism became an integral part of the theories about race that were triggered by Charles Darwin (1809-1882) and his theory of evolution, which tried to show that life is an evolving process of change through a natural selection marked by adaptation, struggle, and the survival of the fittest.[19] Racial theories abound, among them an an-

13. "Race" (2) in *Online Etymological Dictionary,* ed. Douglas Horton (November 2001).

14. Quoted in Paul L. Rose, *Revolutionary Anti-Semitism from Kant to Wagner* (Princeton: Princeton University Press, 1990), p. 96. See Immanuel Kant, *Werke, Briefwechsel, Nachlass,* 23 vols., ed. K. Vorländer (Berlin: Berliner Akademie, 1900-55), vol. 11, p. 321. See also Emmanuel C. Eze, *Race and the Enlightenment: A Reader* (Somerset, NH: Wiley-Blackwell, 2008), pp. 33, 38, 97-103.

15. Eze, *Race and the Enlightenment,* p. 33.

16. Eze, *Race and the Enlightenment,* pp. 96-103.

17. George M. Fredrickson, *Racism: A Short History* (Princeton: Princeton University Press, 2002), pp. 70, 71.

18. Statement on biological aspects of race in *American Journal of Physical Anthropologists* 101 (1996): 570.

19. So argued in Charles Darwin, *On the Origin of Species by Means of Natural Selection* (1859) and *The Descent of Man* (1871).

cient Chinese claim that "barbarians" with blond hair and green eyes "resembled the monkeys from which they descended."[20]

The "father of modern racism" is the French count Arthur de Gobineau (1816-1882), who viewed world history as a struggle between "races." He assumed that there are three races in the world, each exhibiting specific features identified by the colors yellow, black, and white. The yellow race could be recognized as a people concerned with material prosperity, buyers and sellers. But they lacked physical energy and imagination, and tended to be apathetic. The black race had strong animal senses, especially smell and taste, but their intellect was weak. The white race, which included Jews, were endowed with excellence and intelligence, and exhibited noble virtues such as honor, love of liberty, and a strong sense of beauty. This race is best embodied in a strong Nordic race, the "Aryans."[21] "Aryan" is a Sanskrit word meaning "noble." Gobineau assumed that the "Aryans" were the people speaking an Indo-European language; they replaced the aboriginal people in northern India in the second millennium B.C.E.

In 1894, a "Gobineau Society" was founded in Germany by the librarian Ludwig Schemann (1857-1938), who propagated Gobineau's racial theory and transmitted it to the German National Socialists ("Nazis"); Adolf Hitler awarded him with the Goethe Prize for Art and Literature in 1938. Schemann also was a disciple of the composer Richard Wagner (1813-1883), who used Gobineau's theory to justify the society's hatred of Jews. German anti-Semites linked the French racial theory with German nationalism, calling the Germans the strongest and purest race; it had defeated ancient Rome and was destined to lead other nations. Wagner glorified the ancient German sagas and myths in his operas. In his later years, he warned of "race-mixing," and in 1877 he founded the *Bayreuth Leaflets (Bayreuther Blätter)*, a monthly review promoting "folkish" and anti-Semitic views. He claimed that the racial inferiority of Jews prevented them from creating cultured music and

20. Thomas F. Gossett, *Race: The History of an Idea in America* (Oxford: Oxford University Press, 1997), p. 4.

21. Arthur de Gobineau, *The Inequality of the Human Races*, trans. Adrian Collins (New York: G. P. Putman's Sons, 1915; first French edition 1853-55). For a summary of his views and influence see Marvin Perry, "Racial Nationalism and the Rise of Modern Anti-Semitism," in Marvin Perry and Frederick M. Schweitzer, eds., *Jewish-Christian Encounters over the Centuries: Symbiosis, Prejudice, Holocaust, Dialogue* (New York: Peter Lang, 1994), p. 249.

art; they were destined to create only a degenerate culture without any good music and art. Wagner even proposed "annihilation" as the only way to redeem Jews from the terrible curse that hangs over them.[22]

Wagnerian anti-Semitism was enhanced, indeed catapulted to ideological fanaticism, by the British writer Houston Stewart Chamberlain (1855-1927), who admired Wagner, married his daughter, and became a patriotic German. His best-selling book, *The Foundations of the Nineteenth Century,* lists the key arguments for racial purity, embodied in a "folk" that is morally, spiritually, and intellectually superior to any other and consists of blond, blue-eyed, and long-skulled German-Aryans. Chamberlain denied that Christ was a Jew, being rather a descendant of noble Aryans. The fall of Rome was due to a racial mixing that diluted Roman high culture. Miscegenation is the ruin of the world. Keeping themselves pure, Germans will rule the world, but only if they prevent the religious mandate of the Jew "to put his foot upon the neck of all the nations of the world."[23] The German emperor William II praised *The Foundations* as a "hymn to Germanism." Chamberlain became a German citizen and a fanatical supporter of Germany in World War I. The Nazi author of *The Myth of the Twentieth Century* (1930), Alfred Rosenberg, called *The Foundations* "the gospel of the Nazi movement." Chamberlain met Adolf Hitler in 1923; Hitler visited Chamberlain on his deathbed and attended his funeral. Chamberlain had provided the foundation for Hitler's conviction that Jews try to seduce other people to mix their blood with them, thus threatening the survival of the world through racial mixing. In his massive autobiographical book, projecting a racially pure Germany as the only superpower, "My Struggle" *(Mein Kampf),* Hitler constructed an image of racial political rape to warn of the evil intentions of the Jews throughout the world.

> With satanic joy in his face, the dark-haired Jew-boy lies in wait for the unsuspecting girl whom he desecrates with his blood, thus stealing blood from her people. He tries to use every means to de-

22. So stated in the conclusion of his 1869 essay "Judaism in Music." Summarized in Perry, "Racial Nationalism," in Perry and Schweitzer, eds., *Jewish-Christian Encounters over the Centuries,* p. 257.

23. Quoted in Geoffrey G. Field, *Evangelist of Race: The Germanic Vision of Houston Stewart Chamberlain* (New York: Columbia University Press, 1981), p. 90. Houston Stewart Chamberlain, *Die Grundlagen des neunzehnten Jahrhunderts,* 2 vols. (Munich: Bruckmann, 1899). ET by John Lees (London and New York: John Lane, 1911).

stroy the racial basis of the people that are to be subjugated. And as he himself methodically ruins women and girls, so he is not afraid to increase his action by destroying the blood barriers for others.[24]

The French journalist Edouard Drumont (1844-1917) argued in his best-selling anti-Semitic tirade, *Jewish France* (*La France Juive*, 1886) that the inferior race of Jews made them "covetous, scheming, subtle, and cunning," ruining France through commercial exploitation. "The Semitic Jew and the Aryan French represent two distinct races which are irremediably hostile to each other."[25]

Racism also made bewildering turns. Some well-known intellectuals turned the racial anti-Semitic arguments into "pro-Semitic" ones, claiming that Jews were as strong a race as Aryans. The British Prime Minister Benjamin Disraeli (1868 and 1874-80), a native Jew who had been raised as a Christian, described himself as a proud member of the Jewish race, claiming that Jews were the cornerstone of western civilization.[26] The German philosopher Friedrich Nietzsche (1844-1900) echoed the opinion of Disraeli, calling the Jews the "strongest, toughest, and purest race now living in Europe."[27]

Racism became irrational in its attempt to judge the quality of people by their "blood," manifested in genealogies and in physical features. When the Nazis ruled Germany (1933-1945), they mandated that every citizen must prove their non-Semitic, Aryan racial descent through an "ancestral passport" *(Ahnenpass)*, showing the family tree of at least three generations (great-grandfather). The irrational aspect of such legislation is disclosed in the fact that Jews could only be identified by typical Jewish names (Hebrew, Yiddish, or other). A desperate, short-term, unsuccessful measure of "proof" was the use of "phrenology — the detailed study of the shape and size of the cranium as a supposed indication of character and mental ability."[28]

---

24. Adolf Hitler, *Mein Kampf* (1924), trans. Ralph Mannheim (Boston: Houghton Mifflin, 1947), p. 325. The book was written during his brief incarceration (April to December 1924) at Landshut prison.

25. Quoted in Perry, "Racial Nationalism," p. 253. Drumont's book sold over a million copies, over 100,000 in a single year.

26. In his novel *Coningsby*. See Lindemann, *Anti-Semitism before the Holocaust*, p. 45.

27. Lindemann, *Anti-Semitism before the Holocaust*, p. 45.

28. NOAD. The German physician Franz Joseph Gall introduced this "pseudoscience" in 1796. It became popular in the nineteenth century. The Nazis did some ex-

Defenders of anti-Semitic racism claimed to advocate a "racial science" when, in reality, it was a pseudo-science and quackery. That is why the United Nations proposed in 1950 to "drop the term *race* altogether and instead speak of ethnic groups."[29] Such an action is in harmony with the 1776 United States Declaration of Independence, the 1789 Declaration of the Rights of Man and of the Citizen during the French Revolution, and the 1948 Universal Declaration of Human Rights. The term "race" was to be used only in the context of "racial discrimination," according to the United Nations International Convention on the Elimination of All Forms of Racial Discrimination. It was defined in 1966 as

> any distinction, exclusion, restriction or preference based on race, descent, color, or national or ethnic origin which has the purpose or effect of nullifying or impairing the recognition, enjoyment or exercise, on an equal footing, of human rights and fundamental freedoms in the political, economic, social, cultural or any other field of public life.[30]

Scapegoat Mentality

In the Bible a "scapegoat" is "a goat sent into the wilderness after the Jewish chief priest had symbolically laid the sins of the people upon it" (Lev. 16:20-22). The term also describes "a person who is blamed for the wrongdoings, mistakes, or faults of others, especially for reasons of expediency."[31] Similar rituals also existed in the ancient world. The ancient Greeks used human scapegoats. They were blamed for calamities; they were beaten and driven out of cities. Scapegoat mentality has become part of the fabric of culture almost everywhere.

It has been suggested that the phenomenon "blaming the Jews" is

---

periments and quickly abandoned the procedure. I experienced the measuring of my head at age ten in the Hitler Youth in Austria in 1941.

29. *The Race Question*, Par. 6 (Document 791, Paris, 1950). Statement of the United Nations Educational, Scientific, and Cultural Organization (UNESCO).

30. Part I, Article I. Text: HR-NET: http:/hri.org/ICERD66html.2001.

31. NOAD. In the Bible, the Hebrew word for "scapegoat" is *azazel*. Some scholars think the word means the place where the goat was sent, either a desert or a rugged mountain where Satan lives. In the 1530 Bible of William Tyndale *azazel* is read as *ezozel*, meaning "the goat that departs," hence "(e)scapegoat." The King James Version of 1611 used that translation and made it popular.

rooted in the biblical story of Esau and Jacob (Gen. 25:21-35:29).[32] The twins represent two nations (Jacob the Jew and Esau the non-Jew) struggling with each other in the womb of their mother Rebekah. This struggle foreshadows the enduring enmity between the twins, highlighted by the "sin" of Jacob, who cheated Esau out of his birthright as the elder son. But in the mysterious mixture of divine destiny and human sin Jacob becomes the father of Israel as the people of God in a promised land (Gen. 35:9-12). Occasionally, Jewish commentary expressed guilt about the gift of a "promised land" and blamed Jacob's sin for having lost it and for experiencing persecution and exile. "If the reasons for the punishment are unclear, or if the punishment scarcely fits the crime — as is certainly often the case — then a mystical purpose is assumed." In the words of an anonymous Jewish chronicler of the First Christian crusade in 1096, "The fault is ours! . . . Our sins permitted the enemy to triumph; the hand of the Lord weighed heavily upon his people."[33] That is why some modern Jewish thinkers favor exile, not life in a Promised Land; Jews should not become like other nations, corrupted by power. As Isaac Bashevis Singer, the Polish writer and Nobel Prize winner in literature in 1978, put it: "It became clear to me that only in exile did Jews grow up spiritually."[34]

Jews became known as scapegoats, especially among Christians who blamed them for virtually every misfortune in the world, ranging from natural disasters to deadly epidemics such as the Bubonic Plague in Europe (1348-49). This scapegoat mentality was grounded in the devious, irrational theological assumption that Jews had been condemned by God to the realm of evil because they refused to convert to Christianity. This assumption led to specific "teachings of contempt":[35] (1) that the Jews were deprived of a homeland and had to live in dispersion; (2) that Jews were superseded by Christians in the promise of salvation by a new covenant; and (3) that Jews committed "deicide" by crucifying Jesus who, as the "son of God," was God.[36] All three teachings can be easily refuted.

32. Lindemann, *Anti-Semitism before the Holocaust,* pp. 13-15.

33. First quotation Lindemann, *Anti-Semitism before the Holocaust,* p. 14. Second quotation, p. 15.

34. Lindemann, *Anti-Semitism before the Holocaust,* pp. 14-15.

35. See Jules Isaac, *The Teaching of Contempt: Christian Roots of Anti-Semitism,* trans. Helen Weaver (New York: Rinehart & Winston, 1983).

36. As confessed in the Nicene Creed ("true God from true God").

Jews were already dispersed before the Common Era, beginning with the destruction of the Jewish kingdoms: the northern kingdom of Israel by the Assyrians in 722 B.C.E., and the southern kingdom of Judah by the Babylonians in 586 B.C.E. On the other hand, they were not dispersed after the Romans destroyed their temple in 70 C.E. They rebelled against Rome in 132 C.E., and a sizable community lived in Jerusalem during the first Christian crusade in 1099. The continual dispersion of the Jews began in the Middle Ages and extended into the twentieth century, when churches and governments tried to get rid of the Jews.

The "theology of supersession" is the centerpiece of the teachings of contempt. It claims that Jews forfeited all the divine favors granted to them as the "people of God" because they rejected Jesus as the Messiah. Consequently, the old covenant was superseded by a new one, the "new testament," transferring the gift of salvation to Christians. But messianic expectations hardly existed in Diaspora Judaism in the first two centuries of Christianity. They dominated Christian theology in its focus on the second advent of Christ. Jewish messianic spirituality was a Christian straw man. "Whatever conclusions Christian theologians reached, they assumed that their historical victory gave them the right to define Judaism in Christian terms."[37] Moreover, the "theology of supersession" has no solid New Testament evidence. It is refuted by the principal apostolic testimony on Christian-Jewish relations, provided by the leaders in Jerusalem, Peter and James (Acts 15), and by Paul (Rom. 9-11). The council of the apostles in Jerusalem spoke of King David's "new dwelling" where "all other peoples may seek the Lord" (Acts 15:17); and Paul, too, referred to the one and only covenant that unites Christians and Jews (Rom. 11:27). They did not reject Judaism; they believed that Jews and Christians shared the divine promise of salvation. In the mind of Paul, the time of the fulfillment of the promise is an eschatological mystery linked to the "unsearchable" and "inscrutable" ways of God (Rom. 11:33).[38]

---

37. Luke T. Johnson, "Christians and Jews — Why the Real Dialogue Has Just Begun," *Commonweal* (January 11, 2003): 2.

38. See below, pp. 36-39. Detailed study of "supersessionism" in R. Kendall Soulen, *The God of Israel and Christian Theology* (Minneapolis: Fortress Press, 1996). Why the apostle Paul opposes any mission to the Jews is demonstrated by New Testament scholarship. See, for example, Leander E. Keck, *The Letter of Paul to the Romans,* Abingdon New Testament Commentaries, ed. Victor P. Furnish (Nashville: Abingdon, 2005), esp. p. 286.

The charge of "deicide" is unintelligible to both Christians and Jews who respect history and common sense. The crucifixion of Jesus was ordered by the Roman governor Pontius Pilate, motivated by an angry mob that blamed itself for the event ("his blood be on us and our children," Matt. 27:25). Moreover, the apostles accused the Jews of having killed Jesus "in ignorance" (Acts 3:17) — homicide, not premeditated deicide.

Christian scapegoat mentality reached its apex in the thirteenth century when a biblical metaphor of Jews as sons of the devil (John 8:44) attributed to Jews superhuman powers. Christian art and folklore depicted Jews disguised as goats with horns; it was the beginning of "demonization."[39] Since Satan was blamed as the source of everything that goes wrong, the Jews as disciples of Satan were singled out as the scapegoats who carried the world's sins on their backs. They were the most dangerous of all scapegoats because they combined their delivery of misfortunes with satanic rituals. They were accused of infanticide, known as the "Blood Libel" (using the blood of children for healing rituals),[40] of stealing blessed Eucharistic hosts to repeat the killing of Christ, of poisoning water supplies, and of other devious ways to persecute Christians. The gory account of Jewish evil in 1235 in Fulda, Germany, is a case in point.[41] On Christmas of that year, Jews were accused of murdering five sons while their parents attended Mass. It was said that they did it for religious, medicinal, and magical purposes because they siphoned off the blood of the victims into waxed bags to consume it in healing rituals. A Christian mob responded by murdering thirty-five Jews in the town. Although this crime and the myth of Jewish ritual cannibalism were condemned by the German emperor, Frederick II, reports of similar events circulated in Europe. Some official declarations of the church interpreted these reports as evidence of "hatred of the faith of Christ" rather than sa-

---

39. See Frederick M. Schweitzer, "Medieval Perceptions of Jews and Judaism," in Perry and Schweitzer, eds., *Jewish-Christian Encounters over the Centuries*, pp. 145-55.

40. "Blood Libel" refers (1) to the killing of Christians, especially children, to use their blood for matzos at Passover, and (2) to the desecration of the Host, the mystical body of Christ, usually stabbing it. These blood rituals are sheer fantasy without any credible historical evidence. See Lindemann, *Anti-Semitism before the Holocaust*, pp. 10-11, 27.

41. See Schweitzer, "Medieval Perceptions of Jews and Judaism," p. 147. See also Guido Kisch, *The Jews in Medieval Germany: A Study of Their Legal and Social Status* (Chicago: University of Chicago Press, 1949).

tanic rituals — a subtle distinction. In the 1290s and afterwards, host-desecrations were reported almost everywhere. It was a major accusation, resulting in the killing of Jews, between 20,000 and 100,000 in a period of six months in 1298 in Germany. Moreover, Jews were accused of creating a calamitous famine in France in 1315-17. A Christian "Shepherds' Crusade" was organized, consisting of starving, angry peasants who massacred Jews because they were said to have poisoned the water supply with pulverized stolen Eucharistic hosts. As scapegoats for the devastating Bubonic Plague (1348-49) Jews became the main targets of Christian flagellants who beat themselves into penance, and then beat Jews to death as the most God-pleasing act of penance. "The Black [Bubonic] Plague was attributed to a far-flung network of relentlessly conspiring Jews."[42]

An example of a more recent international scapegoat mentality is the infamous booklet, "Protocols of the Elders of Zion," a literary forgery appearing in France in the 1890s, published in Russia in 1903, and widely distributed in Europe after World War I; Henry Ford distributed copies in the United States until 1927.[43] The anonymous author claimed to be a member of the Russian secret police, which was trying to justify the anti-Semitic policy of the tsarist regime. Jews were linked with a fantastic conspiracy theory: the looming international financial crisis was being used by an assembly of Jewish elders in a cemetery in Prague to take over the world. Later it would be rumored that Jews had instigated the Communist Revolution. The killing of some 100,000 Russian Jews between 1918 and 1920 was motivated by the "Protocols." In Germany, anti-Semites began to blame the Jews for starting World War I, for defeating Germany with America's help, and for the revolution that overthrew the monarchy. Readers of the "Protocols" saw the global Jewish conspiracy embodied in the World Zionist Organization, in the League of Nations, and even in the Treaty of Versailles.

Although exposed as a forgery by *The Times* of London in 1921, the "Protocols" continued to shape anti-Semitism. Henry Ford had them reprinted in the 1920s but denounced them in 1927 with an apology to the Jewish community. The Nazis used them; and contemporary Arab enemies of Israel are still using them.[44] When distributors of the "Pro-

---

42. Schweitzer, "Medieval Perceptions of Jews and Judaism," p. 155.
43. See Perry, "Racial Nationalism," pp. 257-59.
44. Lindemann, *Anti-Semitism before the Holocaust*, p. 84.

tocols" were put on trial in Switzerland in 1934, the judge identified the document as a work of forgery and called it "ridiculous nonsense."[45] But the myth of a Jewish global conspiracy survived and became a deadly ideology when the Nazis began to rule Germany. Hitler viewed himself as selected by God for this regime. Whenever he felt he had been saved from danger, especially an assassination attempt, he spoke of "divine providence" *(göttliche Vorsehung)*.[46]

Christian Manifestations

Jews were viewed with suspicion because they were "different," separated from others by their rituals and customs. That is why there was anti-Semitism in ancient Greece and Rome, attested by many Greek and Roman writers.[47] Anti-Jewish riots were recorded in Alexandria, Egypt, in the third century B.C.E. and in 38 C.E.; thousands of Jews died. "Jews accounted for 10% of the total population in the Roman Empire. By that ratio, if other factors such as pogroms and conversions had not intervened, there would be 200 million Jews in the world today, instead of something like 13 million."[48]

Since Jesus and his disciples were Jews, authorities regarded them as a Jewish sect until they attracted a large following through their teachings about Christ as the Messiah. But this teaching, linked to other religious assertions, created enmity between Jews and Christians. Christian anti-Semitism is documented in the New Testament. A Jewish crowd demanded the crucifixion of Jesus, telling Pontius Pilate, "His blood be on us and on our children" (Matt. 27:25); in the Gospel of John Jesus tells the Jews, "You are from your father the devil, and you choose to do your father's desires" (John 8:44). This passage has been used to demonize Jews as part of a "fifth column" of Satan, infiltrating

45. Perry, "Racial Nationalism," p. 259.

46. Hitler used this expression as a substitute for "God." After the assassination attempt of July 20, 1944, in his bunker by military conspirators, he immediately broadcasted his survival as an instance of "divine providence." I heard him use this phrase in his radio address.

47. J. L. Daniels, "Anti-Semitism in the Hellenistic-Roman Period," *Journal of Biblical Literature* 98 (1979): 45-65.

48. Carroll, *Constantine's Sword*, p. 26.

the church to hasten the end of the world.[49] The incident of the striking of Jesus by a guard during the questioning by the high priest (John 18:22) became a proof-text for the myth of the "wandering Jew," representing the Antichrist or Satan combating the Messiah, Christ.[50] Revelation 3:9 speaks of "the synagogue of Satan" that will have to worship the true Messiah. The Acts of the Apostles, written by Luke, condemned Jews for rejecting conversion to faith in Jesus as the Messiah. Peter used his first public sermon at Pentecost to tell the Jews in the audience that they were responsible for killing Jesus (Acts 2:23), "the Author of life" (Acts 3:15). Stephen, one of the seven deacons in the young Christian community, was arrested and tried for blasphemy by Jewish authorities. "You stiff-necked people," Stephen said during his testimony before the high priest, "uncircumcised in heart and ears, you are forever opposing the Holy Spirit, just as your ancestors used to do" (Acts 7:51). An enraged crowd martyred him by stoning (Acts 7:54-60). A popular source for the accusation of deicide is 1 Thessalonians 2:13-16. The text speaks of the killing of Jesus by the Jews who continue "filling up the measure of their sins; but God's wrath has overtaken them at last" (vv. 15-16). But the passage is an interpolation added after the death of Paul, the author of the two letters to the Thessalonians.[51] The New Testament links the death of Jesus to Judas Iscariot (Mark 14:43-44), to Pontius Pilate (John 19:16), to Jewish leaders, and to the people of Jerusalem (Acts 13:27).

49. On anti-Semitism in the Gospel of John see Flannery, *The Anguish of the Jews,* p. 33.

50. Satan, as the "wandering Jew," was said to have an army of cannibalistic Jews plaguing the world before its end. The myth was linked with the legend of Faust, a German astronomer and necromancer (died c. 1540) who sold his soul to the devil (dramatized in plays by Goethe and Marlowe, in an opera by Gounod, and in a novel by Thomas Mann). Similarly, dispersed Jews made a pact with Satan to rule the world with money. Details in Schweitzer, "Medieval Perceptions of Jews and Judaism," pp. 152-53.

51. Besides linguistic evidence through text criticism, there is also evidence that early Christian writers transferred the responsibility for the death of Jesus from Romans (Pontius Pilate) to the Jews. See Daryl Schmidt, "1 Thessalonians 2:13: Linguistic Evidence for an Interpolation," *Journal of Biblical Literature* 102 (1983): 269-79, and Helmut Koester, "Jesus the Victim," *Journal of Biblical Literature* 111 (1992): 3-15. It has been suggested that new translations of the New Testament should offer the interpolation in small print to indicate that it is not from Paul's hand. See Norman A. Beck, "The New Testament and the Teaching of Contempt," in Perry and Schweitzer, eds., *Jewish-Christian Encounters over the Centuries,* pp. 94-95.

The church fathers (significant theologians in the first eight centuries) used the New Testament to defame the Jews, thus laying a biblical foundation for Christian anti-Semitism.[52] Even Paul was a significant part of this foundation despite his exceptional stance on the unity of Jews and Christians. The renowned theologian Cyril of Alexandria (c. 370-444) wrote that Paul "considered [the Law] rubbish" in the light of gaining Christ.[53]

Legal restrictions and forced conversions of Jews began with Emperor Constantine I (c. 274-337) and continued with Theodosius II (401-450) and Justinian I (527-565). Jews were stripped of basic civil rights unless they converted. The Code of Theodosius II in 438 C.E. established Roman Catholicism as the only religion; joining another religion resulted in capital punishment. The church fathers provided the rationale for such actions. In the literary legacy of Tertullian (c. 160-220), the first author of foundational works on Christian life and thought in the Latin western church, twenty-seven out of thirty-two books are anti-Semitic. He wrote them "to construct a Christianity, a Christian social identity, which is centrally, crucially, un-Jewish, anti-Jewish."[54] The major crime of the Jews was the killing of Christ, followed by other crimes that made them "the very antitype of true virtue."[55] Jerome (348-420), representing the golden age of the church fathers, was the first to link Jews with Judas Iscariot and the abuse of money. They are the spiritual sons of Judas. "Iscariot means money and price."[56] Curiously, Jerome also asked his audience to pray for the Jews, referring to Christians as the branches grafted onto Jewish roots. But to add compassion at the end of a long anti-Semitic sermon is a rhetorical oxymoron. The most influential church father, Augustine (354-430), called Jews the "Witness People": they are the descendants of Cain who murdered his brother Abel (Gen. 4:1-16) and symbolize the collective punishment for deicide until they are converted to Christ. They should not be murdered but subjected to Christian rule

---

52. Robert Michael, "Anti-Semitism and the Church Fathers," in Perry and Schweitzer, eds., *Jewish-Christian Encounters over the Centuries*, p. 104.

53. Michael, "Anti-Semitism and the Church Fathers," pp. 105-6.

54. Robert Wilken, *Judaism and the Early Christian Mind: A Study of Cyril of Alexandria's Exegesis and Theology* (New Haven: Yale University Press, 1971), p. x.

55. Robert Wilde, *The Treatment of the Jews in the Greek Christian Writers of the First Three Centuries* (Washington, DC: Catholic University Press, 1979), p. 149.

56. Quoted from the homilies in Michael, "Anti-Semitism and the Church Fathers," p. 112.

without equal rights unless they convert. "Scatter them abroad, take away their strength, and bring them down, O Lord."[57] Gregory of Nyssa (330-395) intensified anti-Semitic polemics, calling Jews "advocates of the devil, criminals, degenerates, enemies of all that is decent and beautiful."[58] The most radical anti-Semite among the church fathers was John Chrysostom (347-407), known as the "golden mouth" because of his popular sermons as bishop of Constantinople. To him, Jewish crimes were endless; they were committed at all times. According to Chrysostom, when the Psalms speak of "sacrifices to demons," they speak of the Jews who reject Christ. And, like obstinate animals, Jews "are fit for killing.... While they were making themselves unfit for work, they grew fit for slaughter."[59] Modern Roman Catholic editions of Chrysostom's works warn readers of his "unchristian" remarks that cannot be excused.[60] This greatest of all preachers in Christian antiquity bequeathed to future generations of students, seminarians, and priests the notion that Jews belong to the "realm of the demonic" and had no place in humanity.[61] Chrysostom's fanatic anti-Semitism may have been one of the reasons why he was expelled by the imperial court in 404 when the Jews were again tolerated.[62] When a Christian crowd, led by a bishop, burned a synagogue in 388 in Callinicum, Mesopotamia, they were punished as arsonists by the Roman governor and ordered to rebuild the synagogue. But the famous bishop of Milan, Ambrose (340-397), defended the arsonists, contending that God had inspired them. By threatening Emperor Theodosius I (346-395) with excommunication, Ambrose had the penalty against the incendiary bishop rescinded.[63]

Christian worship also reflected the anti-Semitism of the church fathers. On Good Friday a prayer spoke of the "perfidious" Jews who need to be led out of their "darkness" through conversion. This part of the prayer prohibited any genuflection and the kiss of peace, because such a liturgical gesture reminds the faithful of the mockery of the

57. Michael, "Anti-Semitism and the Church Fathers," p. 113.

58. Michael, "Anti-Semitism and the Church Fathers," pp. 109-10.

59. Michael, "Anti-Semitism and the Church Fathers," pp. 114-15. Quotation, p. 115.

60. Paul Harkins, ed., *Saint John Chrysostom: Discourses Against Judaizing Christians* (Washington, DC: Catholic University Press, 1979), p. x.

61. Rosemary Ruether, *Faith and Fratricide* (New York: Seabury, 1974), p. 180.

62. Michael, "Anti-Semitism and the Church Fathers," p. 115.

63. Michael, "Anti-Semitism and the Church Fathers," p. 120.

Jews during the Passion of Christ and of the evil kiss of Judas that led to Christ's suffering.[64] The anti-Semitic Good Friday Prayer was removed from the Catholic liturgy in 1965, then reintroduced by Pope Benedict XVI in 2007 under pressure from proponents of the Latin Mass, and removed again in 2008.[65]

Anti-Semitism accelerated with devastating speed between the First Crusade in 1096 and the Spanish Edict of Expulsion in 1492. By 1500, few Jews could be seen in Western Europe.[66] The worst periods of hatred before the Holocaust in the twentieth century were the twelfth and thirteenth centuries, labeled "chimeria."[67] It was "a lapse into the irrational and 'illicit reification'" and "requires a mentality that defies common sense . . . but, enveloped in subjectivity, is susceptible in literal extreme to allegory, myth, and symbol."[68]

The crusades, propagated by secular and ecclesiastical authorities, attracted noble adventurers, seekers of fortune, and large crowds, inspired by preachers who called for the conquest of Jerusalem as the event that would lead to the second coming of the Messiah. A lunatic fringe of millenarians roamed from Germany and France to Palestine to make the world ready for the final kingdom of God. This "messianism of the poor" targeted Jews as the satanic opposition to a God-willed crusade.[69] The first crusading hordes in 1096 were driven on by

---

64. Michael, "Anti-Semitism and the Church Fathers," p. 121.

65. Latin-English text in *Daily Missal* (Charlotte, NC: Catholic Co., 1962). It was approved by the Council of Trent (1545-53). Conservative Catholics revived it, and the pope supported its use in a "Personal Declaration" in July 2007 and ordered its reformulation in February of 2008. See the Vatican newspaper *L'Osservatore Romano* of July 7, 2007, and February 3, 2009. Protestant versions have a prayer about the "glory" of Israel. See *Lutheran Book of Worship* (Minneapolis: Augsburg, 1978), Post-Communion Canticle, p. 73.

66. Summary account with extensive literature in Schweitzer, "Medieval Perceptions of Jews and Judaism," pp. 131-68.

67. From the Greek *chimera*, a mythological description of "a fire-breathing monster with a lion's head, a goat's body, and a serpent's tail," connoting "a thing that is hoped or wished for but in fact is illusory or impossible to achieve." See NOAD and Gavin I. Langmuir, *Toward a Definition of Anti-Semitism* (Berkeley: University of California Press, 1990), pp. 76-77, 302, 334; and *History, Religion, and Anti-Semitism* (Berkeley: University of California Press, 1990), p. 289.

68. Schweitzer, "Medieval Perceptions of Jews and Judaism," p. 131.

69. Schweitzer, "Medieval Perceptions of Jews and Judaism," p. 133. How "messianism" blends with various religious and secular revolutionary movements has been shown by Norman Cohn, *The Pursuit of the Millennium,* 3rd rev. ed. (New York: Oxford University Press, 1970).

the proclamation of Pope Urban II (c. 1042-1099) that the crusade was willed by God. Although he and other church officials did not call for the killing of Jews, leaders of the crusade did, based on the papal declaration, "Let us extirpate them among the nations so that the name Israel will no longer be mentioned."[70] On the way to the "holy land," crusaders destroyed Jewish communities along the Rhine and the Danube. They justified the killing of Jews as an appropriate way of avenging the killing of Jesus. Rome tried to stop the carnage in a "Constitution for the Jews" *(Constitutio pro Judeis),* issued by Pope Calixtus II in 1120. The "Constitution" condemned forced baptism, assaults on Jews, and desecration of synagogues and cemeteries. Moreover, it allowed Jews to govern themselves and to practice their religion — albeit often only in ghettoes.[71] St. Bernard of Clairvaux (1190-1153) was the lonely voice protesting against the persecution of the Jews, on the grounds that they are people "from whom we have our forefathers, and from whom we have Christ of the flesh."[72] But the fanatics won the day, led by such "pillars of the church" as Peter the Venerable (1092-1154), the famous abbot of Cluny. His writings disclose the lethal "chimeria," focusing on alleged usury as a reason for persecution. But despite their clever money dealings, Peter argued with irrational prejudice that they must "be punished, not by killing, but by being preserved in a life worse than death, like Cain the fratricide, for greater torment and greater ignominy."[73] Enslavement, in one form or another, was the result, combined with expulsions.

Church and state prohibited the rabbinical interpretations of the Hebrew Bible, the Talmud (from the Hebrew *talmud,* "instruction"). It was seen as a legalistic collection of self-righteous rules, a human invention, rather than a book of divine revelation, like the Bible.[74] Christian theologians argued against the Talmud in numerous treatises titled "Against the Jews" *(Adversus Judaeos).* Pope Nicholas III ordered the

---

70. Edward A. Synan, *The Popes and the Jews in the Middle Ages* (New York: Macmillan, 1965), p. 71.

71. Synan, *The Popes and the Jews in the Middle Ages,* p. 231. The "Constitution" was issued at least fifteen times by 1450. See Schweitzer, "Medieval Perspectives on Jews and Judaism," p. 135.

72. Schweitzer, "Medieval Perspectives on Jews and Judaism," p. 136.

73. Schweitzer, "Medieval Perspectives on Jews and Judaism," p. 137.

74. Orders by Emperor Justinian I (527-65) and Pope Innocent IV (1243-1254). See Synan, *The Popes and the Jews in the Middle Ages,* p. 112.

Franciscans and Dominicans to summon Jews for conversion efforts that included the burning of the Talmud and other Jewish literature. The Spanish Dominican scholar Raymond Martini published a massive refutation of Jewish and Islamic teachings, *Dagger Against Moors and Jews* (*Pugio fidei*, 1278) as an instrument of mission to the Jews. He even contended that the Jewish plural name for God, *Elohim*, proves the dogma of the Trinity! He also argued that Jews knew that Jesus was the Messiah, but were misled by Satan to reject the offer of salvation.[75] The Franciscan theologian Duns Scotus (1266-1308), known as the "subtle doctor," recommended that Jewish parents be coerced to accept baptism, thus keeping them away from Jewish religion and exposing their children to the Christian faith. "Their descendants, if properly brought up, would become true believers by the third or fourth generation."[76]

Medieval anti-Semitism was also linked to popular magic, or thaumaturgy (from the Greek *thaumaturgos*, "working magic"), but as the evil side of it, namely, "black magic." Listening to Hebrew was perceived to be listening to dangerous sorcery associated with the "ineffable Name of God" in Jewish worship. But since all magic was eventually designated as "satanic" by the church, non-Christian, especially Jewish rituals were condemned. By the thirteenth century, the term "Jews" was automatically equated with sorcery. Its practice was linked to invented stories of host-desecration. "The reserved host" (a blessed Eucharistic wafer) was stolen from a church altar and used for satanic powers and, to make it worse, Jews were driven by Satan to kill Christ all over again, followed by the murder of Christian children and the use of their blood for "black magic." Such a "malignant fantasizing" is recorded in 1494 in Hungary, echoed by the bizarre medieval proverb: "Jews cannot exist or live without the Christian blood."[77]

The accusation of host-desecration and subsequent murder of Jews in the Bavarian village of Deggendorf in 1318 became the occasion for an annual anti-Semitic festival until 1992 when the bishop of Regensburg erected a plaque that described the medieval event as plain

---

75. Detailed analysis of Martini's work in Schweitzer, "Medieval Perceptions of Jews and Judaism," pp. 142-43.

76. Schweitzer, "Medieval Perceptions of Jews and Judaism," p. 144.

77. Schweitzer, "Medieval Perceptions of Jews and Judaism," p. 146. Proverb in Salo W. Baron, *A Social and Religious History of the Jews,* 2nd ed., 18 vols. (New York: Columbia University Press, 1952-83), vol. 11, pp. 153-54. See also Poliakow, *The History of Anti-Semitism,* vol. 1, p. 143, n. 13.

murder and robbery of Jews, not as vengeance for host-desecration.[78] Rumors made such rare events regular occasions, and church officials warned Christians not to buy foodstuff from Jews because they are "enemies who might perfidiously poison it."[79]

It is an extraordinary irony of history, evident in the wild mixing of medieval religious fantasies, that the term "hocus pocus" was used for "magic," Christian or Jewish. The phrase has been traced to the recitation of the Latin Words of Institution of the Roman Catholic Mass (also known as its "Canon"), *"Hoc est meum corpus"* ("This is my body"). Simple worshipers seemed to hear only a contraction of the sentence, sounding like "hocus pocus." In any case, the misheard phrase was later used by magicians and is defined in modern dictionaries as the exact opposite of the original meaning — "meaningless talk, or activity, often designed to draw attention away from and disguise what is actually happening."[80]

When money began to dominate medieval minds, its abuse was quickly ascribed to Jews who, prohibited from owning property, had to make a living through liquid assets. Their honest success was soon labeled "usury" by envious Christians. By the twelfth century, usury was called a "crime" by theologians and Canon lawyers who added it to the list of heresies, sorcery, arson, homicide, and sacrilege. In 1311, Pope Clement V and the Council of Vienne decreed that the practice of usury is to be defined as "heresy" by Canon Law and usurers should be hunted down by the Inquisition.[81] Prominent Jewish jewel merchants were accused of using gems as talismans to ward off evils, or financing wars of Muslims against Christians. In the thirteenth century, German church sculpture depicted Jews as pigs symbolizing deadly sins, especially sloth, greed, and luxury. The "Jewish swine" *(Judensau)* became a permanent symbol of anti-Semitism. It may have originated in Spain, where Jews were ordered to convert. But many *conversos* were nicknamed *marranos* ("swine").[82] Often, the *Judensau* had the features of a

---

78. Schweitzer, "Medieval Perceptions of Jews and Judaism," pp. 149-50.

79. Schweitzer, "Medieval Perceptions of Jews and Judaism," p. 150.

80. "Hocus pocus" in NOAD. An archbishop of Canterbury, John Tillotson (in office 1691-94) has been credited with this explanation. But he may have been influenced by anti-Roman Catholic polemics.

81. Schweitzer, "Medieval Perceptions of Jews and Judaism," p. 154.

82. Scarlett Freund and Teofilo F. Ruiz, "Jews, *Conversos,* and the Inquisition in Spain, 1391-1492: The Ambiguities of History," in Perry and Schweitzer, eds., *Christian-Jewish Encounters over the Centuries*, pp. 169-95.

devil with horns.[83] One of its vilest expressions was the German requirement that Jews engaged in litigation had to stand barefoot on a sow's hide when swearing the oath to tell the truth. Occasionally, the sculpture of the *Judensau* was flanked by a "child-devourers'" well *(Kinderfressenbrunnen)*. In Bern, Switzerland, the well commemorated an alleged ritual murder of children in 1294.[84]

Sometimes, Christian economic greed saved Jews from lethal persecution because political and ecclesiastical authorities used Jews as economic advisers, but usually as servants who were serfs. In 1205, Pope Innocent III decreed that their place in Christian society was "perpetual servitude."[85] The Fourth Lateran Council of 1215 affirmed his papal bull, which ordered Jews to wear a yellow patch; the patch was to be the size of the palm of a hand. More common was a headdress, usually a cone-shaped hat, especially in Germany. Muslims were required to wear a blue patch.[86] The famous *Magna Charta* of 1215 affirmed the constitutional rights of barons who, however, remained the arbiters of Jewish fortunes. Jews remained the enemy of Christian civilization.[87] A picture book for illiterates, *The Antichrist*, shows Jews flocking around the "Antichrist," proclaiming "Yea, God hath come!"[88]

In 1290, King Edward I of England expelled Jews from the land, and in 1492, Ferdinand and Isabella of Spain did the same. "By 1500 European Jewry had either been expelled, forcibly converted, or immured in ghettos; refuge was limited to little more than Christian Poland and the Muslim Ottoman empire, where, indeed, the exiles built up large

---

83. Freund and Ruiz, "Jews, *Conversos,* and the Inquisition," pp. 155-56. See also Isaiah Shachar, *The Judensau: A Medieval Anti-Jewish Motif and Its History* (London: Wartburg Institute, 1974).

84. Schweitzer, "Medieval Perceptions of Jews and Judaism," p. 156.

85. Langmuir, *History, Religion, and Anti-Semitism,* p. 294.

86. Solomon Grayzel, *The Church and the Jews in the Thirteenth Century: A Study of Their Relations During the Years 1198-1254,* 2nd rev. ed. (New York: Hermon Press, 1966).

87. John Mundy, *Europe in the High Middle Ages, 1215-1309* (London: Longman, 1973), p. 91.

88. Heiko Oberman, *The Roots of Anti-Semitism in the Age of Renaissance and Reformation,* trans. James I. Porter (Philadelphia: Fortress Press, 1984; German ed. 1981), p. 42. The picture book appeared in Strasbourg in 1480 without the name of the printer. See also Joshua Trachtenberg, *The Devil and the Jews: The Medieval Conception of the Jew and Its Relation to Modern Anti-Semitism* (New Haven: Yale University Press, 1943; New York: Oxford University Press, 1966).

new communities that flourished for centuries."[89] William Shake-speare popularized the myth of Jewish greed by portraying the Jewish merchant Shylock as an incarnation of the devil.[90]

Sixteenth-century Humanism, and the "rebirth of classical antiquity" known as "Renaissance," continued to spread anti-Semitism, though less driven by irrational propaganda, superstition, and religious ideology. An increasing pamphlet literature, stimulated by an accelerated printing technique developed by Johann Gutenberg about 1450 in Mainz, Germany, advocated religious and social changes in anticipation of the imminent end of the world. The goal was "the renovation of society through the righteous justice of God."[91] Jews, together with Turks (representing Islam) and heretics, were viewed as principal parts of an apocalyptic force, led by Satan and the Antichrist. Economic exploitation of the common people through innumerable taxes, usury, and unfair business practices fueled social unrest, culminating in the German peasant uprising that was crushed by the nobility in 1525. Since Jews had the privilege of charging interest, the medieval complaint of Jewish usury intensified with the spread of paper money linked to improved printing techniques.

Leading Humanists like John Reuchlin (1455-1522) in Swabia and Desiderius Erasmus (1469-1536) in Rotterdam represented different attitudes to Jews. Reuchlin was a lawyer serving as a judge, and an expert in Greek, Latin, and Hebrew as a professor.[92] In 1518, he recommended his great-nephew, Philip Melanchthon,[93] for the chair in Greek at Wittenberg University, where he became Luther's most significant friend and colleague. In 1511, Reuchlin ignited a controversy by the publication of a treatise, "Mirror of the Eyes" *(Augenspiegel),* condemning the destruction of Jewish Talmudic texts. The demand for their destruction had been made by a converted Jew, John Pfefferkorn, in 1507 in a treatise titled "Mirror of the Jews" *(Judenspiegel).* In 1509, he gained the support of Emperor Maximilian I to burn all known copies of the Talmud. Pfefferkorn also advocated a speedy, massive conversion of the Jews as one of

---

89. Schweitzer, "Medieval Perceptions of Jews and Judaism," p. 159.

90. Schweitzer, "Medieval Perceptions of Jews and Judaism," p. 159. Shylock is the principal character in *The Merchant of Venice* (1600).

91. Oberman, *The Roots of Anti-Semitism,* p. 41.

92. See "Reuchlin, Johannes," in OER 3, 425-26. Oberman, *The Roots of Anti-Semitism,* pp. 24-31.

93. A Greek translation of the German family name *Schwarzerd* ("black" — *melan;* "earth" — *chtonos*).

the signs signaling the end of the world. The controversy over the use of Hebrew in biblical studies was fueled by a satirical anonymous publication in 1511, "Letters of Obscure Men" *(Epistolae Obscurorum Virorum).* [94] The "Letters" criticized John Reuchlin's publication of "Letters of Bright Men" *(Epistolae Clarorum Virorum),* authored by independent intellectuals who defended the right to free, critical scholarship, foreshadowing the European Enlightenment in the seventeenth century. Rome judged the publication as a product of Luther's Reformation, and Pope Leo X banned it in 1517, the year when Luther issued his *Ninety-Five Theses* against the abuse of indulgences in the Sacrament of Penance. In 1514, the Dominicans of Cologne had sided with Pfefferkorn and accused his opponents of being "pro-Jewish." But Reuchlin's stance was two-sided: as a lawyer he defended Jews as a tolerated sect in the empire; consequently, their literature may not be confiscated without prior inspection; but they must show signs of improvement, such as forgoing usury, and be willing to receive "reasoned instruction" for conversion to Christianity. Otherwise, they would be expelled.[95]

Erasmus was much more anti-Semitic than Reuchlin. A detailed study of his attitude to Jews concluded that he had a "deeply rooted, unbounded hatred for Jews,"[96] expressed in the often quoted saying, "If to hate the Jews is the proof of genuine Christians, then we are all excellent Christians."[97] Contrary to popular opinion, Erasmus did not advocate religious toleration but the freedom of the individual scholar to engage in research and share it with others.[98] He tolerated only a Christian civilization and thus opposed the threat of paganism, Islam, and Judaism. But the Jews were most threatening because they attacked the core of Christianity, the teachings of Christ, thus being "the most pernicious plague and bitterest foe."[99] Numerous pamphlets fueled hostility against the Jews. Between 1507 and 1521, Johannes Pfefferkorn dis-

---

94. ET in Ulrich von Hutten, ed., *On the Eve of the Reformation: Letters of Obscure Men,* trans. Francis C. Stokes (New York: Harper & Row, 1964).

95. Oberman, *The Roots of Anti-Semitism,* pp. 30-31. For a historical trajectory from the Reformation to the European Enlightenment see also John Edwards, *The Jews in Christian Europe, 1400-1700* (London and New York: Routledge, 1988).

96. Guido Kisch, *Erasmus' Stellung zu Juden und Judentum* (Tübingen: Mohr-Siebeck, 1969), p. 29.

97. Oberman, *The Roots of Anti-Semitism,* p. 40.

98. Oberman, *The Roots of Anti-Semitism,* p. 39.

99. Oberman, *The Roots of Anti-Semitism,* p. 40.

seminated more anti-Semitic pamphlets (in German and Latin) than any other author. But they represented only a small wave in the sea of pamphlets in Germany.[100] Maligned as usurers and social misfits, Jews were expelled from major German cities, most of the time during Lent through sudden mandates. Regensburg was one of the last cities to expel its Jewish population, on February 21, 1519; Jews had to leave within four days. A priest, Balthasar Hubmaier (1481-1528), preached in the streets to a large mob, calling the expulsion of the Jews a liberation from a race that is "idle, lecherous, and greedy."[101] The mob destroyed a synagogue and erected in its place a chapel dedicated to the worship of the Virgin Mary, whom Jews allegedly defamed.

In 1513, the official manual for witch-hunters of 1487, *"Witches' Hammer" (Malleus Maleficarum),* was accompanied by a manual for hunting Jews, known as a "hammer of Jews," with the title *A Quiver of the Catholic Faith (Pharetra catholicei fidei;* in German it was titled *Pharetra contra iudeos. Der Köcher wider die Juden).*[102] The author of the German version was Hans Folz, a "master singer" *(Meistersinger)* from Nuremberg. He used the style of a disputation, with questions and answers, mostly derived from the Old Testament, to convict the Jews, without any interest in their conversion. The medieval demonization of the Jews continued. The *Pharetra* again alleged that Jews called the Virgin Mary a whore, killed Christ again by destroying the Eucharistic host in the tabernacle at altars, and committed ritual murders, targeting Christian children. If Jews were not expelled they were segregated in ghettoes. On April 14, 1519, Georg, the Bishop of Speyer and Duke of Bavaria, justified his order of a complete quarantine of Jews with the comment that the Jews were after all "not humans, but dogs."[103]

Some major and minor reformers displayed constraint.[104] Ulrich

---

100. See the massive collection of Reformation pamphlets, *Flugschriften als Massenmedium der Reformationszeit,* Beiträge zum Tübinger Symposium 1980, ed. H. J. Köhler (Stuttgart: Kohlhammer, 1981).

101. Oberman, *The Roots of Anti-Semitism,* p. 77. Hubmaier became an "Anabaptist" and opponent of Luther. See "Hubmaier, Balthasar," in OER 2, 260-63.

102. The *Malleus Maleficarum* was written by Dominicans; the *Pharetra* discloses Franciscan influences, especially in its defense of the Virgin Mary. See Oberman, *The Roots of Anti-Semitism,* p. 84.

103. Oberman, *The Roots of Anti-Semitism,* p. 96.

104. See Eric W. Gritsch, "The Jews in Reformation Theology," in Perry and Schweitzer, eds., *Jewish-Christian Encounters over the Centuries,* pp. 200-213.

Zwingli (1484-1531) in Zurich urged the conversion of the Jews. John Calvin (1509-1564) maintained that the promise of salvation still belonged to the "children of Abraham," but they must convert to have it fulfilled. But the Strasbourg theologian Martin Bucer (1491-1551) recommended hard labor for Jews. The Lutheran bishop of Calenberg-Göttingen, Antonius Corvinus (1510-1553), who also served as an advisor of Philip of Hesse, stressed the solidarity of guilt because both Christians and Jews share the sin of rebellion against God and need redemption in Christ. In Basel, the Reformed theologian Sebastian Münster (1489-1552) urged conversion by persuasion; he became known as "the father of the Protestant mission to the Jews."[105]

Some non-mainline reformers, later labeled "radical" or "left-wing," extended their demands for religious liberty for Jews. Thomas Müntzer (1489?-1525), the most radical mind of the Reformation, taught that spiritual and physical suffering is a sign of divine election and involves people from all nations, including the Jews. They should join an apocalyptic spearhead, as it were, prophesying a new world. Müntzer joined the Saxon peasant rebellion in 1524 as a means to hasten the end of the old world; he was executed.[106] The Lithuanian unitarian reformer Jacob Paleologus, an apostate Dominican, was the radical proponent of religious liberty. He called for a union of Christians, Jews, and Muslims, led by Jews as the original "people of God"; they should tolerate each other until the arrival of Christ the Messiah, and do deeds of mercy. Rome hunted Paleologus and executed him in Rome in 1585.[107]

On the eve of the Reformation, Jews had been expelled from many territories in Europe: no Jews were allowed to stay in England after 1290, and in Spain after 1492. In Germany, the Jewish population was relatively small after 1520. The wholesale murder of Jews during the Lenten season of 1349 in Thuringia, in Eisenach, Gotha, Frankenhausen, and a month later, in Erfurt, had not been forgotten. The slanderous medieval propaganda against Jews was revived by a best-selling book published in 1530, *The Whole Jewish Faith (Der ganze jüdische*

105. *Antisemitismus* in TRE 3, 149.

106. See Eric W. Gritsch, *Thomas Müntzer: A Tragedy of Errors,* 3rd ed. (Minneapolis: Fortress Press, 2006; 1st ed. 1989).

107. George H. Williams, *The Radical Reformation,* 3rd rev. ed., Sixteenth Century Essays and Studies 15 (Kirksville, MO: Sixteenth Century Journal Publishers, 1992), p. 1153.

Glaub). Its author was Anthony Margaritha, a Jew who had converted to Lutheranism in 1522. He was jailed and expelled from Augsburg when the Jewish community complained about his slanderous statements: that Jesus was the child of Mary, who had relations with a blacksmith, and that the dogma of the Trinity was a lie. The older Luther discussed Margaritha's book in a dinner conversation without, however, referring to its anti-Semitic slander; it reminded him of unnecessary Jewish and Roman Catholic ceremonies that were required for salvation. But Margaritha became a source for Luther's own radical polemics against the Jews.[108] Luther quoted its slanderous polemics regarding Jesus and his mother Mary.[109] There were innumerable other anti-Semitic influences.[110]

But strong supporters of Luther's Reformation did not share his radical anti-Semitism in the treatises of 1543. The Lutheran Hebraist, Andreas Osiander, wrote a tract, published anonymously in 1540, refuting the charge of Jewish ritual murder of children. Kosher laws, he contended, forbade such a crime, including eating meat of animals containing blood.[111] Luther's famous Catholic opponent, John Eck, responded with *Refutation of a Jew-Book,* claiming that he had put his fingers into the wound of a child who was a victim of the Jewish rit-

---

108. "Table Talk" No. 5504. 1542/43. WA.TR 5, 198:19. LW 54, 436. Anthony Margaritha, *The Whole Jewish Faith, together with a thorough and truthful Account of all the Regulations, Ceremonies, and Prayers both for Family and public worship, as observed by the Jews throughout the year, with excellent and well-founded Arguments against their Faith (Der gantz Jüdisch glaub mit sampt einer grundlichen und warhafften anzaygunge Aller Satzungen, Ceremonien/Gebetten Heymliche und offentliche Gebreuch deren sich die/Juden halten durch das gantz Jar Mit schoenen und gegründten Argumenten wider iren Glauben),* 1530. ET of subtitle in LW 47, 130, n. 18. See the study of Luther and Margaritha by Peter von der Osten-Sacken, *Luther und die Juden — neu untersucht anhand von Anton Margarithas "Der gantz Jüdisch Glaub"* (Stuttgart: Kohlhammer, 2002).

109. See LW 47, 257, n. 163.

110. See the instructive study of the formulation and propagation of Jewish stereotypes before the Reformation and their influence on Luther: Ben-Zion Degani, "Die Formulierung und Propagierung des jüdischen Stereotyps in der Zeit vor der Reformatiion und sein Einfluss auf den jungen Luther," in Heinz Kremers, ed., *Die Juden und Martin Luther. Martin Luther und die Juden. Geschichte, Wirkungsgeschichte, Herausforderung,* 2nd ed. (Neukirchen-Vluyn: Neukirchener Verlag, 1987; first ed. 1985), pp. 3-44.

111. ET of the title in Oberman, *The Roots of Anti-Semitism,* p. 35: "Whether It Be True and Credible That the Jews Secretly Strangulate Christian Children and Make Use of the Blood" (original title not listed). See Steven Rowan, "Luther, Bucer, and Eck on the Jews," *Sixteenth Century Journal* 16 (1985): 23.

ual.[112] Justus Jonas, Luther's colleague and best man at his wedding, tried his best (or worst!) to depict Luther as a friendly missionary to the Jews. His Latin translation of "Against the Sabbatarians" (1538) is a case in point. "He introduced his own notions so emphatically that the resultant text distorts Luther's position."[113]

Working Definition

The puzzling variety of hostile attitudes to Jews ever since their first appearance in history confounds all attempts to substitute the designation "anti-Semitism" with terms such as "Judeo-phobia," "Jew-hatred," or any other.[114]

> To have been consistent to the etymology of the term, *anti-Semitism should have referred only to racial hatred, but it almost immediately became used in a blurred, more generic way, and that broader usage has survived to this day.* The tendency to confuse racial and religious belief in the nineteenth century was related to the fact that being Jewish was, and indeed remains, itself a mingled and elusive matter. It is both religious and cultural; one might even say that it retains a "racial" aspect, in the sense that Jewishness has an element of identity by descent. A person with Jewish parents remains Jewish — both in the eyes of traditional Jews and anti-Semites — even when no longer accepting Judaic beliefs.[115]

The nineteenth-century French Jewish intellectual Bernard Lazare maintained that "anti-Semitism" should not be used to describe anti-Jewish attitudes before the nineteenth century; "anti-Judaism" describes theological attitudes. Lazare himself preferred to speak of a racial "modern anti-Semitism" and a nationalist "ethnological anti-Semitism."[116]

The medievalist Gavin Langmuir expressed his dissatisfaction

---

112. See Rowan, "Luther, Bucer, and Eck on the Jews," p. 23.

113. Oberman, *The Roots of Anti-Semitism*, p. 48.

114. Lindemann, *Anti-Semitism before the Holocaust*, p. 9.

115. Lindemann, *Anti-Semitism before the Holocaust*, p. 9. Italics added.

116. Bernard Lazare, *Anti-Semitism: Its History and Causes*, trans. unknown (Lincoln: University of Nebraska Press, 1995; 1st French ed. 1894), pp. 7-9, 116-17.

with the term "anti-Semitism" because it is contaminated with erroneous racist presuppositions. He contended that neither theories of "racism" nor "ethnic prejudice" define the unusual anti-Jewish hostility. He
concluded that "anti-Semitism . . . both in its origins and in its recent
most horrible manifestations, is *the hostility aroused by irrational thinking
about Jews.*"[117] In this sense, "Jews" are defined as a figment of an abu-
sive, irrational imagination, not as the people of Israel. According to
Langmuir, "nonrational" thought characterizes "anti-Judaism," based
on nonrational symbols at the heart of religion, such as the "cross"
with its special Christian meaning; non-Christians view it in nonreligious terms. Such nonrational thinking is not in conflict with rational
thinking. But irrationality is boundless and defies any "proof" for reality. In the case of anti-Semitism, there is no difference between the racist, Nazi "demonologized universe" inhabited by Jews and the theological "demonization" of the Jews by Luther.[118] Robert Michael criticizes
Luther scholars who tone down Luther's views by ignoring the murderous implications of his anti-Semitism.[119] Nazi ideologists, therefore,
saw no difference between Hitler and Luther regarding Jews. As the
Nazi Education Minister put it: "The time is past when one may not say
the names of Hitler and Luther in the same breath. They belong together; they are of the same old stamp."[120] Luther's anti-Semitic writings have been called a "blueprint" for German Lutheran support of
the burning of synagogues at the infamous *Kristallnacht* the night
before Luther's birthday, November 10, 1938.[121] It is an irony of history
that the holocaust made no distinction between converted Jewish

117. Langmuir, *History, Religion, and Anti-Semitism.* By the same author, *Toward a Definition of Anti-Semitism.* He and Lindemann *(Anti-Semitism before the Holocaust)* stimulated my thinking about the inadequacy of religious and racial distinctions, dominant
in studies on Luther's stance toward the Jews. See Eric W. Gritsch, *Martin — God's Court
Jester: Luther in Retrospect* (Eugene, OR: Wipf & Stock, 2009; reprint of 1st ed. in 1983),
p. 145.

118. Lucy Davidowicz, *The War Against the Jews, 1933-1945* (New York: Bantam, 1986;
1st ed. 1975), p. 23.

119. Robert Michael, "Luther, Luther Scholars, and the Jews," *Encounter* 46, no. 4
(1985): 339-56.

120. Quoted in the Nazi paper *Völkischer Beobachter,* August 25, 1933. See Richard
Steigmann-Gall, *The Holy Reich: Nazi Conceptions of Christianity* (New York: Cambridge
University Press, 2003), pp. 136-37.

121. See Diarmaid MacCulloch, *The Reformation: Europe's House Divided, 1490-1700*
(New York: Penguin, 2004), pp. 666-67.

Christians and unconverted Jews; Luther would have welcomed the former and persecuted the latter.

Luther cannot be separated from anti-Semitism as he is sometimes in popular, yet incorrect, hindsight. If this is done, one may have to speak of "two Luthers."

> The first of these is the bold reformer, the liberating theologian, the powerfully eloquent German — this figure is "Jew-free." The other is at best an evil relation who preached hatred to the Germans, codified the truly "German" sensibility, and wrote mainly about the Jews — this Luther is unquestionably an "anti-Semite." If we ever hope to encounter the historical Luther, we will have to overcome this cleavage and reinstate the Jewish question back into its original, contextual framework of Luther's output and impact. This will involve more than reworking the choice tidbits from Luther's writings on the Jews already available in the steadily mounting flood of scholarly literature.[122]

Agreed. But, Luther is responsible for a significant part of a Christianity that, already in his time, was riddled by an irrational anti-Semitism, causing oppression that ranges from expulsion to murder.[123] Luther was just as irrational in his anti-Semitism as were others before and after him.

Albert S. Lindemann speaks of an "eternal anti-Semitism," and a Jewish self-consciousness of being destined to be different from others. The Jewish philosopher Baruch Spinoza (1632-1677) and the Jewish author Arthur Koestler (*Darkness at Noon*, 1940) observed that "hatred of Jews throughout history has been the result of their peculiar kind of separatism, itself related to their sense of superiority to others."[124] But anti-Semitism also reflects a "compound image" and is "multidimensional."[125] Lindemann adds to Langmuir's feature of "irrationality" the notion of an "emotionally-fraught fantasy."[126]

---

122. Oberman, *The Roots of Anti-Semitism*, p. 94. Although Oberman defined Luther's stance as theological "anti-Judaism," he conceded that there are "crossovers and points of transgression" to "anti-Semitism" (p. 22).

123. See the overwhelming evidence in Poliakow, *The History of Anti-Semitism*.

124. Lindemann, *Anti-Semitism before the Holocaust*, p. 4.

125. Lindemann, *Anti-Semitism before the Holocaust*, pp. 6 and 7.

126. Lindemann, *Anti-Semitism before the Holocaust*, p. 10.

But that fantasy is typically intertwined with elements of more accurate or concrete perceptions. It is obviously not a fantasy to say that Jews reject Christ as well as peculiarly Christian messages of universal redemption. Such perfectly accurate observations, it may be noted, provide us already with enough to explain the sometimes raging hostilities of the two groups. Christian sects have murdered one another by the thousands for less. But the further step of asserting that all Jews hate all Christians (or vice versa) is unwarranted by the evidence. To push the matter to a logical and revealing extreme, it is a complete fantasy to say that Jews kill children for their blood to use in matzos at Passover.[127]

Working with historical evidence regarding hostility to Jews, be it rational, nonrational, irrational, or fanciful, is the best way to circumscribe the riddle of anti-Semitism. In researching the meaning of a word (semantics), it has become customary to assume that "the etymology of a word is its history, not its meaning."[128] Be that as it may, anti-Semitism is at its core "hatred of the Jews," or, "the projection of stereotypes on the Jewish people as a whole that portray them as essentially evil."[129]

127. Lindemann, *Anti-Semitism before the Holocaust,* p. 10.

128. James Barr, *The Semantics of Biblical Language* (London: Oxford University Press, 1961), p. 110.

129. *The Cambridge Dictionary of Christianity,* ed. Daniel Patte (Cambridge: Cambridge University Press, 2010).

CHAPTER 2

The Luther Evidence

Since these fifteen hundred years of exile, of which there is no end in sight, nor can there be, do not humble the Jews or bring them to awareness, you may with good conscience despair of them. For it is impossible that God would leave his people, if they were truly his people, without comfort and prophecy so long.[1]

A "Christian" Old Testament and Judaism

Luther's biblical research and teaching concentrated on the Old Testament, thus making him a "Professor of Old Testament" by modern standards.[2] His career of thirty-two years involved only three or four years as lecturer on the New Testament. On the other hand, "he preached thirty times as many sermons on New Testament texts as on

---

1. Martin Luther, "Against the Sabbatarians: Letter to a Good Friend" *(Ein Brief D. Martin Luther. Wider die Sabbather an einen guten Freund)*, 1538. WA 50, 336:1-6. LW 47, 96.

2. Heinrich Bornkamm, *Luther and the Old Testament*, trans. Eric W. and Ruth C. Gritsch (Philadelphia: Fortress Press, 1969; German ed. 1948), p. 7. See also Johannes B. Boendermaker, "Martin Luther – 'ein semi-iudaeus?' Der Einfluss des Alten Testaments und des jüdischen Glaubens auf Luther und seine Theologie," in Heinz Kremers, ed., *Die Juden und Martin Luther. Martin Luther und die Juden. Geschichte, Wirkungsgeschichte, Herausforderung,* 2nd ed. (Neukirchen-Vluyn: Neukirchener Verlag, 1987; first ed. 1985), pp. 45-57. But the author offers little evidence regarding the impact of Hebrew and Jewish culture on Luther's thinking. See also Stefan Schreiner's investigation of how much Luther could know about Judaism, "Was Luther vom Judentum wissen konnte," in Kremers, ed., *Die Juden und Martin Luther,* pp. 58-71. The author concludes that Luther knew "practically nothing that was authentic"; he used only the sources of anti-Jewish polemics (p. 71).

Old Testament ones," concentrating largely on Gospel and Epistle pericopes. His Old Testament sermon texts are based on Genesis and the Psalter.[3] He translated the New Testament in three months while exiled at the Wartburg Castle (May 4, 1521–March 6, 1522). But it took him ten years (twelve, counting the Apocrypha), with assistance from a "linguistic think-tank," for the translation of the Hebrew texts; the assistants were four Wittenberg colleagues, among them two of the best Hebraists, Matthäus Aurogallus and Philip Melanchthon.[4] Luther worked with the best available tools provided by Humanists, who advocated a "return to the sources" (ad fontes). Moreover, he was well versed in the latest ways of biblical exegesis represented by the Franciscan scholar in Paris, Nicholas of Lyra (c. 1270-1340) and by Paul Burgos (1351-1435). Both had used rabbinical methods in their Old Testament interpretation to show that Christ was the Messiah foretold in the Jewish Bible.[5]

When Luther began to read the Old Testament, it became to him "a mirror of life,"[6] filled with the extraordinary stories of the patriarchs, showing spiritual conflicts (Anfechtungen) in the Psalms, the "little Bible,"[7] and offering the consolation of the prophets. "He transferred that world into his own cultural setting better than anyone else since."[8] The struggles of life, be they biological, political, or spiritual, are portrayed in history as the arena of God's activity. The sequence of time reveals how God stays in charge of the world, despite human attempts to create imagined "gods." Luther lectured for years on the Book of Genesis as the prime source of human wisdom grounded in faithfulness to God, the lord of creation and its destiny.[9] But to Luther,

---

3. Bornkamm, Luther and the Old Testament, p. 8.

4. See Eric W. Gritsch, "Luther as Bible Translator," in Donald K. McKim, ed., The Cambridge Companion to Martin Luther (Cambridge: Cambridge University Press, 2003), p. 68.

5. Nicholas of Lyra taught four "senses" of interpretation: "literal," "moral," "anagogical" (pertaining to the end — eschatological), and "allegorical" (figurative). He stressed the "literal" sense. The four "senses" may have originated with the second-century Greek theologian Clement of Alexandria. See "Bible: Biblical Hermeneutics and Exegesis," in OER 1, 153.

6. Bornkamm, Luther and the Old Testament, pp. 11-44.

7. "Preface to the Psalter" (Vorrede auf den Psalter), 1545 (1528). WA.DB 10/1, 99:24-25. LW 35, 254.

8. Bornkamm, Luther and the Old Testament, p. 11.

9. "Lectures on Genesis" (In Primum Librum Mose Enarrationes), 1535-45. WA 42-44. LW 1-8.

the Old Testament also reveals a God who, in Christ, offers universal salvation from sin, evil, and death. The Old Testament prophets proclaim the "good news," the "gospel," as a "new covenant" tied to the old one, thus linking the faith of Abraham to the faith in Christ.

> All history and Word of God are always directed to the coming of Christ who came and in whom everyone had to believe, just as Abraham saw the ram behind the thicket [Gen. 22:13], took it, and sacrificed it — that is, he believed in Christ who was to come afterward and was to be sacrificed.[10]

Other "gods," or other beliefs, are fanciful speculations. "Such prophetic faith is the Old Testament pre-figuration of faith in the God of the new covenant, who can only be found in Christ, the Reconciler."[11] *Here, the Wittenberg Bible scholar defended the church tradition to show the unity of the Bible as the Christ-centered Word of God; he did not use the new, historical-critical hermeneutics of the Humanists.* In this sense, Luther intensified the traditional view of the church that Christ was prefigured in the Old Testament. He summarized this point of view in a simple "instruction and guidance for reading the Old Testament with profit."

> Therefore dismiss your own opinions and feelings, and think of the scriptures as the loftiest and noblest of holy things, as the richest of mines which can never be sufficiently explored, in order that you may find that divine wisdom which God here lays before you in such simple guise as to quench all pride. Here you will find the swaddling clothes and the manger in which Christ lies, and to which the angel points [Luke 2:12].[12]

The premise of a Christ-centered Old Testament led Luther to distinguish between the old pious Israel, with the promise of salvation, and a Talmudic Judaism, cursed by God for its rejection of Christ. This Judaism represented the Jews since the crucifixion of Jesus; Luther knew it well through its Christian anti-Semitic detractors. He shared this anti-Semitism, which saw in the Talmud the rabbinical distortions of the ancient, divine covenant. *This distinction between "faithful Israel,"*

---

10. "Sermon on Septuagint Sunday. Lenten Postil," 1525. WA 17/2, 134:5.

11. Bornkamm, *Luther and the Old Testament,* p. 57.

12. "Preface to the Old Testament" *(Vorrede auf das Alte Testament),* 1545 (1523). WA.DB 8, 13:1-8. LW 35, 236.

known through the prophets, and an anti-Christian Judaism is the foundation of Luther's anti-Semitism. As Heinrich Bornkamm put it succinctly in his classic study, *Luther and the Old Testament:*

> The promise and expectation of Christ and his gospel were the reasons for Luther's affirmation of the Old Testament; the rejection of Christ by the Jews was the reason for his separation from later Judaism. The faith of the Jews had contained the promise. Yet the very same faith became unbelief because it did not accept the coming of the Messiah. As Luther expressed it with classical conciseness in a thesis for a disputation in 1542, "The Jews still believe in vain in a God, who promises a Messiah, by which faith their fathers once believed correctly."[13]

This point of view created an enduring struggle, indeed a theological battlefield, for the hearts and minds of the Jews. It also assumed a "fall" of the Jews into an ethnic sin, as it were, resulting in the distinction between Israel as the "elected people of God" in the Old Testament and later Judaism represented by the "rejected people of God." But like the story of the Fall of Adam and Eve, the Fall of the Jews raises the enduring question, debated since the fifth-century controversy between Augustine and Pelagius, whether God or Jewish human nature caused it. Did God elect, indeed predestine, the Jews to violate the divine covenant, or did they have an innate freedom to do so?

Luther encountered the reflections of the apostle Paul about the fate of the Jews who had deserted the old covenant linked to Abraham and Moses in the Old Testament, his "Bible." Romans 9–11 offers decisive insights, and Luther wrestled with them in his "Lectures on Romans" (1515-16).[14]

Paul begins his reflections by affirming the absolute power of God.

> For the scripture says to Pharaoh, "I have raised you up for the purpose of showing my power in you, so that my name may be pro-

---

13. Bornkamm, *Luther and the Old Testament*, 1. Martin Luther, "The Licentiate Examination of Heinrich Schmedenstede" *(Praesidente reverendo D. Doctore Marti Luthero Respondebit ad haec M. Henricus Lünaeburgensis pro Licentia)*, 1542. Thesis 16. WA 39/2, 188:16. LW 34, 304.

14. *Divi Pauli apostoli ad Romanos Epistola.* WA 56, with Luther's marginal "glosses" and interlinear "scholia." ET of glosses in LW 25, 3-132, and of scholia in 135-524. WA 57 offers extant student manuscripts. They were occasionally consulted by the English editor.

claimed in all the earth." So then he [God] has mercy on whomever he chooses, and he hardens the heart of whomever he chooses [like Pharaoh in Exod. 4:21]. (Rom. 9:17-18)

Paul then reflects on the reasons why.

> Gentiles, who did not strive for righteousness, have attained it, that is, righteousness through faith; but Israel, who did strive for righteousness that is based on the law, did not succeed in fulfilling that law. Why? Because they did not strive for it on the basis of faith, but as if it were based on works. They have stumbled over the stumbling stone. (Rom. 9:30-32)

Paul points to Christ, the stumbling stone, "the end of the law so that there may be righteousness for everyone who believes" (10:4), just as he, Paul, believed and so remained among the elected people of God (11:1).

> But through their [the Jews'] stumbling salvation has come to the Gentiles, so as to make Israel jealous. Now if their stumbling means riches for the world, and if their defeat means riches to the Gentiles, how much more will their full inclusion mean! (Rom. 11:11-12)

Paul concludes his reflections with a fascinating simile of an olive tree and its branches, symbolizing Israel and the Gentiles (Rom. 11:17-24). The olive tree depicts the people of the old covenant, linked to Abraham and Moses. "Some of the branches were broken off . . . because of their unbelief" — unfaithful Jews (17a, 20a). "A wild olive shoot," the Gentiles, was "grafted in their [the unfaithful Jews'] place to share the rich root of the olive tree" (17b). But the "wild olive shoot," the Gentiles, did not replace "the branches [that] were broken off," the unfaithful Jews (19), even though they might think they could boast about it (18b and 20c). God could have decided not to spare the "natural branches," Israel, *and* the unnatural ("wild") ones, the Gentiles. But instead, God reveals a tough love of "severity" for the fallen and of "kindness" for those of new faith.

> Note then the kindness and the severity of God toward those who have fallen, but God's kindness toward you [Gentiles] provided you continue in his kindness; otherwise you will also be cut off. *And*

even those of Israel, if they do not persist in unbelief, will be grafted in, for God has the power to graft them in again. For you have been cut off from what is by nature a wild olive tree and grafted, contrary to nature, into a cultivated olive tree; how much more will these natural branches be grafted back into their own olive tree? (Rom. 11:22-24, italics added)

According to Paul, there is a double grafting: the "broken branches," self-righteous Jews, and the "wild branches," faithful Gentiles, will be joined to the roots of God's covenant with Israel, eternal and still valid by divine love for both Jews and Gentiles. They belong together.

In the glosses for Romans 11:22-24, Luther seemed to have accepted Paul's simile of a double grafting, but in his comment on Romans 11:27 ("when I take away their sins") he added a condition: "that is, when they [the Jews] acknowledge through faith that I [God] am the one who does it, admitting that it is vain for them to think they can do it themselves."[15] In the scholia, he skipped over the symbol of the grafted olive tree (Rom. 11:24).[16] He referred to it in his "Lectures on the Psalms" (1513-16), *but offered an interpretation totally different from that of Paul in Romans 11:17* ("But some of the branches were broken off, and you, a wild olive shoot, were grafted in their place to share the rich root of the olive tree"). This is Luther's interpretation of Paul's simile in his comment on Psalm 52:5 ("God will break you down forever . . . he will uproot you from the land of the living"):

> Four kinds of destruction are listed here to signify that this destruction will be lasting and firm. [First] the synagogue came to an end and fell, never to rise again in a way that it would be a synagogue. Second, they were plucked from their land and scattered throughout every land. Third, they were removed, namely, from this life through various forms of death. Fourth, *they were uprooted from the olive tree and the church, from faith and a true understanding of Scripture.*[17]

15. WA 56, 114:2-3. LW 25, 102, n. 23.
16. WA 56, 436. LW 25, 428-29.
17. "Lectures on the Psalms," 1513-15. WA 3, 296:7-18. LW 10, 245. Italics added. "They were uprooted from the olive tree" reads in the original text *"eradicati de olivia"* — "the ones uprooted from the olive tree." Thus to Luther the text implies that the Jews "broke away" and God punished them with "destruction." Johannes Brosseder (*Luthers Stellung zu den Juden* [Munich: Hueber, 1972], pp. 377-79) concluded that Luther rejected any conversion of the Jews after 1543, but called the conclusion "pure speculation." But

Whereas Paul used the metaphor of the olive tree to show why and how Gentiles and Jews belong together, Luther used only the first part of the metaphor (the "broken off" branches — Rom. 11:17) to *show that the Jews, not the Gentiles, refused the "grafting"; the olive tree is the old covenant with Moses, which already contains the new covenant with Christ.* Since the Jews "uprooted themselves" from the olive tree, a simile for the Word of God incarnate in Christ from the beginning to the end of the world, they have been punished by God.

It should be noted that Luther's view of the divine punishment of the Jews is a leitmotif in his theology from the very beginning, evident in his "Lectures on the Psalms" (1513-15), especially in his exegesis of Psalm 52:5 as an interpretation of Romans 11:17. This leitmotif is accompanied by softer tones, advocating the conversion of the Jew in a "pastoral distance" from Luther's enduring anti-Semitism (1523). But its full blast returned when no conversions were in sight (1538).[18]

In the scholia for the rest of Romans 11, Luther again linked the text with the fall of the Jews as the work of God.

> On the basis of this passage [Rom. 11:22] we teach that when we see the fall of the Jews or heretics or others, we should consider not those who fell *but the work of God in them, so we may learn to fear God by the example of the misery of others and in no way be proud.* For this is the noble teaching of the apostle, who urges us to a consideration more of the one who works by his work than to a comparison of ourselves with others.[19]

But Luther was stumped by Romans 11:25-27:

> I want you to understand this mystery: a hardening has come upon part of Israel, until the full number of the Gentiles has come in. *And so all Israel will be saved;* as it is written [Isa. 27:9; 59:20-21], "Out of Zion will come the Deliverer; he will banish ungodliness from Jacob." "And this is my covenant with them, when I take away their sins."

---

the Luther text leaves no doubt that the Jews were "uprooted" from a "true understanding of Scripture," without which a conversion is impossible.

18. See below, pp. 70-77.

19. "Lectures on Romans," 1515-16. WA 56, 436:7-12. LW 25, 428-29. Italics added.

He could not accept Paul's declaration that "all Israel will be saved," even though the tradition of the church accepted it.

> On the basis of this text, it is commonly accepted that the Jews at the end of the world will return to the faith although the text is so obscure that *unless one is willing to follow the authority of the fathers to explain the apostle in this way, no one would seem to be convinced of this purely on the basis of the text.*[20]

Luther was stumped by this text because of his growing conviction that the Jews' refusal to convert in his own time did not indicate a delay until the end-time, an "eschatological reservation," but the beginning of their divine punishment. For Talmudic Judaism (unknown to Paul!) ignored the Christ-centered ancient covenant with Abraham in favor of a view of salvation constructed with a style of life based on a legalistic self-righteousness. Luther cited Luke 21:23-24 (and other biblical texts) about the wrath against Israel, the fall of Jerusalem, and the conversion of the Gentiles. Then he offered his own interpretation of the "mystery" linked to the prophecy of Isaiah in Romans 11:25-27 (Isaiah 59:20): the "transgression" in Isaiah is "self-righteousness" or "ungodliness," which can only be redeemed in Christ; and Paul's addition to the text of Isaiah, "when I will take away their sins" (Rom. 11:27), only increases the difficulty of interpretation. The addition

> indicates the difference between the two testaments. For the former testament was one in which we increased sin. But the new testament is the one in which God takes away sin. Therefore, he is trying to say: "This is the testament of the remission of sin," in which "He will banish ungodliness from Jacob," just as the other is the testament of the commission of sin, under which men were turned to ungodliness. Therefore Christ has not yet come to the Jews, but He will come, namely, on the Last Day. . . . *Thus it is necessary that we interpret the apostle as speaking of the mystical coming of Christ to the Jews.* In other places this word of Isaiah is clearly fulfilled in the physical coming of Christ. *Therefore I say that the apostle speaks in an unclear way and we could not determine his meaning from the text if we did not be-*

---

20. "Lectures on Romans," 1515-16. WA 56, 438:14-26. LW 25, 429. Italics added. See also Daniel J. Harrington, *Paul on the Mystery of Israel* (Collegeville, MN: Liturgical Press, 1992).

lieve the interpretation of the fathers. Thus in our time "a partial blindness has befallen Israel," but in that future day not a part but all Israel shall be saved. Now only in part they are saved, but then all shall be.[21]

"The passage in Paul [Rom. 11:25-27] remained obscure to him, and he also later sharply rejected appeals to it. He clung to his conviction until his death."[22] Stumped by Paul's views on the "fall" and "rise" of the Jews, Luther concluded that the Jews were destined not to convert, neither in earthly time, nor in the end-time.

> Out of the whole mass, let him hope who will. I do not have any hope here, *and do not have any Scripture for it.* Since we cannot convert the great mass of our Christians, and must be content with the small crowd, how much less possible it is to convert all these children of the devil.[23]

Luther did not assert the solidarity between unconverted Jews and Christian Gentiles *before* the Last Day, as did Paul with his view of an "eschatological reservation" after which Jews and Gentiles will be united on the Last Day as believers in Christ. His distinction between a "Christian" Old Testament and a Jewish Talmud canceled the reservation, as it were. But Luther should not have been stumped by Paul's point of view and should have studied it more carefully without the pressure of anti-Semitism. It blocked Luther's better judgment, namely, that Paul was quite clear in his view of the relationship between Jews and Christians — they are kin in a never-ending covenant. A recent commentary on Romans summed it up.

> Understanding what Paul is saying in this paragraph [Rom. 11:25-32] requires most Christian Gentiles to flush out of their minds what they assume Paul is talking about, namely, the "conversion" of Jews to "Christianity" (a word Paul did not know and which is problem-laden in any case), and their entry into the predominantly

21. "Lectures on Romans," 1515-16. WA 56, 438:14-26. LW 25, 430-31.
22. Bornkamm, *Luther and the Old Testament,* p. 78.
23. "On the Shem Hamphoras and the Genealogy of Christ" *(Vom Schem Hamphoras und vom Geschlecht Christi),* 1543. WA 53, 580:3. Italics added. ET in Gerhard Falk, *The Jew in Christian Theology* (Jefferson, MO: McFarland Co., 1992), Appendix. I am using my own translation.

Gentile church. *From Paul's angle, it is not the Jews who do the "entering" but Gentiles, the wild olive shoots grafted into Israel, yet without becoming converts (proselytes) to Judaism. As Paul sees it, Gentiles abandon their religion when they accept the gospel (1 Thess. 1:9-10), but observant Jews who accept it do not change religions but reconfigure the religion they already have. Together, both groups constitute something new, a new "people," united by a shared conviction about the Christ-event as God's eschatological act.* Given what has happened since Paul, what he envisioned cannot be actualized now; what can, perhaps, be achieved is nonetheless important: a more truly Pauline understanding of the significance of God's indelible covenant with the people of Israel for the authenticity of the faith of Christian Gentiles. Such an achievement requires much more than a tactful "Jewish-Christian dialogue." Important as that is, it requires sustained, serious theological work by both faithful Jews and faithful Christian Gentiles.[24]

Unfortunately, Luther did not relate his view of the Jews to his understanding of history as a carnival of God who uses "masks," "mummery," and "divine games" to direct the sequence of time. Such a view would have prevented Luther from assuming a divine punishment for the Jews; they would be part and parcel of the "carnival" that would reveal them as the elected people of God, but interwoven with others until the end-time (as Paul suggested). After all, Luther told the Lutherans at Riga, Latvia, that their defense against possible Roman Catholic attacks is part of God's work under a mask, just as God conducted all the wars of the people of Israel.

He does the same thing today, wherever the authorities have such faith. . . . Indeed, one could very well say that the course of the world, and especially the doing of his saints, are God's mask, under which he conceals himself and so marvelously exercises dominion and introduces disorder in the world.[25]

Luther found "proof-texts" for the image of God's games in Genesis 42:7 (Joseph hiding his identity from his brothers in Egypt) and in

24. Leander E. Keck, *The Letter of Paul to the Romans,* Abingdon New Testament Commentaries, ed. Victor P. Furnish (Nashville: Abingdon, 2005), p. 286. Italics added.

25. "Exposition of Psalm 127, for the Christians at Riga in Livonia" *(Der hundert und sieben zwentzigt psalm ausgelegt an die Christen zu Rigen in Liffland),* 1524. WA 15, 373:7. LW 45, 331.

Proverbs 8:31 (wisdom delighting in the human race).[26] Switching images, he also described the coming of the gospel to a passing rain shower and a famine. The Germans "should know that God's word and grace is like a passing shower of rain which does not return where it has been. It has been with the Jews, but when it's gone it's gone."[27] And in still another image, Luther described the loss of the Word of God as a terrible spiritual famine, as announced in Amos 8:11 ("I shall send a famine on the land"). That is the lot of the Jews.

> This is the last blow, the most wretched of all. All the rest of the blows would be bearable, but this is absolutely horrible. He is threatening to take away the genuine prophets and the true Word of God, so that there is no one to preach, even if men were most eager to wish to hear the Word of God and would run here and there to hear it. *This happened to the Jews* in the Assyrian captivity and in that last one. We must watch and pray lest that same famine be sent on us, too. Now we are by the grace of God overwhelmed with a manifold abundance of the Word of God.[28]

Luther saw how God uses grace and judgment among nations, illustrated in the Bible, in the old and new "covenants" — a "covenant" being the last will and testament of one about to die.[29] Luther explained the difference in his comments on Deuteronomy 5:1, 3, where Moses summons all Israel to receive the Decalogue.

> Here Moses points out the difference between the New and the Old Testament. The New Testament is the older one, promised from the beginning of the world, yes, "before the ages began," as St. Paul says to Titus (1:2), but fulfilled only under Christ. The Old Testament, promised under Moses, was fulfilled under Joshua. However, there is a difference between the two: the New is founded wholly on the promise of the merciful and faithful God, without our works; but the Old is founded also on our works. . . . Therefore Moses does not

---

26. "Lectures on Genesis," WA 44, 466:22. LW 7, 225.

27. "To the Councilmen in All Cities of Germany That They Establish and Maintain Christian Schools" *(An die Radherrn aller Stedte deutsches land: dass sie Christliche schulen aufrichten und halten sollen),* 1524. WA 15, 32:6. LW 45, 352.

28. "Lectures on the Minor Prophets," 1524. WA 13, 199:21-28. LW 18, 182-83.

29. "The Babylonian Captivity" *(De captivitate Babylonica ecclesiae praeludium),* 1520. WA 6, 513:24. LW 36, 38.

promise beyond the extent to which they keep the statutes and judgments. For this reason *the Old Testament finally had to become antiquated and be put aside; it had to serve as a figure of that New and eternal Testament which began before the ages and will endure beyond the ages. The Old, however, began in time and after some time came to an end.*[30]

Given this perspective, Luther found God's "last will and testament" in Christ. Consequently, there are principal Christian teachings in the Old Testament, above all about Christ and the Trinity. Genesis 3:15 (victory over the serpent) is the "first anticipation of the gospel" *(Protevangelium)* and refers to Christ, not to his mother, Mary.

> For here Moses is no longer dealing with a natural serpent; he is speaking of the devil, whose head is death and sin. And so Christ says in John 8:44 that the devil is a murderer and the father of lies. Therefore, when his power has been crushed, that is, when sin and death have been destroyed by Christ, what is there to prevent us children of God from being saved? In this manner, Adam and Eve understood this text. Their consolation against sin and despair was their hope for this crushing which was to be brought about in the future through Christ. And through the hope based on this promise they will also rise up to eternal life.[31]

Psalm 110 is Luther's most cherished text about Christ because it speaks of one sitting at the right hand of God (110:1).

> This is the excellent knowledge David had about Christ, the Seed who was to come from his tribe and flesh; and he undoubtedly realized and was exceedingly glad that such outstanding glory and honor were being heaped on him in preference to other kings.[32]

Regarding Old Testament predictions about the Trinity, Luther conceded that many were "allegorical," the least reliable of the "four senses of Scripture." Genesis 18:2-5 is a case in point; Abraham's encounter of three strangers in need of hospitality means that "he is re-

---

30. "The Deuteronomy of Moses, with Notes" *(Deuteronomion Mose cum Annotationibus)*, 1525. WA 14, 603:33-36. LW 9, 63. Italics added.

31. "Lectures on Genesis," 1535. WA 42, 142:41–143:7. LW 1, 191. Bornkamm, *Luther and the Old Testament*, pp. 101-20, lists numerous passages as predictions of Christ.

32. "Lectures on Genesis," 1539. WA 43, 261:4-6. LW 4, 173.

ceiving the Lord Himself," and, in a "rhetorical sense, "Abraham had a knowledge of the Trinity from this appearance."[33] When God said, "Let us make human kind" (Gen. 1:26), he did not speak in the "majestic plural," as Jewish interpreters contend, but in a plurality of persons. "Thereby Moses clearly and forcibly shows us that within and in the very Godhead and the Creating Essences there is one inseparable and eternal plurality."[34] When it was difficult to find the "third person," the Holy Spirit, in a text, Luther simply claimed that "whenever Scripture speaks of the two Persons, of the Father and the Son, the Holy Spirit, the third Person is also present; for it is He who speaks those words through the prophets."[35]

According to Luther, the purpose of Mosaic law is to lead to Christ; this is its "second use," namely, to reveal sin and lead to repentance and to the gospel. The "first use" is to keep law and order, to prevent political chaos.[36] In this sense, Moses does the "alien" work of God, as a "minister of death," killing sin through the law and leading to the gospel, the "proper" work of God. He is called "a man of God" in Psalm 90, which is his prayer.

> Therefore the deeds and sayings of Moses must be judged as having divine authority and must be received as sayings of the Holy Spirit, who knows our sad condition better than we ourselves do. . . . Therefore, although Moses kills through his ministry by exposing it and its punishment, nevertheless by calling his psalm a prayer, *he indicates in a veiled but unmistakable language the remedy against death.*[37]

Luther imagined a hearing with Moses, "to test him to see whether we find him to be a Christian," since he wrote about Jesus (John 5:46). The evangelist John and the apostle Paul, "two faithful and reliable legates,"

---

33. "Lectures on Genesis," 1539. WA 43, 14:13-15. LW 3, 178, 195.

34. "Lectures on Genesis," 1539. WA 43, 24-27. LW 1, 58.

35. "On the Last Words of David" *(Von den letzten Worten Davids)*, 1543. WA 54, 41:3-5. LW 15, 282.

36. Luther taught these "two uses" of the law in his "systematic" theology. See Bernhard Lohse, *The Theology of Martin Luther: Its Historical and Systematic Development*, trans. and ed. Roy A. Harrisville (Minneapolis: Fortress Press, 1999; German ed. 1995), p. 287.

37. "Lecture on Psalm 90," 1534-35. WA 40/3, 492:18-19 . . . 493:18-21. LW 13, 80, 81. Luther's distinction between "alien" and "proper work" is based on Isaiah 28:21. See LW 13, 135. Italics added.

should be commissioned to fetch him from his unknown grave. "These two will hit the mark and not miss."[38] Moses is a Christian!

Luther found the clearest evidence of the gospel in the Old Testament in the First Commandment of the Decalogue. "It is the promise of all promises, the fountain and head of all religion and wisdom, *embracing the promise of the gospel of Christ.*"[39] But Christ is present in prophecies, the first in Genesis 3:15 (promising victory over evil) and the last in Luke 24:27 ("Then beginning with Moses and all the prophets, he interpreted to them the things about himself in all the scriptures"). When his friend and colleague Philip Melanchthon expressed doubt about the gospel in Genesis 3:15, Luther contended that both prophecies have "the same structure."[40]

Luther viewed the Word of God in Christ as a timeless truth already present in the Old Testament. The gospel as the new covenant already existed secretly since the Fall of Adam and Eve.

> All history and Word of God are always directed to the coming of Christ who came and in whom everyone had to believe, just as Abraham saw the ram behind the thicket [Gen. 22:13], took it, and sacrificed it — that is, he believed in Christ who was to come afterward and was to be sacrificed.[41]

Luther's Christ-centered view of the Old Testament did not conform with the view of Paul and the early church fathers, who saw the salvation in Christ as "salvation history" *(Heilsgeschichte),* parallel to world history. Paul stressed the course of history as interim between Christ's first and second coming, with Israel being united with Gentiles in the end; and the church fathers, like Augustine (354-430), used the notion of a "spiritual letter" *(litera spiritualis)* in the Bible as pointing to Christ.[42] But Luther "demolish[ed] the whole scheme of a salvation history *(Heilsgeschichte)* in the exegesis of the early church," which saw it as a parallel to world history.[43] He injected a "history of calamity" *(Unheilsgeschichte)* into his view of world history, guided by his

---

38. "On the Last Words of David," 1543. WA 54, 55:12. LW 15, 299.
39. "Glosses to the Decalogue" *(Glossen zum Dekalog),* 1530. WA 30/2, 358:1.
40. "Table Talk" No. 5800 (from various years). WA.TR 5, 361:15.
41. "Sermon on Septuagesima Sunday, Lenten Postil," 1525. WA 17/2, 134:5.
42. Bornkamm, *Luther and the Old Testament,* p. 121.
43. Bornkamm, *Luther and the Old Testament,* p. 255.

Christ-centered view of the Old Testament. Here, Bornkamm's formulation of Luther's position is quite helpful.

> The unbelief of the Jews since the days of Jesus does not nullify the faith with which their fathers listened to the Christ already speaking to them secretly in the words of Moses and the prophets. *To Luther, the later history of Israel became the reverse image of the New Testament. Just as God's promises of grace were fulfilled in Christ and his church, so did the Jews have to experience personally the truth of their prophets' prophecies of damnation and God's threats against any unbelief in his Word.*[44]

"The Uniqueness of Luther's View of the Old Testament"[45] consists in a radical application of a Christ-centered view — "to find the direct testimony, indeed, the work of Christ already in the Old Testament."[46] The Jewish denial of this point of view is the theological premise of Luther's anti-Semitism.

Traditional Polemics (1513-21)

Luther began his academic career with a massive study of his favorite biblical books while leading a reform movement, highlighted by the *Ninety-Five Theses* of 1517, the Leipzig Disputation of 1519, and his hearing and condemnation by church and state in 1521. During this period, he published commentaries on the Psalter (1513-15, 1518-21), on Romans (1515-16), on Galatians (1516-19), and on Hebrews (1517-18).[47] In his exegesis, Luther adhered to the traditional Christian polemics against Jews as enemies of Christ. Using the traditional method of the four senses of Scripture,[48] he used the most powerful one, the "literal," to offer his Christ-centered interpretation of the Bible.

He introduced his *Lectures on the Psalms* with a "Preface of Jesus

---

44. Bornkamm, *Luther and the Old Testament,* pp. 79-80.
45. Bornkamm, *Luther and the Old Testament,* title of the final chapter, p. 247.
46. Bornkamm, *Luther and the Old Testament,* p. 250.
47. There are some doubts about the exact dates and the sequence of Luther's biblical lectures. See Martin Brecht, *Martin Luther,* trans. James L. Schaaf, 3 vols. (Minneapolis: Fortress Press, 1985-99), vol. 1, pp. 128-30.
48. See above, p. 34, n. 5.

Christ, Son of God and Our Lord in the Palter of David."[49] Psalm 1:1 ("Happy are those who do not follow the advice of the wicked . . .") means, in its "literal" sense, that "the Lord Jesus made no concessions to the designs of the Jews." Psalm 1:6 ("the way of the wicked will perish") provided the first occasion to express Luther's agreement with the church's judgment: since Jews do not repent of their self-righteous rejection of Christ, they incur the divine curses and punishments outlined in their own laws (Deut. 28:15-68).

> *Dust* ["chaff"] is dirt, crumbled and dried, weightless, susceptible to every wind, and exposed. This word aptly describes the Jews, who are dry in spirit and abased, and hence incapable of resistance, scattered over all lands and never for one moment secure in their homes. . . . And the curse of Deut. 28:15[-68] upon them is there for all eyes to see. But the church is like a rock on a solid rock and like chosen and precious stones.[50]

Luther used various texts to show how the confession of self-righteousness brings forgiveness, like in the case of David, confessing to Nathan (2 Sam. 12:13-14); or the tax collector (Luke 18:13-14).

> But as the righteous man is the first to accuse himself, so the ungodly man is the first to defend himself. Thus the Jews do not accuse their own ungodliness but defend it. Therefore, if that defense stands, it is impossible for them to rise.[51]

Psalm 5:6 ("the Lord abhors the bloodthirsty") becomes a prooftext for the Jewish crime of the killing of Jesus. "This is said of the Jews, who called down among themselves Christ's blood and also killed him and are abominable in his blood still. . . . To the present day they pour Christ's blood on themselves while they disparage him."[52] Psalm 32:9 ("do not be like a horse and a mule") applies to the Jews because they have "no understanding of faith, they cannot draw near to God, and they also keep others from drawing near."[53]

---

49. Printed at the head of the Psalm texts provided for Luther and his students by Johann Grunenberg. "Lectures on the Psalms," 1513-15. WA 3, 130. LW 10, 6.
50. "Lectures on the Psalms," 1513-15. WA 3, 29:3. LW 10, 30.
51. "Lectures on the Psalms," 1513-15. WA 3, 29:29-33. LW 10, 31.
52. "Lectures on the Psalms," 1513-15. WA 3, 68:4-7. LW 10, 77.
53. "Lectures on the Psalms," 1513-15. WA 3, 176:41–177:9. LW 10, 149.

Psalm 52:5 ("God will break you down forever") says that the Jews, like Judas, were destroyed as an example of God's wrath. Psalm 74:6 (on the destruction of holy places) indicates to Luther that "true" Judaism was destroyed by the "Talmuds."

> At one time there was in the synagogue a known God and spiritual understanding. As the advent of Christ approached, this was thoroughly changed by the interpretation of the scribes into a bare letter. . . . These are their Talmuds, full of lies and alterations, yes, even perversions of Scripture, as Zech. 5:6[-11] prophesies concerning the vessel of wickedness (a vision of a woman in a basket symbolizing evil).[54]

But the Old Testament is a "prefiguration" *(figura)* and "foreshadowing" *(umbra)* of the New Testament united with the New Testament.[55] Using traditional medieval exegesis, Luther "proves" his point in his comment on Psalm 77:1 ("I cry aloud to God"):

> So when this Psalm is spoken in the person of *the faithful synagogue* or the primitive church, the church confesses the works of the Lord Jesus Christ, by means of which He led it out of the spiritual Egypt, out of the rule of sin, the world, and the devil. Hence the spiritual crucifixion and the plagues of Egypt in a moral sense are here beautifully depicted. First the moral Egypt must be stung and humbled and destroyed, and then, finally follows the change of the right hand of the Most High. . . . The whole Psalm has what the Book of Exodus has from the beginning [the liberation from the yoke of self-righteousness].[56]

Luther's basic polemic against the Jews centers in their punishment for having rejected Jesus as the Messiah. Psalm 78:66 ("he put them to disgrace") moved Luther to scatological language in his interpretation of "disgrace."

54. "Lectures on the Psalms," 1513-15. WA 3, 501:4-10. LW 10, 443.

55. How Luther used this Christ-centered hermeneutics is shown by Gerhard Ebeling, "Die Anfänge von Luthers Hermeneutik," in vol. 1 of *Lutherstudien* (Tübingen: Mohr, 1971), pp. 1-68.

56. "Lectures on the Psalms," 1513-15. WA 3, 535:21-28. LW 11, 17. For Luther's use of medieval Old Testament exegesis, leading to the discovery of "the faithful synagogue," see James H. Preus, *From Shadow to Promise: Old Testament Interpretation from Augustine to Luther* (Cambridge, MA: Harvard University Press, 1974).

But at this place, what seems to be more expressly denoted is that their *recta,* their innermost bowels, are sticking out through the rear, because the rear is different from the buttocks on which we sit. . . . Their *recta* stick out, that is, the innermost feelings of their heart and their desires in opposition to Christ they display to the present. Therefore, the *recta* sticking out means that their will to harm and do evil appears, since they are not able to vomit the feces of evils against Him.[57]

In 1514, Luther became involved in the "Pfefferkorn controversy" about the Christian use of ancient Hebrew in biblical scholarship.[58] George Spalatin (1484-1545), an enthusiastic adherent to Humanism and librarian at the new Wittenberg University since 1512, then since 1516 private secretary and spiritual advisor to Frederick III of Electoral Saxony (1463-1525), had contacted Luther's abbot in 1513, John Lang, to ask the new Bible professor for an "opinion" on John Reuchlin's defense of the use of ancient Hebrew. Luther told Spalatin that he found nothing wrong in Reuchlin's stance. Here Luther sided as a scholar with another scholar on the matter of a scientific literary tool, the use of ancient Hebrew for biblical exegesis. He criticized the Dominicans from Cologne for trying "to purify the Jews from blasphemy" through the prohibition of books (like the Talmud). The use of Jewish language, Hebrew, does not make one a Jew, and the attitude to the Jews must be determined from biblical theology.

> I have come to the conclusion that the Jews will always curse and blaspheme God and his King Christ, as all the prophets have predicted. He who neither reads nor understands this, as yet knows no theology, in my opinion. And so I presume the men of Cologne cannot understand the Scripture, because it is necessary for such things to take place to fulfill prophecy [Matt. 26:54, the betrayal and arrest of Jesus]. If they are trying to stop the Jews blaspheming, they are working to prove the Bible and God liars. . . . Conversion of the Jews will be the work of God alone operating from within, and not of man working — or rather playing — from without.

Luther concluded the letter with the observation that the wrath of God has made the Jews incorrigible; such people become worse when others

57. "Lectures on the Psalms," 1513-15. WA 3, 596:28-31 . . . 36–597:4. LW 11, 88.
58. See above, pp. 24-25.

are trying to make them better.[59] But his correspondence clearly distinguished between a divine and human initiative regarding a Christian attitude to the Jews: God remains in charge of their punishment, and conversion attempts only drive Jews further away. Here Luther distanced himself from medieval missionary practices that included forced conversions, especially in Spain. At issue is the interpretation of the Bible by Christians and Jews.

A few years later, in 1519, Luther asked Spalatin to get the approval of Elector Frederick for calling Matthew Hadrian, a converted Spanish Jewish Hebraist to the Wittenberg faculty — "the gifts of God of a most distinguished opportunity to promote the study of Hebrew among us."[60] Hadrian was called in 1520, then transferred to the University of Leipzig.

In the "Lectures on Romans," Luther struggled with the meaning of "righteousness," reflecting his own quest for a gracious God in the face of his inability to please God through "good works" and thus merit salvation. In the glosses, he offered a "summary" before his comments on each chapter; these summaries are derived almost verbatim from the glosses of the renowned medieval scholar Nicholas of Lyra. Luther's Christ-centered exegetical harvest stressed Jewish self-righteousness and Christian faith in Christ. The former is summarized in a gloss to Romans 2:11 ("for God shows no partiality").

> The Jews wanted God to act in such a way that he would bestow the good on the Jews only and the evil on the Gentiles only, as if because they were the seed of Abraham, they should automatically be like Abraham in merit. *Thus the Jews always strive to make God a judge who considers the persons.*[61]

The latter is pointed out in a gloss to Romans 2:13 ("the doers of the law will be justified").

> But no one is looked upon as righteous except the one who fulfills the Law in deed, and *no one fulfills the Law except the man who believes*

---

59. Letter to George Spalatin, February 1514. WA.BR 1, 23:1-24, 46. ET in *Luther's Correspondence and Other Contemporary Letters,* trans. Henry P. Smith (Philadelphia: Lutheran Publication Society, 1913), vol. 1, p. 29. Luther wrote another, shorter letter to Spalatin on August 5, 1514. In it he denounced Reuchlin's opponents without, however, any comments on the Jews. WA.BR 1, 28-29. LW 48, 8-11.

60. Letter of November 7, 1519. WA.BR 1, 532. LW 48, 132.

61. "Lectures on Romans," 1515-16. WA 56, 199:10-13. LW 25, 182. Italics added.

in Christ. Thus the apostle intends to conclude that outside of Christ no one is righteous, no one fulfills the Law.[62]

Most of the summaries of the chapters also reflect this point of view.

Chapter Two. The apostle refutes the faults of the Jews, saying that as far as their guilt is concerned they are the same as the Gentiles and in a certain respect even worse.[63]

Chapter Three. The apostle shows in what way the Jews were better than the Gentiles, demonstrating that the Gentiles as well as the Jews are in need of the grace of Christ.[64]

Chapter Four. Through the example of Abraham the apostle demonstrates that faith is required for salvation, and that the old law does not suffice for salvation.[65]

Chapter Five. The apostle demonstrates the power of faith in the justification of believers, because death reigned from Adam to Christ.[66]

Chapter Eight. He shows that we must firmly cling to the law of Christ, since His law is the law of life and the law of the Spirit.[67]

Chapter Nine. The apostle grieves over the obstinacy of the Jews; he shows that the Jews have not been deprived of the promise of the fathers, and he reminds us that the Gentiles have been called.[68]

Chapter Ten. The apostle prays for the Jews, showing that the righteousness which renders a man worthy of eternal life comes alone from the law of Christ and faith in Him.[69]

---

62. "Lectures on Romans," 1515-16. WA 56, 22, 26-29. LW 25, 19, n. 13. The notes are Luther's marginal glosses. Italics added.
63. "Lectures on Romans," 1515-16. WA 56, 17. LW 25, 15.
64. "Lectures on Romans," 1515-16. WA 56, 29. LW 25, 25.
65. "Lectures on Romans," 1515-16. WA 56, 41. LW 25, 35.
66. "Lectures on Romans," 1515-16. WA 56, 49. LW 25, 43.
67. "Lectures on Romans," 1515-16. WA 56, 74. LW 25, 67.
68. "Lectures on Romans," 1515-16. WA 56, 87. LW 25, 79.
69. "Lectures on Romans," 1515-16. WA 56, 97. LW 25, 88.

Chapter Eleven. The apostle turns back the insulting of the Jews by the Gentiles and describes the present blindness of the Jews; he concludes concerning the wisdom of God.[70]

Only on the gloss to Romans 15:12 (Paul cites Isa. 11:10, prophesying that "the root of Jesse" will survive) Luther struck a positive note on the relationship between Jews and Gentiles.

> They are not in opposition to each other but mutually welcome one another, *just as Christ has welcomed them*. For not only the Jews, *lest they be proud*, but also the Gentiles has He welcomed except out of his pure mercy. Therefore they both have reason to praise God *but none for their own contention*.[71]

But Luther implied that Christ would not welcome "proud Jews" — a signal that they remain rejected. He consistently revealed an exegetical distance between himself and Paul regarding the Jews. Luther continued to use his Christ-centered exegesis and the ecclesiastical tradition that depicts the Jews as detractors of the eternal divine covenant, thus incurring divine punishment; Paul offers a nontraditional exegesis that depicts an eschatological unity of Christians and Jews, manifested in mutual toleration already before the end of time.

"The Lectures on Galatians" deal with Luther's favorite biblical book, and are dedicated to "my Katie von Bora."[72] He also drafted the *Ninety-Five Theses* (1517) while doing the early lectures, with interruptions until 1535. In his summation of the "argument" of Galatians, Luther zealously defended the Christ-centered "doctrine of justification," which was violated by the Galatians who have become "foolish" and "bewitched" (Gal. 3:1). Luther found the "new Galatians" in the "fanatical spirits and sectarians" (people like Thomas Müntzer, called *Schwärmer* by Luther).

> For if the doctrine of justification is lost, the whole of Christian doctrine is lost. And those in the world who do not teach it are either *Jews* or Turks or papists or sectarians. . . . We see this today in the fanatical spirit and sectarians.[73]

---

70. "Lectures on Romans," 1515-16. WA 56, 106. LW 25, 95.

71. "Lectures on Romans," 1515-16. WA 56, 149. LW 25, 122, n. 10. Italics added.

72. "Table Talk" No. 146. December 14, 1531–January 22, 1532. WA.TR 1, 69:18-19. LW 54, 20.

73. "Lectures on Galatians" (*In epistolam Pauli ad Galatas Commentarius*), 1535. WA

Commenting on Galatians 2:16 (justification by Christ, not by works of the Law), Luther accused Jews of using their superstitious belief in the secret name of God, depicted in the "Tetragrammaton" (YHWH).[74]

> But you will never see the name of the Lord more clearly than in Christ. There you will see how good, pleasant, faithful, righteous, and true God is, since He did not spare His own son (Rom. 8:32).

The Galatians are "foolish" because among them (just as among the Jews) "Christ has been crucified among all who put their trust not in Him but in themselves and in the Law; for then the grace of God has been rejected, and Christ does not live in them."[75] Luther interpreted Galatians 3:16-18 (the promises made to Abraham and his "offspring") as a reference to Christ.

> He [Paul] teaches that *the Offspring of Abraham means Christ,* lest the Jews boast that they are the ones in whom the Gentiles are to be blessed — since they are so numerous that it can never be certain in whom the promise is satisfied — lest the promise be imperiled again and God's testament collapse. *Therefore it was necessary to name one offspring to whom this blessing should be given.* . . . So you have the Testator, the testament, the substance of the testament, and those for whom it was made. Now it remains that it be ratified and that, after it has been ratified, it be revealed and distributed, that is, *that the Gentiles receive the blessing of Christ.*[76]

Luther celebrated with Paul the freedom of the Christian faith which transcends human divisions (Gal. 3:28-29, "there is neither Jew nor Greek" in the offspring of Abraham);[77] and there is unity in the fulfillment of the Law through the commandment, "You shall love your

---

40, 48:28-30. LW 26, 9. Reference to Müntzer, 97. ET of Galatians 1-6 (1519) in LW 27, 153-410. Galatians 1-6 (1535) in LW 26 and 27, 3-149. What follows is derived from the commentary of 1519.

74. The "Tetragrammaton" was linked to secret medieval speculations defined as "cabal," meaning "tradition." The Humanist John Reuchlin had written a book about it in 1517, "On the Art of Cabala" *(De arte cabbalistica).* Luther may have used it. Subsequent quotation in WA 2, 491:1-3. LW 27, 221.

75. WA 2, 506:31-38. LW 27, 246.

76. WA 2, 519:32-520:2. LW 27, 265.

77. WA 2, 531. LW 27, 281-82.

neighbor as yourself" (Gal. 5:14). But there is still "Israel after the flesh" among Jews and Gentiles who do not "live by the spirit" (Gal. 6:16).[78]

In the second commentary on the Psalter, Luther returned from the ideal exposition of "justification" in Galatians to the harsh realities of Christian-Jewish relations in 1520. Psalm 14:7 (wishing "deliverance for Israel . . . when the Lord restores the fortunes of his people") moved Luther to complain about Christian attitudes towards Jews. Instead of agreeing with Paul's faith in God's power to graft them in again (Rom. 11:23), so-called "pseudo-Christians" *(Namenschristen)* prevent the conversion of Jews and make them even more hostile to the gospel than they already are, "when, instead, they should attract them with gentleness, patience, prayer, and care." Luther continues:

> Who, I ask, would convert to our religion, no matter how good-natured and patient he would be, if he would see himself treated by us not only with cruelty and in an un-Christian manner, but also with the threat of death. *If hatred of the Jews, or heretics, and Turks make Christians, then we in our rage would truly be most Christian among Christians. . . .* In contrast, the gospel aims to instill in us, fully and completely, the love of God and of Christ in this matter.[79]

On the other hand, Luther remained convinced that, although some Jews convert, most of them remain obstinate. The "proof-text" is Psalm 18:40 ("you made my enemies turn their backs to me, and those who hated me I destroyed").

> The church has suffered no greater hatred than that of its Jewish brothers. . . . This is terrible: the synagogue is conquered and flees, but the church wins and advances. . . . Today, we see with our own eyes that what happens to the Jews cannot be better expressed than with the words "with their backs turned" they are exposed to hatred and all evil.[80]

Luther repeated what he said in connection with Galatians 3:28, namely, that in the end everyone will "turn to the Lord," the living and the dead (Ps. 22:27-29).[81]

78. WA 2, 614. LW 27, 406.
79. "Lectures on Psalms" *(Operationes in Psalmos)*, 1520. WA 5, 429:7-10 . . . 17. Italics added.
80. "Lectures on Psalms," WA 5, 534:13-26.
81. "Lectures on Psalms," WA 5, 667:27-34.

MARTIN LUTHER'S ANTI-SEMITISM

In his early devotional writings, Luther used the image of the Jews to point to the sin of unbelief. In a popular tract for Lent, "A Meditation on Christ's Passion" (1519), Luther wrote that the main benefit of Christ's passion is that one sees one's own true self and becomes terrified and crushed. It is like being an associate in a murder, without being caught, even though the accomplice has been sentenced to death. But when arrested and convicted of having inspired the murder, there is nothing but fear and despair.

> Now the whole world closes in upon you, especially since your conscience also deserts you. You should even be more terrified by the meditation on Christ's passion. *For the evildoers, the Jews, whom God has judged and driven out, were only the servants of your sin; you are actually the one who, as we said, by his sin killed and crucified God's Son.*[82]

Luther continued to speak of the collective guilt of Christians and Jews: "They fall back and cling to their own will, that old knave. Yes, *like the Jews,* they release the criminal Barabbas [Matt. 27:15-23] *and kill the innocent Son of God,* that is, the grace of God, which had just begun to take root in them."[83] In "A Sermon on Preparing to Die," written for a dying friend of George Spalatin, Luther again identified the Jews with the sin and evil that can befall everyone.

> The Jews held the image of sin before Christ when they said to him, "He healed others. If he is the Son of God, let him come down from the cross," etc. — as though they were to say, "His works were all fraud and deception. He is not the Son of God but the son of the devil. . . ." The Lord describes the destruction of Jerusalem in Luke 19[:43-44]. . . . Its enemies . . . will drive them hither and yon. . . . We mark that Christ remained silent . . . and he intercedes for his enemies. . . . We must similarly let these images slip away from us . . . and hold to Christ and firmly believe our sin, death, and hell are overcome in him and no longer able to harm us.[84]

---

82. *Ein Sermon von der Betrachtung des heiligen Leibes Christi,* 1519. WA 2, 138:29-32. LW 42, 10. Italics added.

83. "An Exposition of the Lord's Prayer" *(Auslegung deutsch des Vaterunsers für die einfältigen Laien),* 1519. WA 2, 107:5-8. LW 42, 51. Commentary on the Fourth Petition, "Give Us This Day Our Daily Bread" — the Word of God as comfort. The tract was a best-seller.

84. *Ein Sermon von der Bereitung zum Sterben,* 1519. WA 2, 691:27-33 . . . 692:15-21. LW 42, 107-8.

In a sermon of 1519, Luther joined the discussion on the use and abuse of money-lending, linked to the practice of "usury."[85] Jews were accused of usury. But the charge was linked to an arrangement between Christian princes and Jewish merchants: the Christian political authorities permitted Jews to charge interest rates, but also made the Jews pay considerable sums for protection. It was a form of pawn-broking or of retail trade. Jewish traders offered discount prices, and Christian artisans complained about being cheated, using popular anti-Semitic rhetoric.[86] Roman Catholic Canon Law prohibited usury, referring to Luke 6:35 ("lend, expect nothing in return"). Luther agreed with Canon Law and added the injunctions of the Sermon on the Mount (Matt. 5:40, 42 — give freely and never refuse a borrower) to Jewish law that prohibits "hard-hearted" and "tightfisted" lending of money, especially to those in need (Deut. 15:7-8).

> Look at those who lend wine, wheat, money, or whatever, to their neighbors, then oppress them with annual interest rates that are higher than the sum of money they borrowed. These are the Jewish little tricks. But they constitute an unchristian attitude to the holy gospel of Christ, indeed they violate natural law, as the Lord indicates in Luke 6[:30-31], "do to others as you would have them do to you."[87]

In the first of his "blueprints" for reforms in 1520, "Treatise on Good Works," Luther used popular anti-Semitism about usury and, as was the custom, linked it to two other social abuses: (1) "horrible gluttony and drunkenness"; and (2) "the excessive cost of clothes."

> See, *these are the three Jews, as they call them, which suck the world dry.* On these matters overlords ought not to sleep or be lazy, if they would give a good account of their office to God.[88]

In the other blueprint, "To the Christian Nobility of the German Nation Concerning the Reform of the Christian Estate," Luther associ-

---

85. See "usury," in OER 4, 204-5.

86. See "Jews," in OER 2, 339.

87. "Sermon on Usury" *(Sermon von dem Wucher)*, 1519. WA 5, 3:3-9. See also "Trade and Usury" *(Von Kaufhandlung und Wucher)*, 1524. WA 5, 3:3-11. LW 45, 300.

88. "Treatise on Good Works" *(Von den guten Werken)*, 1520. WA 6, 262:23-263:4. LW 44, 96. Italics added.

ated commerce and the love of money with the people of Israel. That is why God isolated them from other nations. "I do not see that many good customs have ever come to a land through commerce, and in ancient times God made his people Israel dwell away from the sea on this account, and did not let them engage in much commerce."[89]

When Luther attacked the papacy as a tyrannical power trying to create external uniformity and unity, he called it "Jewish" because the Jews expect a Messiah who would create an external kingdom in Jerusalem.

> All those who make the Christian unity or community physical and external, equal to other communities, are true Jews. For they, too, wait for their messiah to establish an external kingdom at a particular external place, namely, Jerusalem. Thus they drop the only faith that makes Christ's kingdom spiritual and internal.[90]

Shortly before his appearance in Worms on April 17, 1521, Luther recommended the inclusion of Jews in the Fourth Petition of the Lord's Prayer ("Give us our daily bread"), together with "heretics and all distressed, desperate, and suffering people."[91] And in a sermon before the journey to Worms, Luther chided those who use the popular meditation on Christ's Passion as an occasion to express their wrath against the Jews. "Some Christians deal with the Passion of Christ as an occasion to be hostile to Jews and to get really angry and slander poor Judas. But this is neither a proper nor useful way to preach or meditate on the Passion of Christ."[92]

While in exile at the Wartburg Castle, Luther sent a brief exposition of Psalm 68:21 ("God will shatter the heads of his enemies") to Melanchthon; Luther viewed it as a "Psalm about Christ."

> It is sufficiently known in public that the Jews have always been the greatest enemies of Christ, even though they wanted to be God's

---

89. *An den christlichen Adel deutscher Nation von des christlichen Standes Besserung,* 1520. WA 6, 461:9-12. LW 44, 213.

90. "On the Papacy in Rome against the Most Celebrated Romanist in Leipzig" *(Von dem Papsttum zu Rom: widder den hochberumpten Romanisten zu Leiptzig),* 1520. WA 6, 294:31-295:1. LW 39, 67. The opponent was Jerome Emser.

91. "A Short Form of the Ten Commandments" *(Eine kurze Form der Zehn Gebote),* 1520. WA 7, 226:16.

92. Sermon on Saturday before Easter, March 29, 1521. WA 9, 651:6-10.

greatest friends. But no one can deny that they experienced what this Psalm says: that their head is destroyed; that they no longer have a kingdom, or rulers, or priests and are always without a head. All this happened shortly after Christ's ascension. This indicates no other misdeed than that they are Christ's enemies and do not let him be God. . . . All this happens because they refuse to believe in him who has taken away sin and death.[93]

When Luther heard that some of his writings were ordered burned by the papal legate Jerome Aleander in Louvain, Cologne, and Mainz, he included his reaction in a lengthy treatise on biblical authority and "justification by faith" against the Louvain theologian James Latomus. Luther approved the burning of "erroneous books," containing "magic" (as recorded in Acts 19:19) or "papist" views, as he himself had done.[94] But they need to be proven "harmful" in order to be burned — a broad definition! Luther opposed the burning of Jewish books just because they were written in Hebrew. "As is said, fire settles no arguments."[95]

An Interlude of Pastoral Evangelism (1521-37)

The tone of Luther's anti-Semitism moderated somewhat after the hearing in Worms in 1521. His translation and commentary on "The Magnificat" (Luke 1:46-55) speaks of a "spiritual Israel" consisting of a certain number chosen by God. In his commentary on Luke 1:54 ("he has helped his servant Israel"), Luther offered his own unique exegesis of Genesis 32:24-28 (the wrestling of Jacob with an angel).

The holy patriarch Jacob wrestled with the angel, who strained the hollow of his thigh out of joint, to show that his children should henceforth not boast of their fleshly birth, as the Jews do. Therefore he also received a new name, that he should henceforth be

---

93. "German Interpretation of Psalm 68" *(Deutsche Auslegung des 68. Psalmes)*, 1521. WA 8, 22:23-23:13.

94. In December 1520 when he joined Wittenberg students and faculty at a bonfire and threw in the papal bull issued against him. See "Why the Books of the Pope and His Disciples Were Burned" *(Warum des Papsts und seiner Jünger Bücher verbrannt sind)*, 1520. WA 7, 161-82. LW 31, 383-95. See also Eric W. Gritsch, *Martin — God's Court Jester: Luther in Retrospect* (Eugene, OR: Wipf & Stock, 2009; reprint of 1st ed. in 1983), pp. 38-39.

95. "Against Latomus" *(Rationis Latomianae confutatio)*, 1521. WA 8, 52:15. LW 32, 150.

called Israel, as a patriarch who was not only Jacob, the father of fleshly children, but Israel, the father of spiritual children. With this the word "Israel" agrees, for it means "a prince with God." That is a most high and holy name and contains in itself the great miracle that, by the grace of God, a man prevailed, as it were, with God, so that God does what man desires. We see the same thing in the case of Christendom. Through Christ she is joined to God as a bride to her bridegroom, so that the bride has the right to, and power over, her Bridegroom's body and all his possessions; *all of this happens through faith. By faith man does what God wills; God in turn does what man wills. Thus Israel means a god-like, God-conquering man, who is a lord in God, with God, and through God, able to do all things.* . . . Israel is a strange and profound mystery.[96]

Luke 1:55 (the promise made to Abraham and his descendants) caused Luther to highlight the divine promise made to Abraham (Gen. 12:3; 22:15-18); it connects him with Christ, "the Seed of Abraham," forever "down to the Last Day." But his descendants lost that connection by trying to take the divine Law into their own hands and thus lost the divine promise, as the prophets testify. "For the prophets well understood the purpose of the Law, namely, that men should thereby know their accursed nature and learn to call upon Christ." They were put to death because of this warning.[97] But Luther distanced himself from a militant anti-Semitism and changed his polemics into a kind invitation for conversion.

Although the vast majority of them [the Jews] are hardened, yet there are always some, however few, that are converted to Christ. . . . *We ought, therefore, not to treat the Jews in so unkindly a spirit, for there are future Christians among them, and they are turning every day.*

Luther then concluded with a sense of pastoral evangelism.

If we lived Christian lives, and led them [the Jews] with kindness to Christ, there would be the proper response. Who would desire to become a Christian when he sees Christians dealing with men in so unchristian a spirit? Not so, my dear Christians. Tell them the truth in all kindness; if they will not receive it, let them go. How many

---

96. "The Magnificat, Translated and Expounded" *(Das Magnificat verdeutscht und ausgelegt),* 1521. Also published with the title "The Holy Virgin's Song of Praise" *(Lobgesang der heiligen Jungfrau).* WA 7, 597. LW 21, 351. Italics added.

97. "The Magnificat," 1521. WA 7, 600:19-21. LW 21, 354.

Christians are there who despise Christ, do not hear his Word, and are worse than the Jews or heathen! Yet we leave them in peace and even fall down at their feet and well-nigh adore them as gods.[98]

In a sermon for St. Stephen's Day (the second day of Christmas on December 26, 1521), Luther again wondered about the conversion of Jews. He agreed with Stephen's judgment that the Jews are a "stiff-necked people" (Acts 7:51), an attitude that Luther called an attempt to please God with "good works." Stephen is to be admired for his prayer of forgiveness when he was stoned to death: "Lord, do not hold this sin against them" (Acts 7:60).

> He [Stephen] goes to confession for them, does penance, as if he wanted to say, as is customary in Confession, "Dear Lord, it is a sin which no one can deny but only confess." Then he prays and sacrifices himself to do satisfaction. So we see how true love is simultaneously a great enemy and friend; there is hard punishment and sweet help, a hard shell which has a sweet fruit, bitter for the old man but very sweet for the new man.[99]

Since Luther expected the Last Day to be imminent, a conversion of Jews could be expected. But in the meantime, they should be granted the secular privilege of intermarriage, based on the views of the apostles Peter (1 Peter 3:1, talking about Christian wives converting non-Christian husbands) and Paul (1 Cor. 7:12-13, prohibiting divorce for religiously mixed couples).

> Marriage . . . is like any other worldly undertaking. Just as I may eat, drink, sleep, walk, ride with, buy from, speak to, and deal with a heathen, Jew, Turk or heretic, so I may also marry and continue in wedlock with him. Pay no attention to the precepts of those fools who forbid it. You will find plenty of Christians — and indeed the greater part of them — who are worse in their secret unbelief than any Jew, heathen, Turk, or heretic.[100]

In another sermon on 1 Peter 1:10-12 (Old Testament prophets speaking of Christ), Luther told his audience that the Old Testament is

---

98. "The Magnificat," 1521. WA 7, 600:29-30 . . . 34-35. LW 21, 355. Italics added.
99. "Church Postil" *(Kirchenpostille)* on Acts 6–7, 1522. WA 10/1, 1, 265:11–266:9.
100. "The Estate of Marriage" *(Uom Eelichen Leben)*, 1522. WA 10/2, 283:9-14. LW 45, 25.

"gospel" in the sense that it mediates Christ through the prophets since they and Moses "described in advance what the apostles preached or wrote later about Christ."[101] As a "figure" of what was to come, the Old Testament is abolished.

> Therefore, the figures are now done away with, for they have served their purpose and have accomplished and fulfilled all they had promised. Henceforth no distinction is to be made of food, clothing, place, and time. Everything is the same in Christ, to whom it was all directed. The Jews were not saved through the Old Testament, for it was not given to them to make them pious; it was given to them to foreshadow them the Christ who was to come.[102]

But any conversion must not be forced.

> My friend, if you wish to drive out heresy, you must find some way to tear it first of all from the heart and completely turn men's wills away from it. With force you will not stop it, but only strengthen it. . . . We learn it also from experience, *for even if all the Jews and heretics were forcibly burned no one ever has been or will be convinced or converted thereby.*[103]

When Luther became acquainted with Bernhardus Gibbingnensis, a Jewish Hebraist who had converted in 1519 and studied at Wittenberg University, he sent him a letter with reflections on Jewish converts. "Almost anywhere in the world," Luther began the letter, "both Christians and Jews regard the conversion of a Jew as infamous." Luther blamed Christian ignorance and rumors about Jews for such an attitude. It is well expressed in the denouncement of the way Pharisees view conversions: they travel great distances to get a single convert but "make the new convert twice as much a child of hell" as they are (Matt. 23:15). "It is as if a procuress teaches a girl prostitution and then accuses her of not being a virgin." Luther sounded quite optimistic in the final portion of the letter.

---

101. "The Catholic Epistles: Sermons on the First Epistle of St. Peter," 1522. WA 12, 275:5-6. LW 30, 19.

102. WA 12, 275:29-34. LW 30, 19-20.

103. "Temporal Authority: To What Extent It Should Be Obeyed" *(Uon weltlicher uberkeytt wie weytt man yhr gehorsam schuldig sey),* 1523. WA 11, 269:10-13 . . . 30-31. LW 45, 115. Italics added.

Now that the golden light of the gospel is rising and shines, there is hope that many Jews might convert and have their hearts carried off to Christ, just as you have been carried off to him, and also others of you who are left from the offspring of Abraham. . . . I wish that your rebirth in God and your work also become known among other Jews.[104]

Luther included a Latin copy of a treatise that discloses his most favorable attitude to the Jews.[105] The occasion for the publication was a rumor that Luther had denied the virgin birth of Jesus and believed him to be only "of the seed of Abraham," together with other siblings fathered by Joseph. Luther intended to prove from Scripture that Christ was a Jew born of a virgin.

I might perhaps also win some Jews to the Christian faith. Our fools, the popes, bishops, sophists [scholastic theologians] and monks — the crude asses' heads — have hitherto so treated the Jews that anyone who wished to become a good Christian would almost have had to become a Jew. *If I had been a Jew and had seen such dolts and blockheads govern and teach the Christian faith, I would sooner become a hog than a Christian.*[106]

Luther blamed "popishness" and "monkery" for an anti-Semitism that treats Jews like dogs, derides them, and deprives them of their property.

I hope that if one deals in a kindly way with the Jews and instructs them carefully from Holy Scripture, many of them will become genuine Christians and turn again to the faith of their fathers, the prophets and patriarchs. They will only be frightened further away from it if their Judaism is so utterly rejected that nothing is allowed to remain, and they are treated only with arrogance and scorn.[107]

---

104. Letter of June 1523. WA.BR 3, No. 629, 101.

105. "That Jesus Christ Was Born a Jew" *(Das Ihesus Christus eyn geborner jude sey)*, 1523. WA 11, 314-36. LW 45, 199-229.

106. "That Jesus Christ Was Born a Jew," 1523. WA 11, 314:23–315:1. LW 45, 200. Italics added.

107. "That Jesus Christ Was Born a Jew," 1523. WA 11, 314:23–315:1. LW 45, 200.

Luther, of course, viewed conversion as a return to the one and only Christ-centered biblical covenant. In this sense, sixteenth-century converts join "Moses the Christian" in the Old Testament.

> When we are inclined to boast of our position we should remember that *we are but Gentiles, while the Jews are of the image of Christ. We are aliens and in-laws; they are blood relatives, cousins, and brothers of our Lord.* . . . God has also demonstrated this by His acts, for to no nation among the Gentiles has He granted so high an honor as He has to the Jews. . . . *And although the gospel has been proclaimed to all the world, yet He committed the Holy Scriptures, that is, the law and the prophets, to no nation except the Jews.*[108]

Luther used three biblical texts to "prove" that Jesus was the promised Messiah.[109] (1) Genesis 49:10-12 ("the scepter shall not depart from Judah") is a prophecy that had been fulfilled in the person of Jesus who is of the tribe of Judah and the royal lineage of David. His rule began fifteen hundred years ago. (2) Daniel 9:24-27 (a numerological prediction of a new covenant) is also a prophecy pointing to the person of Jesus. Using the popular year-week interpretation, Luther calculated the resulting 490 ("seventy weeks/years" — 70 times seven) to be the period between the Persian king Cambyses (529-522 B.C.E.) and the appearance of Christ in his thirtieth year (Luke 3:23). Although these calculations were neither consistent nor precise, Luther found sufficient agreement between Scripture and history to conclude that Daniel spoke of Jesus rather than of anyone else. (3) Haggai 2:9 ("the later splendor of this house shall be greater than the former") and Zechariah 8:23 (Gentiles will join Jews) meant to Luther that there will be a "new Israel," which includes Gentiles under the lordship of Christ. Luther was amazed that Jewish interpreters of Scripture would not agree with such interpretations.

He closed his treatise with advice regarding the conversion of Jews. It should be done very gently. "Let them first be suckled with milk, and begin by recognizing this man Jesus as the true Messiah; after that they may drink wine, and learn that he is true God."[110] Instruction from

---

108. "That Jesus Christ Was Born a Jew," 1523. WA 11, 315:25-27 . . . 29-31 . . . 33-35. LW 45, 201. Italics added.
109. "That Jesus Christ Was Born a Jew," 1523. WA 11, 325:25–336:21. LW 45, 213-29.
110. "That Jesus Christ Was Born a Jew," 1523. WA 11, 336:16-19. LW 45, 229.

Scripture should replace Christian slander and other foolishness. Luther even contended that Jewish usury is the result of unfair Christian treatment, including the prohibition of labor and business.[111]

> If we really want to help them, we must be guided in our dealings with them not by papal law but by the law of Christian love. *We must receive them cordially, and permit them to trade and work with us, that they may have occasion and opportunity to associate with us, hear our Christian teaching, and witness our Christian life. If some of them should prove stiff-necked, what of it? After all, we ourselves are not all good Christians either.*[112]

During the period of territorial reform in Electoral Saxony under the tutelage of Frederick the Wise, Luther maintained his pastoral distance from anti-Jewish polemics. He told new "Lutheran" pastors and congregations to begin any approach to Jews with "love of neighbor" rather than with doctrinal assertions.

> If you should have an opportunity to encounter a Jew who is not poisoned and stiff-necked and bring him to Christ, do not immediately talk about important articles of faith, such as the belief that Christ is the Son of God. Treat him like any other man and let him know that he is a creature of God who sent him and takes care for others. But if he remained stiff-necked and did not listen, you would have to let him go in peace.[113]

In this spirit of toleration, Luther responded to a request by the Electoral Court chaplain George Spalatin on the contemporary validity of Mosaic law for non-Jews. Luther told Spalatin that it is a "civil law" like any other law in a country. "The laws of Moses were binding for the Jewish only in the country which God had chosen for them. Now they are a matter of choice. Were all the laws [of Moses] to be kept, then there is no reason why we should not also be circumcised and observe all the laws concerning ceremonies."[114]

When the Peasant Rebellion of 1524/25 and other turbulent events

---

111. "That Jesus Christ Was Born a Jew," 1523. WA 11, 336:27-29. LW 45, 229.
112. "That Jesus Christ Was Born a Jew," 1523. WA 11, 336:30-34. Italics added.
113. Sermon on February 14, 1524, on Matthew 4:1-11 (the temptation of Jesus). WA 15, 447:11-23.
114. Letter of March 14, 1524. WA.BR 3, 254. LW 49, 74.

reminded Luther of the imminent end of the world, he preached about false Jewish expectations, based on Matthew 24:15-28 (final words of Jesus on the end, especially the appearance of "false Messiahs"). Gone was the pastoral distance from anti-Semitism. The Jews were accused of the false assumption that their kingdom would last forever. They did not hear the prophecy about the destruction of Jerusalem, with all its gruesome details. In his collection of Lenten Sermons in 1525, Luther used John 8:46-59 (Jesus' dialogue with Pharisees about his identity) to tell his listeners that Christ is an enduring scandal for the Jews, who become the prototype for all spiritually blind people.[115]

> Thus the death of Christ and of all the prophets was most dreadfully avenged because they unceasingly raged against the Word of God and, in addition, persecuted and drove away the apostles, as Paul says in 1 Thessalonians 2[:14-16].[116]

In his 1525 "Lectures on Deuteronomy" 15:1 (the canceling of debt every seventh "sabbatical" year), Luther used the stipulation to reflect on Jewish usury. He recalled that Jews had been permitted to lend on interest. But such privilege was not granted by God "because of their own merit or by common law," but because God used them as "instruments of his wrath."

> Thus if you view the matter properly, *it is not the Jews themselves who are usurers, but God* who persecutes the Gentiles through the usury of the Jews. *This was sufficiently demonstrated when He, in turn, handed over the Jews, who were disobedient to Him and sinned, to the Gentiles,* not only to be burdened by usury but to be troubled by every sort of shame, a good deal more dreadfully than the Gentiles had been when He gave them over to the Jews.[117]

Israel was hoisted with its own petard, as it were!

The rise of "sectarian" views in his own camp, embodied in Dean

---

115. "Lenten Postil" *(Fastenpostille)*, 1525. WA 17/2, 236:36–237:11.

116. "A Sermon on the End of the Jewish Kingdom and the End of the World" *(Ein Sermon von des jüdischen Reichs und der Welt Ende)*, 1525. WA 15, 742-47. Luther may have read historical details of the fall of Jerusalem in 70 C.E. in the account of the Roman historian Flavius Josephus, *The Jewish War (De bello Judaico,* 77-78), Book VII, Chapters 8-9.

117. "Lectures on Deuteronomy" *(Deuteronomium Mosi cum annotationibus),* 1525. WA 14, 656. LW 9, 146. Italics added.

Carlstadt (Andreas of Bodenstein) who was banned from Electoral Saxony in 1523, and Thomas Müntzer who was executed with rebellious peasants in 1525, prompted Luther to identify them with Jewish "legalism," which tried to earn salvation through a casuistic fulfillment of the Law. So Luther preached a sermon on "How Christians Should Regard Moses."[118] Its main point: God preached two sermons, one on the Law (Decalogue) recorded in Exodus 19–20, the other one on the Gospel (Christ) at Pentecost through the Holy Spirit in Acts 2:2-4; both must be properly distinguished (not identified with each other as the "sectarians" do). But Mosaic law, with its detailed stipulations about how to live, is no longer valid after the advent of Christ.

> What God said to Moses by way of commandment is for the Jews only. But the gospel goes through the whole world in its entirety; it is offered to all creatures without exception. . . . *We read Moses for the sake of the promises about Christ, who belongs not only to the Jews but also to the Gentiles; for through Christ all the Gentiles should have the blessing, as was promised to Abraham* [Gen. 12:3].[119]

But no matter how hard Luther tried to be different in his attitude than the established church, to create a more realistic atmosphere for "Christian-Jewish relations" in the Lutheran reform movement, he ended up in total frustration about the Jewish rejection of Christ. His "Psalm of Comfort" (Ps. 109), sent in 1526 to the recently widowed Queen Mary of Hungary, is a case in point. Psalm 109:17 (on "curses") made Luther think of Matthew 27:25 ("his blood be on us and on our children"), "a curse which is still bearing down hard on them." Psalm 109:18 ("He clothed himself with cursing as his coat, may it soak into his body like water, like oil into his bones") showed Luther how hard the curse really is. "It does no good to preach to them or admonish them, to threaten them, sing to them, or speak to them." The "coat" symbolizes Jewish love for stubbornness; it has soaked into their bodies and has become part of their nature; and like "oil," it penetrates the skin.[120]

---

118. *Eyn Unterrichtung wie sich die Christen ynn Mosen sollen schicken*, 1525. WA 16, 363-93. LW 35, 161-74.

119. WA 16, 390:5-8 . . . 10-14. LW 35, 172, 173.

120. "Four Psalms of Comfort for the Queen of Hungary" *(Vier tröstliche Psalmen für die Königin zu Ungarn)*, 1526. Ps. 109. WA 19, 606:22-23. LW 14, 267. WA 19, 607:20-25. LW 14, 268.

We see this in our daily contacts with the Jews. How stiff and stubborn they are from one generation to the next! *They are incredibly venomous and spiteful in their language about Christ.* What we believe and teach about Christ they regard as sheer poison and as curse. They suppose that Christ was nothing more than a criminal who, because of His crime, was crucified with other criminals. . . . For since they believe that Jesus was a criminal, it is inevitable that they should regard us Christians as the most foolish and filthy people under the sun. . . . The oil has soaked into their bones, and they go on soaking up the water. *What a terrible judgment and illustration of divine wrath!* [121]

Luther told his audience in a sermon and his dinner guests in a "Table Talk" that he had talked with three learned rabbis about the Old Testament prophecy of the coming of Christ, Jeremiah 23:5-6 (a descendant of David will be a king called "The Lord is Our Righteousness"). The visit occurred probably in 1526.

I held up this text for them. But they could not overcome me. Finally, they said that they would only believe their Talmud which says nothing about Christ. They did not stick to the text and sought for excuses. Had they stuck to this text alone, they would have been defeated. [122]

In 1530, Luther once gave a pastor detailed instructions concerning the baptism of a young Jewish girl. Listing all the liturgical features, he closed with a warning.

Make sure that this girl does not pretend a belief in Christ. For these people are astonishing in their deceit. Saying this, I do not doubt that a remnant of Abraham will be left and will belong to Christ. But so far Jews have in various ways pretended to have our faith. So admonish her to avoid the misfortune not to deceive herself. If she is honest I wish her grace and perseverance. [123]

Luther increasingly spoke of the Christian church as "the new Israel," a designation linked to a "theology of supersession," one of the

121. WA 19, 607:32–608:4, 18-20. LW 14, 269-70. Italics added.
122. Sermon of November 25, 1526. WA 20, 569:36-37. "Table Talk" No. 5026. May 21–June 11, 1540. WA.TR 4, 620:5-8.
123. Letter to Pastor Heinrich Gnesius, July 9, 1530. WA.BR 5, 452:1-28.

popular anti-Semitic "teachings of contempt."[124] In a Preface to Ezekiel 38–39 (Gog and Magog, with the prophecy of the restoration of Israel in 39:25), Luther said that "the Jewish apostles and other Jewish disciples of Christ were true Israelites and have inherited the name 'Israel' from the whole people of Israel. That is why now holy Christendom, and all of us who believe the word of the apostles, are called 'Israel.'"[125]

In the "Lectures on Isaiah" (1527-30), Luther acknowledged that Paul spoke of a remnant of Jews that would survive through Christ (Rom. 9:29); but Isaiah predicted their destruction (Isa. 24:23, "the sun will be ashamed"). "The ruined and still living Jews will not see the brightness of the sun and the moon when Christ will reign. . . . *This prophecy expresses the destruction of the Jews.*"[126] In Isaiah 63:3 ("I have trodden the winepress alone") Luther imagined a "personification of Christ" who declares "I am the cause of the destruction of this people. I had to do it because they refused to believe."[127]

After the creation of Lutheran territories that adhered to *The Augsburg Confession* of 1530, Luther heard rumors about Jewish proselytizing. Various stories were told about the infiltration of Jews. During a dinner conversation, Luther stated his approval of the reaction to Jews in the city of Prague: it was reported that Jews could not sit next to Christians, and that they had to wear capuchin coats; if they did not wear them, they could be beaten up in public.[128]

Luther agreed with the decision of Elector John Frederick in 1536 to expel Jews from his territory. When the most famous German Jewish leader, Josel of Rosheim, asked Luther to use his influence at the Saxon court for permission to travel through Electoral Saxony, Luther declined. Although they were friends, being a Jew made a difference. Luther told his dinner guests: "Why should these rascals, who injure people in body and property and who withdraw many Christians to their

---

124. See above, pp. 10-12. Luther represents a "punitive supersessionism": the rejection of Jesus as the Jewish Messiah effects the divine condemnation, transferring the promises made to the Jews to Christians. See R. Kendall Soulen, *The God of Israel and Christian Theology* (Minneapolis: Fortress Press, 1996).

125. "Preface of Martin Luther to Ezekiel 38–39 about Gog" (*Vorrede Martin Luthers auf das 38 und 39. Kapitel Hesekiel vom Gog*), 1530. WA 30/2, 224:24.

126. "Lectures on Isaiah," 1532. WA 31/2, 136:12-24. LW 16, 192, 193. On the remnant, 14. Italics added.

127. WA 31/2, 534:27-28. LW 17, 354.

128. "Table Talk" No. 3512. December 18, 1536. WA.TR 3, 370.

superstitions, be given permission? . . . I'll write this Jew not to return."[129] In the letter, Luther was polite but firm in his anti-Jewish stance. He told his friend that being captive to anti-Christian Jewish propaganda, instead of being liberated in Christ, makes all the difference; it is a parting of the ways. "I would have liked to bring your concern [safe travel] to my gracious Lord [the Elector]. . . . But since your side abuses my services and presents things that we Christians cannot tolerate, they take away any demands I could otherwise have negotiated with princes and lords. . . . They should not be confirmed in their error through my favor and become worse." Luther then once again listed his theological grievances about Judaism, culminating in the Jewish rejection of Jesus. He closed the letter with a refusal to help his friend.

> Please accept this as a friendly advice and admonition. For the sake of the crucified Jesus, whom no one can take from me, I would have liked to do the very best for you Jews. But you would use my favor for your stubbornness. You know that. That is why others may take your letters to my gracious Lord. May God be with you.[130]

A Tragic Conclusion (1538)

In the late 1530s, Luther became increasingly convinced that Jews, besides Muslims (Turks), "papists," and unitarian (anti-Trinitarian) "radicals,"[131] were Satan's fifth column, trying to destroy the Christian foundations of the world. He probably was not influenced by rumors about assassination plots against him.[132] When the pope and the emperor advocated war against schismatic territories, and Lutheran princes responded with the formation of the military "Smalcald League" of 1537, Luther wanted the members of the League to know

129. "Table Talk" No. 3597. Between May 27 and June 18, 1537. WA.TR LW 54, 239.

130. Letter to Josel of Rosheim, June 11, 1537. WA.BR 8, 89-91.

131. "Anti-Trinitarian" radicals became well known through the Spanish physician Michael Servetus, who published a book on the errors of the Trinity in 1531. These radicals were also called "Socinians" (named after their Italian leaders, the brothers Fausto and Lelio Sozzini) and known through the Rakow Catechism of 1575. See "Servetus, Michael," in OER 4, 48-49, and "Socinianism," in OER 4, 83-87.

132. In a letter of January 23, 1535, he reported to Nicholas Amsdorf, an early disciple and good friend, that a Polish physician had been sent to Wittenberg to poison him but had been arrested before he could carry out his plan. WA.BR 3, 428:14-17.

what they might die for; he wrote his "theological testament," as it were, known as the "Smalcald Articles."[133] It centers in the Christ-centered "chief article of faith," with its message of "justification" as the spiritual wedge against "the pope, the devil, and the world."[134] In a separate publication, Luther defended the dogma of the Trinity as the cornerstone of a true monotheism weakened by Muslim and especially Jewish teachings about Jesus as one of the children of Mary, denying his divinity. "O clever people who judge God's unsearchable, eternal substance in the manner of mortal human beings — or of dogs!"[135]

Frustrated by his failure to create a cadre of Jewish converts by exegetical-theological argumentation, especially among the intelligentsia, and disappointed by the lack of Jewish response to his pastoral advances, Luther looked for *historical evidence* to "prove" his case. Like a prosecuting attorney in a court of law, he tried to show that the Jews had committed a mortal sin, as it were, by refusing to admit that they had abandoned Mosaic law with its promise of salvation in Christ. Such Jewish stiff-necked stubbornness had caused the destruction of Jerusalem in 70 c.e. and the dispersion of the Jews. *Luther interpreted these and other calamities as principal evidence of the divine punishment "prefigured" by Old Testament prophets.* He could have followed Paul's advice to live with the divine "mystery" regarding the relationship between Jews and Christians. But Luther did not. Instead, he offered his concluding argument for this divine verdict in 1538 when he heard about Jewish attempts to infiltrate Christian communities, indeed to proselytize.

Luther's anger about the news put a chill on his moderate, pastoral attitude to Jews. When he learned that some Christians had become "Sabbatarians," representing a movement committed to Jewish Sabbath observances,[136] he was ready to argue for a verdict of "guilty" at the court of history. He did so in the treatise "Against the Sabbatarians: Letter to a Good Friend" in 1538;[137] and he argued his case point by point.

133. They were added to the normative Lutheran Confessions of 1580. See BSLK 405-68; BC 295-328.
134. II, 5. BSLK 416. BC 301.
135. "The Three Symbols or Creeds of the Christian Church" *(Drei Symbola oder Bekenntnis des Glaubens Christi),* 1538. WA 50, 286:14-15. LW 34, 209.
136. See "Sabbatarianism," in OER 3, 459-60.
137. "Against the Sabbatarians: Letter to a Good Friend" *(Ein Brief D. Martin Luther. Wider die Sabbather an einen guten Freund),* 1538. WA 50, 312-37. LW 47, 65-98. The

1. The power of the rabbis has overwhelmed the Jewish people, just as the pope and his decrees dominate Christians. But historical evidence should change their minds. Luther summarized his argument from history.

> This is the argument. The Jews have been living away from Jerusalem in exile for fifteen hundred years, bereft of temple, divine service, priesthood, and kingdom. Thus their law has been lying in the ashes with Jerusalem and the entire Jewish kingdom all this time. *They cannot deny this, for it is proven clearly and emphatically by their wretched situation and experiences and by the place itself, which is even today called Jerusalem and which lies desolate and devoid of Jewry before the eyes of all the world.* However, they cannot observe Moses' law anywhere but in Jerusalem.[138]

Consequently, the Jews are in a quandary, Luther contended: on the one hand, God's promise to Abraham is still valid; on the other hand, God has not granted any fulfillment of the promise for fifteen hundred years.

> Since it is nonsense to accuse God of not keeping his promise and of having lied for fifteen hundred years, you must ask what is wrong, for God cannot lie or deceive. *They will and must reply that this is due to their sins.* As soon as these are atoned for, then God will keep his promise and send the Messiah.[139]

2. In the face of Jewish sin, God made a new promise, clearly stated in Jeremiah 31:31-40 (there will be a new covenant "with the law written on their hearts"); it is a new promise of forgiveness for their sin against the first covenant. The second covenant is no longer linked to obedience of specific laws, but is grounded in gracious forgiveness granted by faith.

> God here declares that he will make a new covenant or law, unlike Moses' covenant or law, and that he will not be prevented from doing this by the fact that they have sinned. *Indeed, precisely because*

"friend" is Count Wolfgang Schlick in Falkenau, who reported Judaizing tendencies among Christians in Moravia (now Czechoslovakia).

138. "Against the Sabbatarians," 1538. WA 50, 313:12-20. LW 47, 66. Italics added.

139. "Against the Sabbatarians," 1538. WA 50, 313:35-314:2. LW 47, 67. Italics added.

they failed to keep the first covenant, he wants to establish a new covenant, which they can keep. Their sin or their breaking of the previous covenant will not deter him. He will graciously forgive their sin and remember it no more.[140]

3. The new covenant has been implemented, but is still not yet accepted by the people of the old covenant. That is why God is punishing them with an exile in which they have no divine consolation, a "Roman exile," totally different from the exiles in Babylonia and Egypt. Luther tried to show, with reference to numerous biblical passages, how the Jews have forfeited being Jews according to the covenant made with Abraham and Moses. Then he stated the verdict.

In brief, since these fifteen hundred years of exile, of which there is no end in sight, nor can there be, do not humble the Jews or bring them to awareness, *you may with good conscience despair of them. For it is impossible that God would leave his people, if they truly were his people, without comfort and prophecy so long.*[141]

Luther concluded: *"it is evident that he [God] has forsaken them, that they can no longer be his people, and that the true Lord, the Messiah, must have come fifteen hundred years ago."*[142]

Luther's verdict, based on chronological and historical calculations, assumed that God had forsaken Israel because they rejected the promised Messiah, Christ. Once God left them alone, they were exposed to suffering without any divine comfort. This assumption, expanded into an anti-Semitic verdict, raises the question whether Luther spoke of the "hidden God" *(deus absconditus)* in contrast to the "revealed God" *(deus revelatus)* — a key element in Luther's theology. A decade earlier, Luther had made this distinction as a criterion for theological reflection, when the Humanist Erasmus of Rotterdam defended the "freedom of the human will" to accept or to reject divine grace on the basis of the "image of God" in every created human being (Gen. 1:27). Luther totally denied any such freedom in an extensive treatise.[143]

---

140. "Against the Sabbatarians," 1538. WA 50, 316:5-12. LW 47, 70. Italics added.

141. "Against the Sabbatarians," 1538. WA 50, 336:2-6. LW 47, 96. Italics added.

142. "Against the Sabbatarians," 1538. WA 50, 336:15-18. LW 47, 97. Italics added.

143. "The Bondage of the Will" *(De servo arbitrio)*, 1525. WA 18, 635. LW, 33, 60. ET of Erasmus's "Diatribe or Discourse Concerning Free Will" *(De libero arbitrio diatribe sive collatio)*, 1525. Gordon E. Rupp and Philip S. Watson, eds., *Luther and Erasmus: Free Will*

> The human will is placed between the two [God and Satan] like a beast of burden. If God rides it, it wills and goes where God wills. . . . If Satan rides it, it wills and goes where Satan wills; nor can it choose to run to either of the two riders or to seek him out, but the riders themselves contend for the possession and control of it.[144]

Consequently, the Christian theologian must concentrate on what God has revealed rather than on what is mysteriously hidden.

> We have to argue in one way about God or the will of God as preached, revealed, offered, and worshiped, and in another way about God as he is not preached, not revealed, not offered, not worshiped. *To the extent, therefore, that God hides himself and wills to be unknown to us, it is no business of ours. . . . God must therefore be left to himself in his own majesty, for in this regard we have nothing to do with him, nor has he willed that we should have anything to do with him. But we have something to do with him insofar as he is clothed and set forth in his Word, through which he offers himself.*[145]

The "Word" points to the mysterious divine dialectic of grace and judgment, God working through opposites, also disclosed in the dialectic of law and gospel, the law creating order against chaos and repentance of sin (the two "uses");[146] and the gospel promising salvation through Christ without any merits by the works of the law — thus "justification by faith alone."[147]

Although Luther would permit theological statements about the second use of the law (how it causes anxiety and penance), he would not allow any description of the painful state of penance as divine punishment through the wrath of God; this would be sheer speculation. But he offered a detailed description of a divine punishment for the unrepentant Jews: the destruction of the temple, their dispersion, and their calamities experienced through the hatred of anti-Semites. *Luther assumed to know the will of the hidden God in regard to the historical fate of the Jews.*

---

and Salvation, Library of Christian Classics 17 (Philadelphia: Westminster Press, 1969). See also Lohse, *The Theology of Martin Luther,* pp. 215-18.

144. "The Bondage of the Will." WA 18, 635:17-22. LW 33, 65-66.

145. "The Bondage of the Will." WA 18, 685:3-6, 140-46. LW 33, 139. Italics added.

146. See Lohse, *The Theology of Martin Luther,* pp. 267-73.

147. Lohse, *The Theology of Martin Luther,* pp. 258-66.

Luther was otherwise quite consistent. A student once asked him, "What did God do before the creation of the world?" Luther replied: "God was making hell for those who are inquisitive."[148] He also told students in a lecture, "To seek God outside Jesus is the devil."[149] When Luther talked later about the treatise "On the Bondage of the Will," he recalled his own personal trouble about divine punishment and likened any speculation about the mystery of God to a life-threatening accident.

> I was troubled by the thought of what God would do with me, but I repudiated such a thought and threw myself entirely on his revealed will. *We can't do any better than that. The hidden will of God can't be searched out by man.* God hides it on account of that very clever spirit, the devil, in order that he may be deceived. For he learned the revealed will from us, but God keeps the hidden will to himself. *We have enough to learn about the humanity of Christ, in whom the Father revealed himself. But we are fools who neglect the revealed Word and the will of the Father in Christ and, instead, investigate mysteries which ought only to be worshiped. As a result many break their necks.*[150]

One could surmise that Luther's constant, but fruitless, exegetical and theological attempts to prepare Jews for conversion may have made him succumb to the "rage of theologians" *(rabies theologorum),* as his friend Melanchthon dubbed unnecessary controversies.[151] But Luther's "rage" consisted of a tragic conclusion: that the Jewish rejection of Jesus as the Messiah resulted in a devastating, specific divine punishment, namely, the annihilation of religious Judaism as it was known in the world — with a temple, a body of law, and a land. Luther claimed to know that this punishment was willed by the God of Israel who also was the Father of Jesus Christ.

> Luther did not let the apostasy of later Judaism confuse the fact of the election of the ancient people of Israel and the uniqueness of their history as recorded in the Old Testament. Election found its natural conclusion in the crucifixion of Jesus. Moreover, God visibly

---

148. "Table Talk" No. 5010, 1538. WA.TR LW 54, 377.
149. "Lectures on Psalms" (Ps. 130:1), 1532-33. WA 40/3, 337:11.
150. "Table Talk" No. 5070, 1540. WA.TR 4, 641:14-18, 20–642:2. LW 54, 385. Italics added.
151. See Eric W. Gritsch, *A History of Lutheranism,* 2nd rev. ed. (Minneapolis: Fortress Press, 2010), p. 98.

confirmed the fact that Israel was no longer his nation by the destruction of Jerusalem and the expulsion of the Jews from the Holy Land. Nor did they have any promise of a return to Palestine.[152]

Luther made it clear that such divine punishment signaled the end of the "old" covenant made with Abraham. As he put it in his "final solution" of the Jewish question:

> Indeed, if God had not allowed the city of Jerusalem to be destroyed and had them driven out of their country, but had permitted them to remain there, no one could have convinced them that they are not God's people, since they would still be in possession of temple, city, and country regardless of how base, disobedient, and stubborn they were. . . . Why, even today they cannot refrain from their nonsensical, insane boasting that they are God's people, although they have been cast out, dispersed, and utterly rejected for almost fifteen hundred years. By virtue of their own merits they still hope to return there again. *But they have no such promise with which they could console themselves other than what their false imagination smuggles into Scripture.*[153]

Luther may have expected Jewish conversions to his reform movement rather than to the Roman Catholic Church (their worst enemy). But the lack of such conversions may also have convinced him that the reconciliation of Israel with the gospel was God's affair rather than the church's obligation. His hopes for his own kind of improved Jewish-Christian relations died in 1538. Jews, together with "papists" and radicals in his own camp *(Schwärmer)*, embodied the hardened hearts that God seemingly permitted as the final sign of the struggle between good and evil that would soon come to an end. Luther therefore viewed the time between the crucifixion of Jesus and his own time fifteen hundred years later as "proof" that God had forsaken the Jews; therefore, all Christians should forsake them, indeed should participate in their divine punishment (as Luther recommended later in his treatise "On the Jews and Their Lies," 1543).

In contrast to the apostle Paul, his model theologian, Luther fell

---

152. Bornkamm, *Luther and the Old Testament*, p. 77.
153. "On the Jews and Their Lies" *(Von den Jüden und ihren Lügen)*, 1543. WA 53, 447:27-31 . . . 34-448:1. LW 47, 174. Italics added.

for the temptation (which he had linked to the devil) of speculating about the "mystery" of the hidden God (Rom. 11:25).[154] Unlike Paul, he interpreted the post-Pauline time of ardent Christian anti-Semitism as a sign that Jews had separated themselves from Christians after the resurrection of Jesus. He also could have concluded that Christians had initiated the separation. In both cases the reason would be hatred — Christian, for the Jewish killing of Jesus, and Jewish, for the Christian claim of a Jewish Messiah. *Paul refused to offer any conclusions regarding the mystery of Jewish-Christian relations after the crucifixion of Jesus during the time before the Last Day; he contended that in the interim Jews and Christians should find some historical configuration to exist together without any mutual hatred.* Such a stance preserved faith in the one and only covenant between God and his people, a covenant on the way to its perfect completion at the end of time. But, after fifteen hundred years of Christian anti-Semitism, Luther felt forced to conclude that the existing hatred of the Jews revealed the hatred of God. *This conclusion is a violation of his own rule, so vehemently established and enforced against Erasmus in 1525, that to speculate about the hidden God "is no business of ours." To do so is against Luther's better judgment.*

Demonizing Attacks (1539-46)

In his final years, Luther often mused about Jews in "Table Talks," reflecting the popularity of anti-Semitism and other topics at dinner tables. He also told people in sermons that the Last Day was truly at hand because of lack of penance everywhere, exemplified by the Jews.[155] He bemoaned the destruction of Jerusalem, imagining how sad Christians would be if they experienced such a loss. But God had to do it:

154. Luther's disagreement with Paul has also been noted by Jewish scholars. See Pinchas E. Lapide, "Stimmen jüdischer Zeitgenossen zu Martin Luther," in Kremers, ed., *Die Juden und Martin Luther,* p. 184. Good insights regarding Luther's problem with Paul are offered by Brosseder, *Luthers Stellung zu den Juden,* pp. 377-79: Luther called the reference to a conversion of the Jews "dark" *(dunkel)* and abandoned it in 1543, assuming that the Jews are the "broken-off branches" (Rom. 11:17) and are rejected by God. The reason for this conclusion is his own view of the imminent end of the world, without any evidence of Jewish conversions. But this is said "in the realm of pure speculation" (p. 379).

155. Sermons on Matthew 24, 1539/40. WA 20, 230:31-33 (Brecht, *Martin Luther,* vol. 3, p. 328).

"[T]he destruction of Jerusalem was more terrible than all the plagues on earth. But it was too much that his [God's] people took his Son outside the city and crucified him."[156] When he heard that Jews slandered the Virgin Mary, he told his guests that he would advise the authorities "to chase all the Jews out of their land. . . . If I were a lord I'd take them by their throat. . . . They are wretched people. I know of no stronger argument against them than to ask them why they've been in exile so long."[157] Luther reminded his guests that the Jews prayed to God in vain; God remained silent, the worst aspect of divine wrath. "I am not surprised that God does not answer their prayers. It is wrath, a great, great, ineffable wrath."[158]

Luther resolved to end his massive anti-Jewish campaign, since it did not accomplish its objective, convincing the Jews that Jesus is the Messiah. But he could not remain silent, and in 1543 he composed his longest writing about the Jews for his correspondent Count Schlick, as a sequel to the treatise on the "Sabbatarians."[159]

> I had made up my mind to write no more either about the Jews or against them. But since I have learned that these miserable and accursed people do not cease to lure to themselves even us, that is, the Christians, I have published this little book *so that I may be found among them who opposed such poisonous activities of the Jews and who warned the Christians to be on their guard against them.*[160]

Luther also felt compelled to respond to a Jewish treatise engaging a Christian in dialogue, hoping to "destroy the basis of our faith with perverted scriptural passages" about Christ and Mary, his mother.[161] He neither wanted to quarrel with Jews nor convert them, but provide information, especially to Germans, "in order to strengthen our faith."[162] "If someone wanted to talk with Jews, it is enough to remind them of the fifteen hundred years as the people forgotten by God. Let

---

156. "Table Talk" No. 4466, April 3, 1539. WA.TR 4, 327:16.
157. "Table Talk" No. 5462, Summer or Fall, 1542. WA.TR 5, 166:30. LW 54, 426.
158. "Table Talk" No. 5544a. Winter 1542/43. WA.TR 5, 235:22.
159. "On the Jews and Their Lies," 1543. WA 53, 417-552. LW 47, 137-306.
160. "On the Jews and Their Lies," 1543. WA 53, 417:2-9. LW 47, 137. Italics added.
161. "On the Jews and Their Lies," 1543. WA 53, 417:17-18. LW 47, 137. Neither the Jewish author nor the treatise has been identified.
162. "On the Jews and Their Lies," 1543. WA 53, 417:19-21. LW 47, 140.

the Jews bite into this nut and dispute the question as long as they wish."[163]

> For such ruthless wrath of God is sufficient evidence that they assuredly have erred and gone astray. Even a child can comprehend this. For one dare not regard God as so cruel that he would punish his people so long, so terribly, so unmercifully, and in addition keep silent, comforting them neither with words nor with deeds, and fixing no time limit and no end to it. Who would have faith, hope, or love toward such a God? *Therefore, this work of wrath is proof that the Jews, surely rejected by God, are no longer his people, and neither is he any longer their God.*[164]

"On the Jews and Their Lies" was meant to be an instruction to other Christians in four parts. (1) An exposition of the "crass follies of the Jews," exhibited in their ethnic pride of having a special land, lineage, and a covenant of special laws and circumcision; but it is a self-righteousness contrary to the Word of God in the Bible and to the fundamental teaching of the Reformation, namely, salvation by faith through divine grace embodied in Christ. (2) An instruction on the correct interpretation of biblical texts, focusing on the Messiah, based on the Christ-centered exegesis of the Old Testament, as it was begun in the New Testament and continued by revered teachers in the church. Luther chose the four classic texts of Genesis 49 (Jacob's legacy), 2 Samuel 23 (the legacy of David), Haggai 2 (the future glory of the temple), and Daniel 9 (prayer for true righteousness and a prophecy about a new covenant). (3) An uncritical account of some of the grossest Jewish slander against Jesus and Mary, combined with a summary of Jewish "lies" and the worst medieval superstitions concerning the Jews. (4) Finally, Luther presented the now famous recommendations to secular and ecclesiastical authorities for the exclusion of the Jews from Christian civilization.

---

163. "On the Jews and Their Lies," 1543. WA 53, 417:19-21. LW 47, 140. Luther refers to chronological calculations he had established in a tabular outline of world history from the creation of the world to the year 1540 and revised in 1545. In these calculations, Luther assumed the date of 74 C.E. for the destruction of Jerusalem. He also followed a medieval scheme of a succession of millennia analogous to the seven days of creation. See "Reckoning Years of the World" *(Supputatio annorum mundi),* 1541. WA 53, 418:13. See also Gritsch, *Martin — God's Court Jester,* p. 100.

164. "On the Jews and Their Lies," 1543. WA 53, 418:15-22. LW 47, 138-39. Italics added.

1. Luther described Jewish ethnic pride, linked to Abraham, Jacob, and the twelve patriarchs, as foolish self-righteous boasting.

God has to endure that in their synagogues, their prayers, songs, doctrines, and their whole life, they come and stand before him and plague him grievously (if I may speak of God in such a human fashion). . . . And there is no limit about their descent and their physical birth from the fathers.[165]

Luther recounted how Jewish prophets censured their people for such pride, especially the last prophet before Christ, John the Baptist, who called the Pharisees "a brood of vipers" before God, who can raise up children of Abraham from stones (Matt. 3:7, 9). Jesus called them sons of the devil (John 8:44) who accept only a Messiah as a justification for their ethnic pride in a nobility of blood and lineage.

This is just as though a king, a prince, a lord, or a rich, handsome, smart, pious, virtuous person among us Christians were to pray thus to God: "Lord God, see what a great king and lord I am! See how rich, smart, and pious I am. . . . Be gracious to me, help me, and in view of all this save me! The other people are not as deserving, because they are not so handsome, rich, smart, pious, noble, and highborn as I am." What, do you suppose, should such a prayer merit? It would merit that thunder and lightning strike down from heaven and that sulphur and hellfire strike from below.[166]

Why not boast about being children of Adam and Eve, or being circumcised and inflicting its pain on infants, Luther asked.[167] Summarizing his previous exegetical work, Luther got angry and called the Jews "real liars and bloodhounds," who yearn to deal with Gentiles as they did at the time of Esther (chapter 9, which describes the killing of 75,000 enemies).

Oh, how fond they are of the Book of Esther, which is so beautifully attuned to their bloodthirsty, vengeful, murderous yearning and hope. *The sun has never shone on a more bloodthirsty and vengeful*

---

165. "On the Jews and Their Lies," 1543. WA 53, 419:42-43. LW 47, 140.
166. "On the Jews and Their Lies," 1543. WA 53, 422:24-32. LW 47, 143-44.
167. "On the Jews and Their Lies," 1543. WA 53, 420:3. LW 47, 148, 153. Luther learned about the physical procedure of circumcision from Anthony Margaritha, *The Whole Jewish Faith.*

people than they are who imagine that they are God's people who have been commissioned and commanded to murder and to slay the Gentiles. In fact, *the most important thing they expect of their Messiah is that he will murder and kill the entire world with their sword.* They treated us Christians in this manner at the very beginning throughout all the world. They would still like to do this if they had the power and often have made the attempt, for which they have got their snouts boxed lustily.[168]

A Messianic holocaust of Gentiles?

Luther warned his readers to expect nothing but a "den of devils" in synagogues, a crowd of blasphemers and usurers.[169] He saw the same pattern on the part of the Turks, the papists, and the radicals. They abound everywhere. They are the foxes of Samson, which are tied together tail by tail but whose heads turn away in different directions (Judg. 15:4 — three hundred foxes, with lit torches between each pair of tails, were driven into Philistine territory to destroy the harvest).

2. Luther wanted to assure his readers that, regarding the Messiah, he offered a better and surer knowledge of Scripture: "all the devils shall not deprive us of it, much less the miserable Jews."[170] Genesis 49:10, "the scepter shall not depart from Jacob," is a clear text, saying that the tribe of Judah will rule until the advent of the Messiah, when the rule will be extended to all people on earth.[171] Luther again attacked Jews for denying this, twisting and perverting the text.

> Their glosses remind me very much of an evil, stubborn shrew who clamorously contradicts her husband and insists on having the last word although she knows she is in the wrong. Thus these blinded people also suppose that it suffices to bark and to prattle against the text and its true meaning; *they are entirely indifferent to the fact that they are lying impudently.*[172]

Luther could not resist citing and refuting specific Jewish interpretations of words and phrases, despite his intention not to do so, and

---

168. "On the Jews and Their Lies," 1543. WA 53, 433:18-26. LW 47, 157. Italics added.

169. "On the Jews and Their Lies," 1543. WA 53, 446:10. 448:19. 448:28-30. LW 47, 172.

170. "On the Jews and Their Lies," 1543. WA 53, 450:17. LW 47, 178.

171. "On the Jews and Their Lies," 1543. WA 53, 450:19-22. LW 47, 179.

172. "On the Jews and Their Lies," 1543. WA 53, 450:25-30. LW 47, 178. Italics added.

comparing them to equally wrong Christian commentaries (one group was linked to the model exegete Nicholas of Lyra), calling their interpretation "humbug."[173] He recalled his encounter with "three learned Jews." They expressed their hope for better relations between Jews and Christians because Luther and other colleagues in Wittenberg read biblical texts in Hebrew. Luther disagreed with their rabbinical exegesis, which they used to deny that Jesus was the Messiah. Luther accused them of "blasphemy" and "lying."

> I took pity on them and gave them a letter of recommendation to the authorities, asking that for Christ's sake they let them freely go their way. *But later I found out that they had called Christ a tola, that is, a hanged highwayman. Therefore I do not wish to have anything more to do with any Jew.*[174]

2 Samuel 23:2-5 ("the Spirit of the Lord speaks through me. . . . Does not my house stand with the Lord?") was for Luther another irrefutable prophecy of an everlasting divine covenant linked to the House of David.

> They [the Jews] are convinced and won over, and yet refuse to admit it. They are like the devil, who knows very well that God's word is the truth and yet with deliberate malice contradicts and blasphemes it. The Jews feel distinctly that these verses are solid rock and their interpretation nothing but straw or spiderweb. But with willful and malicious resolve they will not admit this.[175]

Luther seemed to relish the image of Jews throwing opposite biblical texts at him and he dodging them, accompanied by victorious pieces of exegesis! He packs them into explosives of superstitious hatred.

> Therefore, dear Christian, be advised and do not doubt that next to the devil, you have no more bitter, venomous, and vehement foe than a real Jew who earnestly seeks to be a Jew. There may perhaps be some among them who believe what a cow or a goose believes,

---

173. "On the Jews and Their Lies," 1543. WA 53, 459:24. 460:32. LW 47, 188.

174. "On the Jews and Their Lies," 1543. WA 53, 461:28–462:5. LW 47, 192. Italics added. The exact date of the meeting is not known, but could have been close to 1540, when Luther mentioned the encounter in a "Table Talk." No. 5026. WA.TR 4, 619-20. For details see LW 47, 191, n. 63. See also above, p. 68.

175. "On the Jews and Their Lies," 1543. WA 53, 468:36–469:2. LW 47, 200.

but their lineage and circumcision infect them all. *Therefore the history books often accuse them of contaminating wells, of kidnapping and piercing children,* as for example at Trent, Weissensee, etc. They, of course, deny this. Whether it is true or not, *I do know that they do not lack the complete, full, and ready will to do such things either secretly or openly where possible.*[176]

Luther added the crime of usury as the devious Jewish method to avoid working for a living.

They do not work, and they do not earn anything from us, nor do we give or present it to them, and yet they are in possession of our money and goods and are our masters in our own country and in their exile. A thief is condemned to hang for the theft of ten florins, and if he robs anyone on the highway, he forfeits his head. *But when a Jew steals and robs ten tons of gold through his usury, he is more highly esteemed than God himself.*[177]

When Luther turned to Haggai 2(:6-7), "I will shake the heavens and the earth, and all the nations," his exegesis related the text to the conflict between the serpent and the "seed" of a woman (Gen. 3:15), presumably because of the universal conflict prophesied by Haggai. The "seed," of course, is Christ. In the context of a historical sketch leading to the destruction of the temple, Luther repeated popular anti-Semitic accusations directed against rabbis.

It is no sin for a Jew to kill a Gentile, but it is only a sin for him to kill a brother Israelite. Nor is it a sin for a Jew to break his oath to a Gentile. Likewise they say that it is rendering God a service to steal or rob from a Goy, as they in fact do through their usury.[178]

Luther wanted readers to know that such language is not unfounded slander but justified demonizing.

---

176. "On the Jews and Their Lies," 1543. WA 53, 482:8-18. LW 47, 217. Luther used the anti-Semitic hate literature about the "blood libel," claiming that Jews continued to kill Jesus by piercing consecrated hosts and killing children. See Eric W. Gritsch, *Toxic Spirituality: Four Enduring Temptations of Christian Faith* (Minneapolis: Fortress Press, 2009), pp. 14-16.

177. "On the Jews and Their Lies," 1543. WA 53, 483:3-8. LW 47, 218. Italics added.

178. "On the Jews and Their Lies," 1543. WA 53, 489:31-35. LW 47, 226-27.

Someone may think that I am saying too much. I am not saying too much, but too little; for I see their writings. They curse us Goyim. In their synagogues and in their prayers they wish us every misfortune. . . . *No pagan ever acted thus; in fact, no one acts thus except the devil himself, or whomever he possesses, as he has possessed the Jews.*[179]

Daniel 9:24 ("seventy weeks," with a vision of "everlasting righteousness") is at the top of texts used in the Jewish and Christian traditions to point to the Messiah. But Luther chided Jews for regarding Christ as a "false Messiah." "They [the Jews] stubbornly insisted on having their own Messiah in whom Gentiles should not claim a share, and they persisted in trying to exterminate this Messiah in whom both Jews and Gentiles gloried."[180] Luther repeated the worst medieval anti-Semitic lies: the life of Jews "abounds with witchcraft, conjuring signs, figures," and usury for which "they should be hanged on the gallows seven times higher than other thieves."[181] The beautiful text of Daniel 9:24 is torn apart by "these holy, circumcised ravens."[182] Luther claimed to have uncovered ten exegetical lies about the text, but conceded that any refutation of these lies would take him longer than two thousand years. The Jews and the papacy are beyond any reform.[183]

3. In this part of the treatise, Luther wanted to expose Jewish lies "against persons," Jesus, Mary, and Christians in general. Such lies are used by the devil when he cannot refute doctrine, just as the "papists" did in his, Luther's case, in saying that he was possessed by the devil, that he was a changeling, and that his mother was a whore.[184]

Luther relied on popular anti-Semitic sources, among them the notorious work of Anthony Margaritha, *The Whole Jewish Faith*, 1530. He had also read a popular anti-Semitic work of the Italian Carthusian monk Salvagus Porchetus.[185] Margaritha provided the description of Mary, "a whore, who conceived him [Jesus] in adultery with a black-

179. "On the Jews and Their Lies," 1543. WA 53, 491:5-12. LW 47, 228. Italics added.

180. "On the Jews and Their Lies," 1543. WA 53, 495:9-11. LW 47, 233.

181. "On the Jews and Their Lies," 1543. WA 53, 502:2-11. LW 47, 242.

182. "On the Jews and Their Lies," 1543. WA 53, 505:3. LW 47, 246. "Ravens" (*Raben* in German) is a wordplay on "rabbis" *(Rabinen)*.

183. "On the Jews and Their Lies," 1543. WA 52, 511:18-24. LW 47, 254.

184. "On the Jews and Their Lies," 1543. WA 52, 511:25-34. LW 47, 254.

185. "The Victory over the God-less Hebrews" *(Victoria adversus impios Henbraeos),* c. 1300. Luther may have used the Paris edition of 1520.

smith."[186] "She conceived him at an unnatural time . . . during the female's menstrual uncleanness," a violation of Jewish law (Lev. 20:18).[187] Such attacks against the holiest article of the Christian faith, God's incarnation in Christ, brought forth a punishment worse than physical suffering. Luther saw it in the fulfillment of the Mosaic prophecy in Deuteronomy 28 (a long list of afflictions) that the Jews will become mentally deranged, spiritually blind, and confused.[188]

Luther accused Jews of attacking Christians because of their reverence for "these despicable, dead persons," Christ and Mary;[189] and they want to see Christians dead.

> This gives you a clear picture of their conception of the fifth commandment ["You shall not kill"] and their observation of it. They have been blood-thirsty bloodhounds and murderers of all Christendom for more than fourteen hundred years in their intentions, and would undoubtedly prefer to be such with their deeds. *Thus they have been accused of poisoning water and of kidnapping children, of piercing them through with an awl; of hacking them into pieces, and in that way secretly cooling their wrath with the blood of Christians.*[190]

Luther agreed with the expulsion of the Jews because they held countries captive with their practices of usury. They complain, Luther declared, that they have lost their freedom. "Indeed, we hold them in captivity just as I hold my gallstone, my bloody tumor, and all the other ailments and misfortunes which I have to nurse and take care of with money and goods and all that I have."[191] But Jewish hatred of Christians justifies Christian revenge.

> So we are even at fault in not avenging all this innocent blood of our Lord and of the Christians which they have shed for three hundred years after the destruction of Jerusalem, and the blood of the children they have shed since then. . . . *We are at fault for not slaying them.*[192]

---

186. "On the Jews and Their Lies." WA 53, 514:18-19. LW 47, 257.
187. "On the Jews and Their Lies," 1543. WA 53, 516:31-32. LW 47, 260.
188. "On the Jews and Their Lies," 1543. WA 53, 518:13-15. LW 47, 262.
189. "On the Jews and Their Lies," 1543. WA 53, 519:19-23. LW 47, 264.
190. "On the Jews and Their Lies," 1543. WA 53, 520:8-14. Italics added.
191. "On the Jews and Their Lies," 1543. WA 53, 521:24-25. LW 47, 266.
192. "On the Jews and Their Lies," 1543. WA 53, 522:9-12. LW 47, 267. Italics added.

4. Finally, Luther advised secular and ecclesiastical authorities to implement a specific program against the Jews, a middle course between conversion and vengeance, labeled "sharp mercy" (scharfe Barmherzigkeit).

> Since they live among us, we dare not tolerate their conduct, now that we are aware of their lying and reviling and blaspheming. Thus we cannot extinguish the unquenchable fire of divine wrath, of which the prophets speak, nor can we convert the Jews. *With prayer and the fear of God we must practice a sharp mercy to see whether we might save at least a few from the glowing flames. We dare not avenge ourselves.* Vengeance a thousand times worse than we could wish them already has them by the throat.[193]

Luther's "advice" consists of seven actions against the Jews.

> First, to *set fire to their synagogues or schools* and to bury and cover with dirt whatever will not burn, so that no man will ever again see a stone or cinder of them. *This is to be done in honor of our Lord and of Christendom, so that God might see that we are Christians, and do not condone or knowingly tolerate such public lying, cursing, and blaspheming of His Son and of His Christians.* For whatever we tolerated in the past unknowingly — and I myself was unaware of it — will be pardoned by God. But if we, now that we are informed, were to protect and shield such a house for the Jews, existing before our very nose, in which they lie about, blaspheme, curse, vilify, and defame Christ and us, it would be the same as if we were doing all this and even worse as we very well know.[194]

Luther cited Mosaic law (Deut. 13:12-18, punishment of idolatry by fire) to support his advice.

> Second, I advise that their houses also be razed and destroyed. For they pursue in them the same aims as in their synagogues. *Instead they might be lodged under a roof or in a barn, like the gypsies.* This will bring home to them the fact that they are not masters in our country, as they boast, but that they are living in exile and in captivity, as they incessantly wail and lament about us before God.[195]

---

193. "On the Jews and Their Lies," 1543. WA 53, 522:29-38. LW 47, 268. Italics added.
194. "On the Jews and Their Lies," 1543. WA 53, 523:1-2. LW 47, 268-69. Italics added.
195. "On the Jews and Their Lies," 1543. WA 53, 523:24-29. LW 47, 269. Italics added.

Third, I advise that all their prayer books and Talmudic writings, in which such idolatry, lies, cursing, and blasphemy are taught, be taken from them.[196]

Fourth, I advise that their rabbis be forbidden to teach henceforth on pain of loss of life and limb.[197]

Fifth, I advise that safe-conduct on the highways be abolished completely for Jews. For they have no business in the countryside, since they are not lords, officials, tradesmen, or the like. Let them stay at home.[198]

Sixth, I advise that usury be prohibited to them, and that all cash and treasure of silver and gold be taken from them and put aside for safekeeping.[199]

Luther proposed that a specific sum of money should be used for sincere conversions and to maintain family life and the care for the old and feeble.

Seventh, I recommend putting a flail, an ax, a hoe, a spade, a distaff, or a spindle into the hands of young strong Jews and Jewesses and letting them earn their bread in the sweat of their brow, as was imposed on the children of Adam [Gen. 3:19]. For it is not fitting that they should let us accursed Goyim toil in the sweat of our faces while they, the holy people, idle away their time behind the stove, feasting and farting, and on top of it all, boasting blasphemously of their lordship over the Christians by means of our sweat. No, *one should toss out these lazy rogues by the seat of their pants.*[200]

"God's anger with them is so intense," Luther summarized his advice, "that gentle mercy will only tend to make them worse, while sharp mercy will reform them but little. *Therefore, in any case, away with them!*"[201] Since secular authorities often did profitable business with

---

196. "On the Jews and Their Lies," 1543. WA 53, 523:30-31. LW 47, 269.

197. "On the Jews and Their Lies," 1543. WA 53, 523:32-37. LW 47, 269.

198. "On the Jews and Their Lies," 1543. WA 53, 524:6-9. LW 47, 270.

199. "On the Jews and Their Lies," 1543. WA 53, 524:18-19. LW 47, 270.

200. "On the Jews and Their Lies," 1543. WA 53, 525:31–526:6. LW 47, 272. Italics added.

201. "On the Jews and Their Lies," 1543. WA 53, 526:14-16. LW 47, 272.

Jews, Luther invited them for better advice, but only for the purpose of getting rid of the Jews who blaspheme against Christ and his mother. "Do not grant them protection, safe conduct, or communion with us. . . . With this faithful counsel and warning, I wish to cleanse and exonerate my conscience."[202]

Luther, then, turned to the ecclesiastical authorities, especially pastors. They should support the secular authorities in their actions against Jews. If Jews are in their midst, they should inform these authorities who must enforce the law. Luther reminded pastors that they must "save our souls from the Jews, that is, from the devil and from eternal death."[203] He, then, offered his advice in "spiritual" matters, consisting of four features:

> First, *that their synagogues be burned down*, and that all who are able toss in sulphur and pitch; it would be good if someone could throw in some hellfire. That would demonstrate to God our serious resolve and be evidence to all the world that it was in ignorance that we tolerated such a house, in which the Jews have reviled God, our dear Creator and Father, and his Son most shamefully up till now, but *that we have now given them their due reward.*[204]

> Second, *that all their books* — their prayer books, their Talmudic writings, also *the entire Bible — be taken from them*, not leaving them one leaf, and that these be preserved for those who may be converted.[205]

> Third, *that they be forbidden on pain of death to praise God*, to give thanks, to pray, and to teach publicly among us and in our country.[206]

> Fourth, *that they be forbidden to utter the name of God within our hearing.* For we cannot with a good conscience listen to this or tolerate it, because their blasphemous and accursed mouth and heart call God's Son *Hebel Vorik.*[207]

---

202. "On the Jews and Their Lies," 1543. WA 53, 527:15-31. LW 47, 274.
203. "On the Jews and Their Lies," 1543. WA 53, 536:19-22. LW 47, 285.
204. "On the Jews and Their Lies," 1543. WA 53, 536:23-28. LW 47, 285. Italics added.
205. "On the Jews and Their Lies," 1543. WA 53, 536:29-33. LW 47, 285. Italics added.
206. "On the Jews and Their Lies," 1543. WA 53, 536:34-35. LW 47, 286. Italics added.
207. "On the Jews and Their Lies," 1543. WA 53, 537:6-9. LW 47, 286. *Hebel Vorik* means "316" in Hebrew and was said to be used as a curse. Luther read about it in Anthony Margaritha, *The Whole Jewish Faith.*

Luther told the pastors to end all relationships with Jews because "they say and practice far worse things secretly than the histories and others record about them."[208] If he had power over the Jews, he would "assemble their scholars and leaders and order them, *on pain of losing their tongues down to the root,*" to convince Christians of their "truth" within eight days, or, if they failed, to be punished for their lies. But Luther's proposal was rhetorical polemics, because he predicted that Jews would never be able to disprove the Christian dogma of the Trinity![209]

Luther repeated his advice to secular rulers, telling them not to be merciful to the Jews. Rulers "must be like a good physician who, when gangrene has set in, proceeds without mercy to cut, saw, and burn flesh, veins, bone, and marrow. . . . If this does not help, we must *drive them out like mad dogs.*"[210] He added a personal note: "Finally I wish to say this for myself: If God would give me no other Messiah than such as the Jews wish and hope for, I would much, much rather be a sow than a human being."[211] Then, once again, he cited and interpreted biblical passages to "prove" that Jesus was the Messiah and praised the Gentiles for accepting him. He closed his long tirade:

> My essay, I hope, will furnish a Christian (who in any case has no desire to become a Jew) with enough material not only to defend himself against the blind, venomous Jews, but also to *become the foes of the Jews' malice, lying, and cursing, and to understand not only that their belief is false but that they are surely possessed by all devils.*[212]

Such language prompted some cautious criticism from traditional Luther research: there is a "deep contradiction in his [Luther's] argumentation," namely "to defend his non-violent Christ with the power of the Christian state"; and he "violated his own exegetical principles."[213]

---

208. "On the Jews and Their Lies," 1543. WA 53, 538:30-32. LW 47, 288.

209. "On the Jews and Their Lies," 1543. WA 53, 539:31-34. 540:8-10. LW 47, 289-90.

210. "On the Jews and Their Lies," 1543. WA 53, 541:25-28 . . . 36-542:1. LW 47, 292. Italics added.

211. "On the Jews and Their Lies," 1543. WA 53, 542:5-7. LW 47, 292.

212. "On the Jews and Their Lies," 1543. WA 53, 532:29-36. LW 47, 305-6. Italics added.

213. Brecht, *Martin Luther,* vol. 3, pp. 346, 351. In his summary of Luther's stance, Brecht still defends the view that "Luther, however, was not involved . . . with later racial anti-Semitism" (p. 351); in the German text: "Luther had nothing to do with it": *(hatte an sich nichts zu tun).* But "racist" anti-Semitism is an integral part of anti-Semitism; "rac-

Some time later (in March and August 1543), Luther felt compelled to compose two more treatises against rabbinical biblical interpretations. The first dealt with the mystical "secret" Jewish rituals about the Tetragrammaton (YHWH) known as *Shem Hamphoras* ("the ineffable name" [of God]); the practice was linked to the Jewish tradition known as "Kabbalah."[214] The second interpreted again 2 Samuel 23:1-7 (the last words of David) in order to "prove" the deity of Christ.[215]

"The Shem Hamphoras and the Genealogy of Christ" consists of two parts: the refutation of the rabbinical "cabala," and proof that Jesus descended from David. Luther wanted to warn Christians of Jewish machinations against Christianity.

(1) The refutation began with a description of the "Shem Hamphoras" legend, which Luther presented in a translation of Part I, chapter 11 in the account of Porchetus:[216] Jesus appears in Israel at the time of Empress Helena, the mother of Constantine I (c. 274-337). On a piece of paper he copied the secret formula that was inscribed on a stone altar for the Ark of the Covenant. Knowing that it would give him miraculous power, he hid the paper in a self-inflicted wound that would heal immediately. That prevented his forgetting the secret formula when the two bronze dogs of the priests scared intruders into forgetting it. With the help of the formula, Jesus performed miracles, including a resurrection from the dead, attracted disciples, and many followers. Finally, Jewish wise men caught him and hanged him on a stump of cabbage; cabbages had grown in the sanctuary ever since.

Then Luther revealed the secret formula inscribed on the stone supporting the Ark of the Covenant in the temple of Jerusalem. It listed 216 letters that interpreted the miraculous crossing of the Red Sea (Exod. 14:19-21). Luther read about the meaning of the formula in Margaritha, *The Whole Jewish Faith:* One divides the 216 letters into three lines, each containing seventy-two letters. Then one takes the first let-

---

ism" cannot be segregated from anti-Semitism. See above, pp. 29-31. Moreover, Hitler and the Nazis ranked global Jewish commerce as the greater danger; Nazis also included Slavs (Polish and Russian), gypsies, and other "non-Aryan" races in their polemics.

214. See above, p. 54, n. 74. The "cabala" involved the use of esoteric methods using ciphers. "The Shem Hamphoras and the Genealogy of Christ" *(Vom Schem Hamphoras und vom Geschlecht Christi),* March 1543. WA 53, 573-648.

215. "The Last Words of David" *(Von den letzten Worten Davids),* August 1543. WA 54, 16-100. LW 15, 267-352.

216. See above, p. 84. "The Shem Hamphoras . . . ," March 1543. WA 53, 581:7-586:18.

ter in the first line and adds the last letter of the second line and the first letter of the third line; the result is a word with three letters. If one does the same with the rest of the letters, one gets seventy-two words, each consisting of three letters. Each of the group with seventy-two letters represents one of seventy-two angels. If one substitutes for each group of angel numbers another sum of numbers amounting to the same sum, the resulting letters mean an attribute or an activity of God. But instead of saying what one reads, one must simply say "My Lord" *(Adonai)*.[217] Luther commented:

> This is the unfolded name, "Shem Hamphoras." Such foolery may do well in Hebrew. . . . Now you have the "Shem Hamphoras" totally. Now you are not only a true, uncircumcised Jew but one who can do various miraculous signs just like the seducer Jesus. But how is it that they [the Jews] did not use the art and power of the "Shem Hamphoras"? After all, they had been defeated by the Romans under Emperor Vespasian [69-79] — this was the time to perform miracles, and afterwards when they were beaten and dispersed under [Emperor] Hadrian [117-38] with their Messiah Kochba. The rabbis reply: they were pious enough; they suffered misfortune and God's disgrace in strange lands; and, for a long time, they had forgotten about the power of the 72 angels.[218]

Luther taunted the Jews as liars who make big claims they cannot realize.

> Where are they now, these circumcised saints, who boast against us Christians that they alone honor the one, righteous God while the cursed "Nozrim" [adherents to Jesus of Nazareth] pray to three gods? Here they attribute so much divine power and honor to merely dead letters in the "Shem Hamphoras" that also those who are god-less and seduced against the will of God [in the Decalogue] can do God's own majestic work. Oh, they are holy children of God who make so many gods beyond the one God as there are letters in the "Shem Hamphoras," supposedly 216.[219]

Luther suggested a simple explanation of the origins of the "Shem Hamphoras" for ordinary people not interested in the mystical ciphers.

217. "The Shem Hamphoras . . . ," March 1543. WA 53, 594:24–595:4.
218. "The Shem Hamphoras . . . ," March 1543. WA 53, 598:16-17; 599:5-20.
219. "The Shem Hamphoras . . . ," March 1543. WA 53, 592:9-16.

He described the popular medieval relief depicting a "Jew sow" (*Judensau*) at the Wittenberg Town Church.[220]

> There is here in Wittenberg at our parish church a sow carved in stone. Under her there are suckling pigs and Jews. A rabbi stands behind the sow, lifting her right hind leg and drawing the tail over himself with the left hand, crouches and looks with great diligence into the Talmud, as if he wanted to read or see something sharp and special. There they [the Jews] certainly have their "Shem Hamphoras." For there were very many Jews in these lands in former times as verified by Hebrew names of towns and villages, also of burghers and peasants, still today. Perhaps a learned and honest man, who hated the filthy lies of the Jews, might have arranged to create the relief. For there is a German proverb about someone who discloses good sense without any reason: "Where did he learn it? In the arse of a sow" (*Wo hat er's gelesen? der Sau im Hintern*). One could easily interpret the word "Shem Hamphoras" that way and turn it around, namely, "peres schamha," or, as they do, have the courage and turn it into "Scham Haperes," meaning "here filth" (*hier Dreck*) — not the filth in the streets, but the filth that comes from the stomach.[221]

Luther interrupted his polemical tirade, thinking of Christians who might be offended by it. "Oh Lord God," he answered his own concern, "I am much too incompetent to mock these devils. I'd love to do it, but they are much superior in their mocking" of God, Christ, and Christians.[222]

(2) The proof of the descent of Jesus from David consisted of an interpretation of the accounts in Matthew 1(:1-16), which starts with Abraham and stresses the relation to David, and Luke 3:23-38, which begins with Adam and neglects the Jewish heritage of Jesus. Mixing his

---

220. It was made of sandstone and was attached to a wall in the beginning of the fourteenth century. The inscription "Rabbini and Shem Hamphoras," seen today, was added two hundred years after Luther's treatise on this topic. Many European cities ornamented churches with such reliefs. See Isaiah Shachar, *The Judensau: A Medieval Anti-Jewish Motif and Its History* (London: The Wartburg Institute, 1974). After 1945, a metal plaque, surrounded by stones, was placed on the ground under the sow carved in stone; its inscription mentions the Nazi holocaust of six million Jews.

221. "The Shem Hamphoras . . . ," March 1543. WA 53, 600:7-601:13.

222. "The Shem Hamphoras . . . ," March 1543. WA 53, 590:23-27; 590:33-591:1.

interpretation with a repetition of earlier anti-Semitic polemics (Jews are spies, they poison wells, steal children, commit arson, and represent the worst evils in the world),[223] Luther offered a lengthy defense of Mary's virginity, based on Isaiah 7:14 ("Behold, a virgin [young woman] shall conceive a son . . . Immanuel"). Jews and some Hebraists understood the Hebrew *alma* to mean "young woman"; Luther insisted on "virgin." But the "damned rabbis" perverted Scripture, which belongs neither to them nor to the Gentiles, but to God alone; here Luther seemed to pretend to know the divine meaning that cannot be contested.[224] He ended the treatise with frustration: "I am done with the Jews. I shall no longer write against them."[225]

But he did — in the treatise "On the Last Words of David."[226] In it Luther translated and interpreted 2 Samuel 23:1-7 to show that it is a prophecy about Christ as a descendant of David, "the anointed of the God of Jacob" (2 Sam. 23:1), through whom the Spirit of the Lord speaks (v. 2). Luther therefore viewed the passage as an Old Testament proof-text for the Trinity rather than just as a spiritual elevation of the house of David by the God of Israel. Jews, Turks, and heretics misread Scripture when they deny the Trinity.[227] Old and New Testament texts are united to "prove" the point. Luther identified three speakers in the text: the Holy Spirit (2 Sam. 23:2); the God of Israel; and the Son of God through whom everything was made (John 1:3, referring to Gen. 1:3). "His [God's] word is the person of the Son through which Word 'all things were made' (John 1:3). The same Son the Spirit by the mouth of David [speaks]. . . . Thus all three persons speak, and yet there is but one speaker, one Promise, just as there is but one God."[228]

Luther could not hold back his anger about Jews and the Jewish designation "Goyim" for "Gentiles," who are to be blessed through the seed of Abraham (Gen. 22:18).

However, they, these circumcised saints, want to see us Gentiles damned and claim they are the only seed of Abraham. But be-

223. "The Shem Hamphoras . . . ," March 1543. WA 53, 613:16-32.
224. "The Shem Hamphoras . . . ," March 1543. WA 53, 644.
225. "The Shem Hamphoras . . . ," March 1543. WA 53, 579:11-12.
226. "On the Last Words of David," 1543. WA 54, 28-54. LW 15, 267-352.
227. "On the Last Words of David," 1543. WA 54, 67:39-68:20. LW 15, 295. Luther interpreted the reference to the temple ("house" in 2 Sam. 7:11) as a reference to the Messiah.
228. "On the Last Words of David," 1543. WA 54, 36:1-9. LW 15, 276.

cause they curse the Gentiles and want to be a seed through which all the Gentiles are cursed, it is manifest that they are not Abraham's but the devil's seed. For God, whose judgment is just and certain, says that Abraham's seed will not curse the Gentiles, as they do, but that all the Gentiles will be blessed through Him. And this has now been true for approximately 1543 years, and it will be true forever.[229]

Luther concluded the treatise with a call for continued study of Hebrew by theologians of the Reformation ("our theologians"). The call shows the radical hermeneutical difference between Luther and the rabbis in their use of the "literal sense" of a text.

> May God grant that our theologians boldly apply themselves to the study of Hebrew and retrieve the Bible for us from those rascally thieves. And may they improve on my work. They must not become captive to the rabbis and their distorted grammar and false interpretation. Then we will again find and recognize our dear Lord and Savior clearly and distinctly in Scripture.[230]

While writing these final treatises, Luther also made some bitter remarks at table regarding Jewish youth, physicians, and usurers. When a dinner guest reported that the sons of a Jew from Eisleben had called the chaplain of the Mansfeld princes a "Goy," Luther said, "If I had been in his place, I would have resigned immediately and not remained in their [the princes'] service." Another guest said that Jewish physicians ingratiated themselves with noblemen and aristocrats because of their medical skills, which were superior to those of Christian physicians. Luther retorted, "The devil can do much." Still another guest asked Luther whether a private individual could punch a blaspheming Jew. He responded: "Certainly! *I would slap his face and, if I could, fling him to the ground and, in my anger, pierce him with my sword.* For since human and divine law permit to kill a highway robber, it is much more so permitted to kill a blasphemer." Regarding a comment on Christian usury being worse than Jewish usury, Luther said: "This is true. In the city of Leipzig Christian usurers are worse than Jewish ones — except that Jews teach that it is right. This we do not do; indeed, we preach against it

---

229. "On the Last Words of David," 1543. WA 54, 75:18-24. LW 15, 323.
230. "On the Last Words of David," 1543. WA 54, 100:21-23. LW 15, 352.

and loathe usury in our hearts."[231] In this "Table Talk," Luther *seemed willing to kill a Jew with his own hand!*

In a sermon on John 10:12-16 (how the good shepherd cares for all sheep) from his final collection of "Sermons for the Christian Home" *(Hauspostille)* in 1544, Luther regretted that the devil prevented the conversion of all people to the Christian faith; but he hoped that even Jews and Christians might be united in the care of the one and only shepherd. "For the only, right and true religion is to follow this shepherd and his voice."[232] In the same year, Luther reinterpreted a stanza in a Wittenberg hymnal bemoaning the betrayal of Jesus by Judas Iscariot (Matt. 26:47-50): "Oh, you poor Judas, what did you do . . . ?" His guilt is also the guilt of Christians.

> Our great sin and heavy misdeeds have crucified God's true Son indeed. We may not, like enemies, scold you, poor Judas and the Jewish crowd. For the guilt, to be sure, is ours, clear and loud.[233]

It seems that Luther threw up his theological hands, as it were, in the face of Christian apathy and Jewish opposition. Now, at the end of his life, he expressed a unity of Christian and Jewish guilt.[234] But this stance did not mark Luther's final days. In one of the last letters to his wife, Luther told her that fifty Jews still lived in his native Eisleben and about four hundred in Rissdorf [a neighboring town]. He spent the fi-

---

231. "Table Talk" No. 5576, Spring 1543. WA.TR 5, 257:11-31. Italics added.

232. WA 52, 282:34.

233. *Unsere grosse Sünde und schwere Missetat*
  Jesum, den wahren Gottessohn ans Kreuz geschlagen hat.
  Darum wird dich, armer Judas, dazu der Juden Schar
  nicht feindlich dürfen schelten, die Schuld ist unser zwar.

See WA 35, 576, and Markus Jenny, ed., *Luthers geistliche Lieder und Kirchengesänge*, Archiv zur Weimarer Ausgabe. Texte und Untersuchungen 4 (Cologne and Vienna: Böhlau, 1985), pp. 123-24, 312-13.

234. Heiko A. Oberman (*Luther: Man Between God and the Devil*, trans. Eileen Walliser-Schwarzbart [New Haven: Yale University Press, 1989], p. 297) used this stanza for his thesis that the Jews are the "mirror" in which Christians should see their anti-Semitic polemics. See also below, pp. 135-36. It could be said that Luther's revision of the hymn about the "Christ-killers" indicated a sense of his better judgment, or "his better instincts." See Denis R. Janz, *Martin Luther,* The Westminster Handbook (Louisville: Westminster/John Knox Press, 2010), p. 78. But this glimpse of guilt is drowned in the sea of Luther's anti-Semitism.

nal days of his life in Eisleben to settle a dispute between the two counts of Mansfeld.

> Count Albrecht, who owns all the area around Eisleben, has declared that the Jews who are caught on his property are outlaws. But as yet no one wants to do them any harm. . . . Today I made my opinion known in a sufficiently blunt way if anyone wishes to pay attention to it. Otherwise it might not do any good at all.[235]

During his last sermon in Eisleben, February 15, 1546 (three days before his death), he was too weak to finish preaching, but managed to read the text of an "Exhortation Against the Jews" *(Eine Vermahnung wider die Juden)*. In it, he repeated his call for their conversion, but called them "public enemies," "poisoners," and "blood-suckers." He warned his audience to refrain from participating in the "strange sin" *(fremde Sünde)* — to live with Jews — and to cling to the Lord as he, Luther, always did.

> This is what I wanted to tell you, as a final admonition not to become part of a strange sin. . . . If the Jews want to convert to us and cease to blaspheme, and from whatever else they have done, we will be happy to forgive them. *But if not, we should neither tolerate nor accept them among us.*[236]

Luther's final public words were anti-Semitic — against his better judgment.

---

235. Letter of February 7, 1546. WA.BR 11, 286-87. LW 50, 302-3. The editors of WA and of LW are uncertain whether Luther referred to a sermon or to another occasion for making his opinion known. See LW 50, 303, n. 19.

236. WA 51, 196:12-17. Italics added.

CHAPTER 3

After-Effects

Whoever writes anything against the Jews, no matter what the mo-
tives are, believes to have the right to refer triumphantly to Luther.[1]

Incentive for Mission

The immediate effect of Luther's final attacks against the Jews was min-
imal. "The danger which he [Luther] conjures up is not at all as great as
the contemporary Jews initially fear, who consider themselves threat-
ened in their very existence."[2] Only in Electoral Saxony, Luther's home
territory, were his radical steps against Jews partially implemented. Jews
could no longer travel through the territory in 1543 because of alleged
attempts to convert Christians. But in Hesse and Brandenburg, Luther's
advice, communicated in letters, was ignored.[3] "There is no trace of enthusiastic approval."[4] The renowned Jewish leader Josel von Rosheim
lobbied successfully for an imperial "privilege" granting Jews basic
rights.[5] The Swiss successor to Ulrich Zwingli, Henry Bullinger, warned
that Luther would be remembered as "a man of inexcusable passions."[6]

---

1. Reinhold Lewin, *Luthers Stellung zu den Juden. Ein Beitrag zur Geschichte der Juden*
wahrend des Reformationszeitalters, Neue Studien zur Geschichte der Theologie und
Kirche 10 (Aalen: Scientia Verlag, 1973; first ed. 1911), p. 110.
2. Lewin, *Luthers Stellung zu den Juden,* p. 100.
3. Lewin, *Luthers Stellung zu den Juden,* pp. 104-5.
4. Lewin, *Luthers Stellung zu den Juden,* pp. 97-98.
5. Lewin, *Luthers Stellung zu den Juden,* p. 101.
6. Lewin, *Luthers Stellung zu den Juden,* p. 98.

The body of normative Lutheran teachings, generated between 1529 and 1580, has only one reference to the Jews as the prime example of divine punishment for "contempt for his [God's] Word in a nation or people . . . as can be seen with the Jews."[7] Thus, Lutheran pastors, who are bound to adhere to the teachings of the Lutheran Confessions, were not instructed to be anti-Semitic. On the other hand, Luther's rejection of Muslims is affirmed in *The Augsburg Confession* of 1530 and its defense, *Apology*, in 1531, both drafted by Philip Melanchthon.[8] He may have been influenced by the dangerous though unsuccessful Turkish siege of Vienna in 1529. Luther's famous hymn, "Lord, Keep Us Steadfast in Your Word" (1541), rhymes with "Curb the murder by Pope and Turk," the "double Antichrist." After the Lutheran defeat in the Smalcald War of 1548, "Satan" was substituted for "Pope and Turk"; today it reads "Curb those who by deceit and sword."[9] Moreover, the medieval link of Christ's passion to the Jews as "murderers of Christ" is absent in Lutheran hymnody. In seventeenth-century Lutheran hymns, Muslims are viewed as bound by the devil; Jews are seen as spiritually blind. The best-selling book of John Arndt, *Four Books of Christianity* (1605-10), contains no anti-Jewish references, and in another popular publication, *Little Garden of Paradise (Paradiesgärtlein)*, Arndt offers prayers against the Turks as blaspheming enemies of Christendom.[10] Lutheran pastors, who are bound to adhere to the Lutheran Confessions, learned to reject Muslims rather than Jews as enemies of Christ.

The first Luther biographer, John Matthesius (1504-1585), a frequent dinner guest of Luther and pastor of a Saxon congregation of miners, had nothing critical to say about Luther. He depicted the re-

7. "Formula of Concord" (Solid Declaration), XI:58 (on divine election). BSLK 1080. BC 650. But the short version of the "Formula" (Epitome) omitted the reference.

8. In "The Augsburg Confession" of 1530, I:5 (on God). BSLK 51. BC 36. "Apology of the Augsburg Confession," 1531, XV:18 (on "human traditions") refers to Mohammed as "Antichrist" together with the papacy. BSLK 300. BC 225.

9. Luther called it "a song for children *(Kinderlied)* to be sung against the two arch-enemies of Christ and his holy church, the pope and the Turks." See Johannes Wallmann, "The Reception of Luther's Writings on the Jews from the Reformation to the End of the 19th Century," in Harold Ditmanson, ed., *Stepping-Stones to Further Jewish-Lutheran Relations* (Minneapolis: Augsburg Fortress, 1990), pp. 124-25. See also Rudolf Mau, "Luthers Stellung zu den Türken," in Helmar Junghans, ed., *Leben und Werk Martin Luthers von 1526-1546*, Festgabe zu seinem Geburtstag, 2 vols. (Göttingen: Vandenhoeck & Ruprecht, 1983), vol. 1, pp. 647-62; vol. 2, pp. 956-66.

10. Wallmann, "The Reception of Luther's Writings on the Jews," p. 125, n. 20.

former's life in seventeen sermons between 1562 and 1564, later published as *Luther's Life in Sermons (Luthers Leben in Predigten)*.[11] The fourteenth sermon deals with Luther's attitude to the Jews. He viewed the writings as attempts to convert the Jews who, according to the witness of the Old Testament, are stubborn and lie about Christianity. Matthesius reminded his listeners that this "old" and "fragile" people who, like Luther, suffered and fought the devil, should be honored in their wisdom; God will judge them in the end.

But in the 1570s Luther's radical anti-Semitism was revived. In 1570 the Saxon Lutheran pastor Georg Nigrinus published a work that recommended Luther's radical "suggestions" for dealing with Jews, *Enemy Jew,* subtitled: "Concerning the Noble Fruits of the Talmudic Jews who now reside in Germany, a Serious Well-Grounded Writing that Shows Briefly that they are the Greatest Blasphemers and Despisers of our Lord Jesus Christ, in Addition Being Committed and Irreconcilable Enemies of the Christians. On the Other Hand, they are Friends and Relatives of the Turks. . . . That is why they should not be Tolerated by any Christian Government, or be Treated According to the Way God Himself has Established Secular and Spiritual Law."[12] In 1577, the Leipzig professor of theology and coauthor of the Lutheran "Formula of Concord" (1577), Nicholas Selnecker, followed with an anthology of Luther's works on the Jews, including a reprinting of three of his final publications. It is interesting to note that Selnecker published these three treatises because "Luther's works against the Jews have up to now been suppressed, and that it is now necessary to make them available to the people again."[13] The

11. Johannes Mathesius, *D. Martin Luthers Leben. In siebzehn Predigten dargestellt* (Berlin: Evangelischer Buchverlag, 1885). The sermons are also in vol. 3 of Matthesius' *Ausgewählte Werke,* ed. Georg Loesche (Prague, 1906), pp. 340-69. See also Johannes Brosseder, *Luthers Stellung zu den Juden* (Munich: Hüber, 1972), pp. 44-46. I am relying on his massive collection of about 105 ways of "reception" and "interpretation" between 1564 and 1970.

12. Wallmann, "The Reception of Luther's Writings on the Jews," p. 125, n. 21. *Jüden Feind. Von den Edelen Früchten der Thalmudischen Juden/so jetziger Zeir in Deutschland wohnen/eine ernst/wohlgegründete Schrift — Darin kurtzlich angezeiget wird/Das sie die gröste Lesterer und Verechter unsers Herrn Jesus Christi/Dazu abgesagte und unversünliche Feinde der Christian sind. Dargegen Freund und Verwande der Türcken . . . Derhalben sie billig von einer jeden Christlichen Oberkeit nicht geduldet werden solten/oder dermassen gehalten/wie in Gott selbs/die weltlichen und Geistliche Recht auferleget.*

13. Wallmann, "The Reception of Luther's Writings on the Jews," p. 125.

three writings are "On the Jews and Their Lies," "The Shem Hamphoras of the Jews and the Genealogy of Christ," and "Against the Sabbatarians," "By Dr. Martin Luther. About the Daily Blasphemies of the Jews Against our Lord Jesus Christ, Against our Dear Government, and Against all Christians. Now all this is Communicated to New, Pious, True Christians."[14]

Nigrinus called on the political authorities in Hesse to banish Jews from the territory. He (and also Selnecker) viewed them as secret allies of the Turks. Luther's measures should be implemented, Nigrinus contended, and, if they are ineffective, the Jews should be driven out. Selnecker addressed the businessmen in large cities and marketing centers. They should stop all contacts with the Jews. Selnecker also wanted to add the Jews to the list of those groups that had been condemned in the "Formula of Concord" (published in the same year).[15] In 1595, another edition of Luther's treatise "On the Jews and Their Lies" is said to have been published in Dortmund, but was confiscated by the Emperor Rudolf II when Jews objected. A local history of the Jews in Frankfurt am Main mentioned the title of the publication: "Dr. Martin Luther's Instruction about the Lies of the Jews Against the Person of our Lord Jesus Christ" *(D. Martini Luther Christlicher Unterricht von der Jüden Lügen wider die Person unseres Herrn Jesu Christi)*.[16] In 1613 and 1617, Selnecker's lead was followed in the publication of Luther's three late treatises in Frankfurt am Main. The 1613 publication was titled *Treatise on the Jews and Their Lies . . . Once printed in Wittenberg but now again for the Faithful Memory of all Christian Governments that have Jews Living in their Realm and Should Banish them.*[17] The

14. Wallmann, "The Reception of Luther's Writings on the Jews," p. 125. *Von den Jüden und ihren Lügen. Vom Schem Hamphoras der Juden/und vom Geschlecht Christi. Wider die Sabbather/under der Jüden Lügen und Betrug. Durch D. Martin Luther. Item/Von den teglichen Gotteslesterungen der Jüden wider unsern HERRN Jhesum Christum/wider unsere liebe Obrigkeit/und wider alle Christen. Alles jetzt auff ein newes fromen rechten Christen . . . mitgeteilet.*

15. In the Preface to his edition of Luther's treatises. See Wallmann, "The Reception of Luther's Writings on the Jews," p. 126. Wallmann conjectures that Selnecker may have added the only reference to the Jews as enemies of Christ in the "Formula of Concord" (p. 126).

16. Wallmann, "The Reception of Luther's Writings on the Jews," p. 126.

17. *Tractat von den Jüden und ihren Lügen . . . Zu, andernmal zu Wittenberg gedruckt: Jetzo aber widerumb auff erhalter guthertziger frommer Christen auffs neuere übersehen/und zu treuherziger Christlicher Erinnerung aller und jeglicher Obrigkeit/so Jüden unter sich wohnen haben/die abzuschaffen.*

1617 publication had the title *Treatise on the Jews and Their Lies,* with the subtitle *Three Christian Treatises, Well Grounded in the Word of God (Drey Christliche/in Gottes Wort wolgegründete Tractat).*[18] Both editions appeared at the time when Jews had been banned from Frankfurt and Worms, "the single large-scale expulsion of Jews from Lutheran cities in Germany known to have occurred before the 20th century."[19]

There were no reprints of these treatises before the twentieth century, although Luther's "suggestions" of 1543 were kept alive in German anti-Semitism. Converted Jews advocated this anti-Semitism and re-published its most scandalous source, the work of the convert Antonius Margaritha *The Whole Jewish Faith* (1530), in 1544, 1561, 1686, and 1705. Other converts published their anti-Semitism with such titles as "Scourge of the Jews," "Mirror of the Jews," and "Cast-Off Jewish Snakeskin." So the medieval propaganda against the Jews continued. But only one of the authors, Christian Gerson, a Lutheran pastor in Saxony, referred to Luther, albeit to the moderate treatise of 1523, "That Jesus Christ Was Born a Jew." He tried to refute the Talmud in *The Noblest Content of the Talmud and Its Refutation (Der Jüden Talmud Fürnembster innhalt/und Widerlegung,* 1607). The work became popular and appeared in five editions until 1689. In a "Dedicatory Letter" *(Epistola Dedicatoria),* he cited Luther's proposal to treat Jews well so that they are not compelled to become usurers; Gerson was well respected among contemporary Lutherans.[20]

This tolerant attitude, based on Luther's treatise of 1523, prevailed for a while. In 1611, the magistrate of the city of Hamburg requested an "opinion" *(Gutachten)* from the Lutheran theological faculties in Jena and Frankfurt am Main whether or not Jewish refugees from Portugal could reside in the city. The theological faculties approved such residence, citing long passages from Luther's 1523 treatise, but adding certain conditions: no public worship, and restrictions of certain civil rights.[21] The toleration of Jews created a lengthy discussion among Lutherans. The renowned theologian John Gerhard summarized and refined the discussion in his magnum opus of 1619, *Loci Theologici:* Jews should be compelled to attend Christian worship services; they should

18. Wallmann, "The Reception of Luther's Writings on the Jews," p. 126.
19. Wallmann, "The Reception of Luther's Writings on the Jews," p. 126.
20. Wallmann, "The Reception of Luther's Writings on the Jews," p. 127.
21. Wallmann, "The Reception of Luther's Writings on the Jews," pp. 128-29.

not be allowed to have books in Hebrew (one of Luther's stipulations of 1543 cited by Gerhard).[22]

In 1644, a popular work on the Jews by Pastor Johannes Müller of Hamburg used Luther's treatise "On the Jews and Their Lies" as a basis for some toleration: *Judaism or Jewry. An Extensive Report about the Unbelief of the Jewish People, their Blindness and Stubbornness. For the Fortification of our Christian Faith, Thwarting of Jewish Blasphemy. Also a Necessary Instruction of Christians who deal daily with Jews.*[23] But Müller rejected Luther's demand for the burning of Jewish books, and he had a literary dialogue with a rabbi.[24] The limited toleration enabled some Jewish families to become accepted, successful merchants in Germany.[25]

The least tolerant attitude came from the pen of a Calvinist scholar, Johann Andreas Eisenmenger, a native of the Palatinate, who spent his entire life attacking Jews and their literature — a "monomaniacal anti-Jew" whose book *Judaism Unmasked* (1711) fed radical anti-Semitism well into the twentieth century. The subtitle discloses the author's intention: *A Thorough and True Report How the Obdurate Jews Slander and Dishonor most Horribly the Holy Trinity, Despise the Holy Mother of Christ, Scoff at the New Testament, and do their utmost to Reject and to Curse all of Christendom. All this Becomes Evident when one Reads with great Effort their many Books.* Eisenmenger never mentioned Luther even though his hatred of the Jews echoed the old Luther. But he supplanted Luther, whose radical anti-Semitic writings were ignored until the twentieth century.[26]

22. Wallmann, "The Reception of Luther's Writings on the Jews," pp. 129-30.

23. *Judaismus oder Judenthumb. Das ist ausführlicher Bericht von des jüdischen Volkes Unglauben/Blindheit und Verstockung . . . Zur befestigung unseres Christlichen Glaubens/Hintertreibung der Jüdischen Lästerung — auch notwendigen Unterricht derer Christen — die täglich mit Jüden umgehen* (Wallmann, "The Reception of Luther's Writings on the Jews," p. 130).

24. Wallmann, "The Reception of Luther's Writings on the Jews," p. 141, n. 50.

25. See the seventeenth-century memoir of the wife of a Jewish merchant, Glückel von Hameln, *Denkwürdigkeiten der Glückel von Hameln* (Darmstadt, 1979; reprint of the 4th ed. of 1923). Cited in Wallmann, "The Reception of Luther's Writings on the Jews," p. 130.

26. Wallmann, "The Reception of Luther's Writings on the Jews," pp. 127-28. *Entdecktes Judenthum/Oder Gründlicher und Wahrhafter Bericht/Welchergestalt Die verstoeckte Juden die Hochheilige Drey-Einigkei erschreckender Weise lästern und verunehren/die Heil. Mutter Christi verschmähen/das Neue Testament spöttisch durchziehen/und die gantze Christenheir auff das äusserste verachten und verfluchen . . . Alles aus ihren eigenen/und zwar sehr vielen mit grosser Mühe durchlesenen Bücher. . . .* This work of 2000 pages was published again in Dresden in 1893.

Lutheran interpreters of Luther, however, continued to exhibit a tolerant attitude, mixed with mild criticism and hope for Jewish conversions. The Jena professor Johann Walch, known for his massive edition of Luther's works,[27] declared that Luther "saved the truth of the Gospel on the one side, and refuted the slander and lies of the Jews on the other side."[28] He also noted two different attitudes in Luther between 1523 and 1543: "[I]n the beginning, he [Luther] hoped for the conversion of the Jews, afterwards he had no trouble to reject such a hope as unwarranted."[29] But Walch also criticized Luther.

> It cannot be denied that there [in his outbursts] too, Luther was human and had his weaknesses. . . . He advised to destroy their homes and synagogues, to take their Bibles from them, and to prohibit them to engage in business: to drive them from the land. Here he [Luther] showed such zeal that he went beyond bounds and overdid it.[30]

Eighteenth-century Pietism either ignored or criticized Luther's anti-Semitism, and radical Pietists were committed to the conversion of Jews. The founder of Pietism, Philip Jacob Spener (1635-1705), had read all of Luther's works, but ignored Luther's massive anti-Jewish statements. A sermon preached in Frankfurt am Main in 1682 stressed the virtues of the Jewish people as the most noble of all people. Spener used Luther to support this judgment.

> And just as our dear Luther thought it right that we should love all Jews for the sake of the one Jew, Jesus, in the same way we are to hold their whole race in high esteem for the sake of this most noble of the Jews: Jesus.[31]

The leader of eighteenth-century Pietism, Count Nicholas of Zinzendorf (1700-1760), supported his respect for the Jews with a reference to Luther: "Jesus was a Jew, and for that reason, one should love all

---

27. *Martin Luthers sämmtliche Schriften,* 25 vols., 2nd ed. (St. Louis: J. J. Gebauer, 1880-1919; 1st ed. 1747). See also Brosseder, *Luthers Stellung zu den Juden,* pp. 46-48.

28. Brosseder, *Luthers Stellung zu den Juden,* p. 46.

29. Brosseder, *Luthers Stellung zu den Juden,* p. 48.

30. Brosseder, *Luthers Stellung zu den Juden,* p. 47.

31. Quoted in Wallmann, "The Reception of Luther's Writings on the Jews," p. 131.

MARTIN LUTHER'S ANTI-SEMITISM

Jews, as Luther writes to the Jew, Rosel of Rosheim."[32] The source for such a pro-Jewish Luther is his treatise "That Christ Was Born a Jew" (1523). It is quoted in detail by the radical Pietist Gottfried Arnold (1666-1714), the author of the famous *Impartial History of the Church and Its Heretics (Unparteiische Kirchen- und Ketzerhistorie*, 1700). Arnold criticized Luther for revoking his positive stance of 1523.[33]

This image of a pro-Jewish Luther changed radically during the early age of the European Enlightenment in the eighteenth century. Now the old, radical anti-Semitic Luther is revived. The Hamburg Pastor Erdmann Neumeister outdid everyone since the time of Luther in his hatred of Jews; he repeated all the medieval accusations, including the charge of the ritual murder of Christian children. His view became popular when it was used in 1735 in the entry "Jews" *(Juden)* in the *Comprehensive Universal Encyclopedia (Grosses vollständiges Universallexikon)*, edited by Johann Heinrich Zedler. "The eleven pages on the Jews in the fourteenth volume of 1735 are unique in their own way. They read like an inflammatory sermon, echoing the propaganda for a crusade by medieval, religious zealots."[34] Neumeister and the encyclopedia did refer to Eisenmenger, but not to Luther.

A pro-Jewish attitude prevailed during the age of Enlightenment. Its two most important German Lutheran theologians at the renowned University of Halle, the center of Pietism, S. Jacob Baumgarten (1707-1757) and Salomo Semler (1725-1791), rejected any anti-Jewish tendencies. Baumgarten did so in a "Theological Opinion on the Conscientious Toleration of the Jews and Their Worship Among the Christians" *(Theologische Bedenken von gewissenhafter Duldung der Juden und ihres Gottesdienstes unter den Christen*, 1745). He even admonished Christians to recall their own persecution and "to actively express their disgust for the acts of violence against the Jews which had been committed by Christians to their gross dishonor."[35] Semler was even more critical of anti-Semitism. In his "Answer to the Fragments of an Unknown" *(Beantwortung der Fragmente eines Ungenannten*, 1779),[36] he wrote:

32. Quoted in Wallmann, "The Reception of Luther's Writings on the Jews," p. 131.
33. Wallmann, "The Reception of Luther's Writings on the Jews," p. 131.
34. Quoted in Wallmann, "The Reception of Luther's Writings on the Jews," p. 141, n. 59, from Barbara Suchy, *Lexikographie und Juden im 18. Jahrhundert* (Cologne and Vienna, 1979), p. 239. Much of the entry consists of quotations from Neumeister.
35. Wallmann, "The Reception of Luther's Writings on the Jews," p. 132.
36. The publication was also known as "The Wolfenbüttel Fragments" (the name

> The scorning of the Jews . . . is truly inappropriate for a dignified hu-
> manitarian. . . . Unfortunately the Christians have always inflicted
> great trouble, misery, and oppression on this nation, to whom we
> owe so much. . . . For many centuries papal and imperial orders were
> needed to somewhat impede and restrain the foolish human zeal, the
> spirit, the oppression and cruel persecution by the Christians. The
> Jews were much better off under the Romans, Greeks, and Moslems
> than was usually the case under the Christians.[37]

Both Baumgarten and Semler never mention Luther when dealing with
Jews. Baumgarten's well-known *History of Religious Parties (Geschichte der
Religionsparteien),* edited by Semler in 1766, contains a wealth of pri-
mary and secondary sources on Judaism — again, no reference to Luther's writings. "From the early 18th century almost all traces of a further influence of Luther in this area disappeared. Whoever writes
about Jews no longer mentions Luther's writings on them."[38] None of
the famous philosophers of German Idealism in the eighteenth century did: Immanuel Kant, Georg Friedrich Hegel, Friedrich Wilhelm
von Schelling, and Immanuel Hermann von Fichte. When Fichte
made anti-Semitic comments in 1793, critics called him "Eisenmenger
the second" because Eisenmenger had outdone Luther in his hatred
of Jews.[39] Johann Georg Hamann (1730-1788), a philosopher of Roman-
ticism, who attacked Enlightenment rationalism and was an eager
student of Luther, criticized any form of diminishing Judaism: the
German Jewish philosopher Moses Mendelsohn, for his attempt to
merge Jewish religion with Enlightenment reason; and Immanuel
Kant, who had expressed his dislike of Lessing's hero Nathan.[40] The

---

of a Saxon town with the famous library of the Duke of Herzog), published by the German dramatist Gotthold E. Lessing (1729-1781), whose popular play "Nathan the Wise"
(*Nathan der Weise,* 1780) portrayed total religious toleration. A controversy was begun by
the "unknown" author Hermann S. Reimarus (1694-1768), a "deist" and rationalist who
argued, on the basis of his biblical studies ("fragments"), that there should only be "a religion of pure reason" since the historicity of Jesus cannot be proven. His position
prompted the famous "quest for the historical Jesus" in subsequent generations of his-
torians and theologians.

37. Quoted in Wallmann, "The Reception of Luther's Writings on the Jews,"
p. 132.
38. Wallmann, "The Reception of Luther's Writings on the Jews," p. 133.
39. Wallmann, "The Reception of Luther's Writings on the Jews," p. 133.
40. Wallmann, "The Reception of Luther's Writings on the Jews," p. 133.

philosopher and Lutheran cleric Johann Gottfried Herder (1744-1803), a powerful preacher, made one comment on Luther's complaint about Jewish refusal to convert: Luther was "too harsh," in the manner of his time.[41]

The revival of anti-Jewish sentiments in the nineteenth century was fed by the fanatical anti-Semite Andreas Eisenmenger, not by Luther. An otherwise unknown author in Berlin, Carl Wilhelm Grattenauer, published a "warning" about the Jews: *Against the Jews: A Word of Warning to All Our Christian Fellow Citizens* (*Wider die Juden: Ein Wort der Warnung al alle unsere christliche Mitbürger,* 1803). His anti-Semitic source is the French philosopher Voltaire (the pen name of François-Marie Aruet, 1694-1778), "the last who knew and described the Jews in Berlin from this perspective."[42] The German political philosopher Jacob Heinrich Fries (1773-1843) at the University of Jena wrote about the Jewish threat to Germany: *On the Danger That Arises to the Prosperity and Character of the German Nation through the Jews* (*Über die Gefährdung des Wohlstands und Charakters der Deutschen durch die Juden,* 1816). At the Wartburg (castle) Festival of German students at the 300th anniversary of Luther's *Ninety-Five Theses* he participated in the burning of Jewish books, with the shout, "Woe to the Jews!" But no one mentioned Luther's anti-Jewish writings. A Jewish critic of the event, Saul Ascher, complained that Luther's name had been used in the invitations to the event — a touchy sentiment in the face of an event remembering Luther![43] The well-known German patriot, poet, and opponent of the Jews, Ernst Moritz Arndt (1769-1860), was steeped in Luther's writings. But his study notes on the Walch edition jump over the volumes containing Luther's writings against Turks and Jews.[44] It is astonishing that the icon of German historiography, Leopold von Ranke, wrote the classic work *German History in the Age of the Reformation* (1839-47) without saying anything about Luther's attitude to the Jews when dealing with their persecution!

It seems that "the ban of oblivion"[45] on Luther's late anti-Jewish writings was not lifted until the publication of volume 32 of the

41. Wallmann, "The Reception of Luther's Writings on the Jews," p. 142, n. 68.
42. Quoted in Wallmann, "The Reception of Luther's Writings on the Jews," p. 142, n. 69.
43. Wallmann, "The Reception of Luther's Writings on the Jews," p. 142, n. 71.
44. Wallmann, "The Reception of Luther's Writings on the Jews," pp. 133-34.
45. Wallmann, "The Reception of Luther's Writings on the Jews," p. 134.

Erlangen Edition in 1832.[46] Soon thereafter, a publication appeared in Leipzig in 1838, authored by a Ludwig Fischer and titled "Dr. Martin Luther. On the Jews and their Lies. A Crystallized Excerpt from his writings on the Delusion, Misery, Conversion, and Future of the Jews. A Contribution to the Character of this people."[47] The title is misleading because Fischer cited only passages in which Luther opposes the glorification of reason. "In our days of tolerance and emancipation," Fischer wrote at the beginning of his study, "we cannot adopt the fanaticism of Luther."[48] Fischer opposed the cultural influence of Jews in the movement of nationalist intellectuals, "Young Germany" *(Jungdeutschland),* especially the popular poet Heinrich Heine (1797-1856), even though he had converted to Christianity. An anonymous Jewish author responded in the "Common Newspaper of Judaism" *(Allgemeine Zeitung des Judentums),* contending that Luther still remains "the great genius" who deserves admiration, but without any reference to his dealings with the Jews.[49] Another Jewish author, D. Honigmann, wrote an essay in 1845, "The Reformation and the Jews," which is no longer extant.[50]

The German Lutheran churchman Ernst Wilhelm Hengstenberg (1802-1869), founder of the influential church paper *Evangelische lutherische Kirchenzeitung,* published a series on the Jews and the church; they appeared in book form, *The Victims of Holy Scripture* (*Die Opfer der Heiligen Schrift,* Berlin 1859).[51] Hengstenberg was motivated by reports from America that Lutheran synods had referred to Luther in their abandonment of hope for the conversion of the Jews in the final millennium of world history. He called attention to Luther's 1523 treatise "That Jesus Christ Was Born a Jew," which disclosed a "spirit of heartfelt love for the Jews." The old Luther is criticized for his radical treatises.

---

46. This volume contains the late writings against the Jews. See *Dr. Martin Luthers sämmtliche Werke,* 65 vols. (Erlangen: Heyder & Zimmer, 1857).

47. *Dr. Martin Luther. Von den Jüden und ihren Lügen. Ein crystallisierter Auszug aus dessen Schriften über der Juden Verblendung, Jammer, Bekehrung und Zukunft. Ein Beitrag zur Charakteristik dieses Volkes* (Leipzig, 1838). See Wallmann, "The Reception of Luther's Writings on the Jews," p. 134.

48. Quoted in Wallmann, "The Reception of Luther's Writings on the Jews," p. 143, n. 77.

49. Wallmann, "The Reception of Luther's Writings on the Jews," p. 143, n. 77.

50. See Brosseder, *Luthers Stellung zu den Juden,* pp. 41-42.

51. Wallmann, "The Reception of Luther's Writings on the Jews," p. 134 (with excerpts).

The attitude toward the Jews which Luther had late in his life is certainly very appropriate to make clear the difference between him and the apostles and to show how dubious it would be to follow such a master wholeheartedly without examining the Scriptures, a mistake the Lutheran church has never made.[52]

The spirit of anti-Semitism was revived by Adolf Stoecker (1835-1909), who founded the Christian-Socialist Labor Party in 1878 in order to stem the tide of Marxism. But his anti-Semitism was neither religious nor racist but social-political. He rejected the "unbridled capitalism" embodied in Judaism, threatening the German Christian culture. He never referred to Luther's anti-Jewish writings; Luther was to him a great German reformer in line with Otto von Bismarck (1815-1898).[53] But he advocated a mission to the Jews in order to integrate them into society and to defuse their materialism.

Leading German Lutheran biographies of Luther continued the historical trajectory of focusing on the friendly, younger Luther of the 1520s and the angry older Luther of the 1540s. The Erlangen author Theodor Kolde depicted Luther as conditioned by time and culture. "He was unable to rise above his time, as in regards to other issues, for example, the belief in witches and demons. For what he said was the common opinion of Protestants and Catholics."[54] The massive Lutheran biography by Julius Köstlin and Gustav Kawerau repeats the notions of hope and disappointment of the young and old Luther regarding the mission to the Jews. He wrote his final anti-Jewish tracts with "inner agitation" *(Erregung)* and "energy" *(Energie)*.[55]

The popular *Encyclopedia for Protestant Theology and Church (Enzyklopädie für protestantische Theologie und Kirche,* 1880) lists entries on "Luther and the Jews" *(Luther und die Juden)* and "Missions among the Jews" *(Missionen unter Juden),* lifting up Luther's friendly attitude of 1523 and regretting his "merciless advice."[56] Roman Catholic treatments of

52. Quoted in Wallmann, "The Reception of Luther's Writings on the Jews," p. 135. On Lutheran millennialism in the United States, see Eric W. Gritsch, *A History of Lutheranism,* 2nd rev. ed. (Minneapolis: Fortress Press, 2010).

53. See Brosseder, *Luthers Stellung zu den Juden,* p. 74, n. 16.

54. Theodor Kolde, *Martin Luther. Eine Biographie,* 2 vols. (Gotha, 1889), vol. 2, p. 533. See also Brosseder, *Luthers Stellung zu den Juden,* p. 67.

55. Quoted in Brosseder, *Luthers Stellung zu den Juden,* p. 78.

56. Julius Köstlin and Gustav Kawerau, *Martin Luther. Sein Leben und seine Schriften,*

Luther's attitude to the Jews appear in the context of harsh polemics, exemplified by Ignaz Döllinger who accused Luther of trying to start a "war of extermination" against the Jews in Germany.[57] The most radical critic of Luther, Heinrich Denifle, only mentioned the bawdy language in the treatise on the Schem Hamphoras.[58] Jewish views pointed to Luther's "Christian" Old Testament as the key issue of his anti-Semitism.[59]

The critical reception of Luther's anti-Semitism between the end of the sixteenth and the beginning of the twentieth centuries is best illustrated by an essay of Friedrich Lezius, a Lutheran professor at the University of Königsberg: "Luther's Attitude as Regards the Jews" (*Luthers Stellung zu den Juden*, 1892). He praised the younger Luther for being friendly to the Jews in 1523, and he called the "suggestions" of 1543 "scandalous measures, clearly contrary to the spirit of the Gospel."

> It is obvious that Luther does not argue in concordance with the spirit of the New Testament and the Reformation. . . . The Protestant Church has therefore rejected the errors of the aging reformer as not binding for the church and only regards Luther's treatise "That Jesus Christ Was Born a Jew," which was published in 1523, as a true expression of the spirit of the Reformation. . . . The German nation did not want to follow . . . Luther's suggestions because they do not agree with the Gospel and the concept of modern humanitarianism. . . . It was therefore beneficial to Christendom to ignore the admonitions of the mighty man.[60]

Secular anti-Semites, like the founder of "practical anti-Semitism," Theodor Fritsch, published a "Catechism for Anti-Semites" *(Antisemiten-*

---

2 vols. (1875; 3rd ed. Berlin, 1905). Quotation in vol. 2, p. 591. See also Brosseder, *Luthers Stellung zu den Juden,* pp. 77-78.

57. Johann Joseph Ignaz von Döllinger, *Die Reformation, ihre innere Entwicklung und ihre Wirkungen im Umfange des Lutherischen Bekenntnisses,* 3 vols. (1848). Quoted in Brosseder, *Luthers Stellung zu den Juden,* p. 80.

58. Heinrich Denifle, *Luther und Luthertum in der ersten Entwicklung* (Mainz, 1906). Brosseder, *Luthers Stellung zu den Juden,* p. 88.

59. For example, Ludwig Geiger, "Die Juden und die deutsche Literatur," *Zeitschrift für die Geschichte der Juden in Deutschland* 2 (1888): 197-374. See also Brosseder, *Luthers Stellung zu den Juden,* pp. 93-94.

60. Excerpts quoted in Wallmann, "The Reception of Luther's Writings on the Jews," pp. 135-36.

Katechismus) in 1887 in which he described Luther as seeing the error of his ways when he changed his pro-Jewish position of 1523 to the attitude he really felt in his heart in 1543, rejecting the Jews as a people cursed by God.[61]

There is a continuing historical trajectory, focusing on the tolerant, friendly, younger Luther in the 1520s and on the intolerant, angry, older Luther in the 1540s. In the trajectory, Luther appears as a disappointed missionary who could no longer hope for Jewish conversions. The Erlangen theologian Gustav Plitt continued the interest in Luther as missionary to the Jews in an essay, "Luther's Attitude to a Mission to the Jews" (*Luthers Stellung zur Judenmission*, 1870) as part of a history of Lutheran Jewish mission.[62] Luther did not succeed, Plitt wrote, because his mildness caused the opposite of what he wanted to achieve, a lack of Jewish response. So he called for "sharp mercy" in his late writings on the Jews in order to move some to conversion. Luther's outbursts are excused with an interesting psycho-historical observation.

When he [Luther] offered hard advice he did so only to excuse his conscience. With an aching heart he thought of the Jews in whom he saw the terrible consequences of God's wrath. . . . Just as his heart had spoken before with friendly words, so did his hard speaking later become a matter of conscience. We may doubt whether this final choice was the right one. But that much is clear: Luther stuck to his mission to the Jews and pursued it to the end. . . . That this was the case can only be seen and by one who knows, as Luther did, *that it is infinitely more important and valuable to save the immortal soul than to lead here a life in freedom, honor and well-being.*[63]

An echo of the classic mentality of fanatical crusaders who justify their terrorism with the excuse that killing the bodies of heretics saves their souls!

---

61. Brosseder, *Luthers Stellung zu den Juden*, p. 100. After thirty editions, the catechism was published in 1931 as *Hand-Book of the Jewish Question (Handbuch der Judenfrage)*.

62. In a journal created for a mission to the Jews, *Seed of Hope (Saat der Hoffnung)* 7 (1870): 279-95. The essay was part of a series of lectures published as *A Brief History of Lutheran Mission (Kurze Geschichte der lutherischen Mission*, Erlangen, 1871). See also Brosseder, *Luthers Stellung zu den Juden*, pp. 52-55.

63. Quoted in Brosseder, *Luthers Stellung zu den Juden*, pp. 54-55. Italics added.

Embodiment of German Nationalism

The focus on mission was merged with the notion of Luther as the quintessential German patriot. He was so portrayed in an anonymous essay of 1881 in Leipzig, titled "Luther and the Jews" *(Luther und die Juden),* with the subtitle "Dedicated to the German Students by a Fellow-Student" *(Den deutschen Studenten gewidmet von einem Kommilitonen).*[64] It was to be a contribution to the "anti-Semitism Controversy" in the early 1880s (during the rule of Otto von Bismarck) dealing with the issue whether or not Jews may be in public positions. Nationalist anti-Semites opposed such a move; eventually, the anti-Semitic spirit prevailed.[65] The author made it clear as crystal that German Protestant Christians must see Luther as their model and therefore cannot live side-by-side with Jews.

> *A Jew cannot be a German because a true German can only be someone who is a Christian. . . .* How can we allow among us a people that slanders and derides every day our Lord and Savior? And because Christ stands in the center for our Dr. Martin Luther, he speaks with a true, holy wrath against the Jews.[66]

When Luther discovered this evil character of Jews, the author wrote, he abandoned any notion of mission and warned Germans of the Jewish threat. That is why the political support of anti-Semitism in Germany breathes the spirit of Luther.

But Luther was still linked to a mission to the Jews in the first comprehensive treatment of his attitude to the Jews by the German rabbi Reinhold Lewin in a doctoral dissertation, honored with the annual prize of the Lutheran Theological Faculty in Breslau.[67] Lewin's thesis: Luther's interest in a mission to the Jews was the result of an encounter with two Jews during his journey to Worms in 1521; the encounter motivated him to write the "missionary treatise" *(Missions-*

---

64. According to Brosseder (*Luthers Stellung zu den Juden,* pp. 55-60), the author could have been a Luther biographer named G. Buchwald.

65. See the sketch of anti-Semitism in the nineteenth century, Brosseder, *Luthers Stellung zu den Juden,* p. 56, n. 2.

66. Quoted in Brosseder, *Luthers Stellung zu den Juden,* pp. 58, 59. Italics added.

67. Lewin, *Luthers Stellung zu den Juden.* Lewin and his family became victims of the Nazi holocaust in the 1940s. See Brosseder, *Luthers Stellung zu den Juden,* pp. 112-14.

schrift) "That Jesus Christ Was Born a Jew" (1523); but a lack of response
and rumors about Jewish attempts to convert Christians drove Luther
into his radical anti-Semitic outbursts in 1543. This thesis is weakened
by the discovery that reports about Luther's encounter with Jews in
Worms proved to be an unreliable legend. Moreover, Lewin did not ana-
lyze Luther's extensive exegetical and theological reflections about the
Jews.[68]

But "the German Luther" dominated. As the renowned Jena philosopher Wilhelm Wundt put it, "The work of Martin Luther made
possible the rebirth of Christian faith through the German spirit."[69]
But the quadricentennial of Luther's *Ninety-Five Theses* in 1917 continued the interest in missionary efforts. The leader of such efforts was
the Berlin pastor Ernst Schaeffer, who advocated his views as the Director of the Society for Furthering Christianity Among Jews in Berlin. He
summarized his views in a book, *Luther und die Juden* (1917). Like others
before, Schaeffer cited Luther's friendly treatise of 1523 as evidence for a
mission and, when no conversions were in sight, Luther became a German patriot who wanted to defend "a German national Christian religion"; but this was not a satisfactory rationale for a change from
"prophet" to "patriot."[70]

The "missionary Luther" was drowned in a sea of propaganda centered in the idea of "folk" and "race." Houston Stewart Chamberlain
(1855-1927), an Englishman who became a German citizen, was a principal voice in praising Germans as a world-class race that would put the
entire world on the right track.[71] The darling of German high society
and the new racist ideologists, ranging from Emperor William II to
Adolf Hitler, Chamberlain viewed Luther as the political reformer
whose patriotism should have created a substitute for the rule of Ro-

68. See the critique in Brosseder, *Luthers Stellung zu den Juden,* p. 113. The Worms
legend appeared in 1575. See text in Walter Bienert, *Martin Luther und die Juden* (Frankfurt
am Main: Evangelisches Verlagswerk, 1982), p. 56.

69. Quoted in Günther B. Ginzel, "Martin Luther: 'Chief Witness of Anti-
Semitism,'" in Heinz Kremers, ed., *Die Juden und Martin Luther. Martin Luther und die
Juden. Geschichte, Wirkungsgeschichte, Herausforderung,* 2nd ed. (Neukirchen-Vluyn: Neu-
kirchener Verlag, 1987; first ed. 1985), pp. 192-93.

70. Brosseder, *Luthers Stellung zu den Juden,* p. 220.

71. So argued in the book *Foundations of the Nineteenth Century,* written in German
as *Die Grundlagen des neunzehnten Jahrhunderts* (1899). See Brosseder, *Luthers Stellung zu den
Juden,* pp. 100-101. Chamberlain married the daughter of the nationalist musician Richard Wagner.

man Catholicism. Not "dogmatic subtleties" *(dogmatische Tüffeleien)* but German nationalism propelled the Reformation. "Unconditional patriotism and conditional theology made him [Luther] throw off his monastic habit."[72]

The discussion about anti-Semitism in the 1920s motivated some Luther interpreters to defend Luther's use of the Old Testament as necessary evidence that the Jews had a wrong view of it because they saw it through Talmudic glasses. The Leipzig theologian Wilhelm Walther had dealt with this issue in a series of essays on Luther and the Jews in the weekly *Allgemeine evangelische Kirchenzeitung;* the essays also appeared in book form, *Luther und die Juden und die Anti-Semiten* (1912).[73] Walther defended Luther as "pro-Semitic" in his use of the Old Testament and in his 1523 treatise on Christ as a born Jew. For Luther, "the religious question is everything! Decisive is one's attitude about Christ."[74] Luther wrote his anti-Jewish treatises against the religious disposition of the Jews, Walther contended, not against their actions. But Walther echoed a nationalist tone in his description of the Russian Revolution in 1917 as an event in which Jews spilled Christian blood. Luther's outbursts should be ignored because the rejection of Christianity is more evident in the "liberties" established after the French Revolution of 1789.

> One senses hostility against Christianity as well as Jewish business habits no longer as specifically Jewish and unbearable. Since the French Revolution one has moved exactly in the opposite direction that Luther proposed as right: Freedom for Jews, complete coordination with Christians. Have the consequences been more favorable than those he had to experience, based on similar ideas he had expressed in his writing of 1523 which was friendly towards Jews?[75]

Walther did not answer the question. He was attacked by anti-Semitic German nationalists, led by a Munich author, Alfred Falb, who published a book, *Luther and the Jews: Germany's Leading Men and Judaism* (*Luther und die Juden: Deutschland's führende Männer und das Judentum,* 1921). Falb addressed "all teachers, educators, and mothers of German

72. Quoted in Brosseder, *Luthers Stellung zu den Juden,* p. 101.
73. See Brosseder, *Luthers Stellung zu den Juden,* pp. 114-20.
74. Brosseder, *Luthers Stellung zu den Juden,* p. 116.
75. Brosseder, *Luthers Stellung zu den Juden,* p. 118.

youth and of the German future." The Preface hails Luther as a patriotic liberator.

At a time when the pagan-Jewish spirit in the Roman Church had conquered the West, when Jewish loaning of money dominated Europe and slowly gave birth to capitalism . . . there arose in the most dire circumstances the liberator in Luther's fighting heroism. *Pure German in his blood and born in poverty, he carried the fate of Germany in his chest.* But this fate is yet to be fulfilled! He foresaw what is happening now; posterity ignored his warnings. Only the future will complete what he already felt in his anxious soul. . . . A pointer in this book.[76]

Falb supported Luther's outburst of 1543 with a description of Jews as being nervous, bustling, and contradictory in their thinking — "a hereditary, pernicious mental faculty in a people that, more than any other, inclines to be mentally ill, perverse, etc."[77] Falb combined anti-Semitism with racism and anti-Roman Catholicism; Luther had become the father of a "German religion."[78]

Luther's image as a role model for German patriotism became very popular and appeared in various publications linked to anti-Semitic organizations, such as the "Tannenberg Covenant" *(Tannenbergbund)* in the late 1920s,[79] and the "German Faith Movement" *(Deutsche Glaubensbewegung)* in the early 1930s. The latter advocated the creation of a "third" religious community (besides Roman Catholicism and Protestantism), marked by a "free Germanic spirituality" *(freie germanische Gläubigkeit).* In this context, Luther became the precursor of a global struggle for a new world dominated by an "eternal German spirit" *(ewiges Deutschtum).*[80] Advocates of this image of Luther declared that his 1543 treatise "On the Jews and Their Lies" should have become a

76. Quoted in Brosseder, *Luthers Stellung zu den Juden,* p. 156. Falb was a physician and died in 1925 at age thirty-five, praised by leaders of the nascent movement of National Socialism ("Nazism").

77. Brosseder, *Luthers Stellung zu den Juden,* p. 160.

78. Brosseder, *Luthers Stellung zu den Juden,* p. 163.

79. Named after the place of a successful German battle against Russia in the first year of World War I. The victor was General Erich Ludendorff, who became the Chief of Staff of the German armed forces.

80. So argued by the nationalist Walther Linden and repeated by others. See Brosseder, *Luthers Stellung zu den Juden,* p. 176.

"folk book" *(Volksbuch)*, instructing readers about the Jewish threat to civilization. "His [Luther's] literary attacks against Judaism are the fruit of an enduring struggle for the birth of an unlimited, European Christian way of thinking and feeling; they are a legacy of the eternal German spirit that shall never be forgotten."[81]

The "Nazi" underground movement, before and after its political victory in 1933, propagated a fanatic, racist anti-Semitism in its weekly journal, *Der Stürmer* ("the Assailant"), advertised as a "special paper for the battle for the truth" *(Sonderblatt zum Kampf um die Wahrheit)* and edited in Nuremberg by Julius Streicher, the most radical anti-Semite of the movement. He began referring to Luther in 1925 as one whose "German spirit" fights the devil in the Jews. On the 450th birthday of Luther in 1933, Streicher complained about the lack of references to Luther's anti-Semitism.

> Luther stands before us as the warrior against the international power of the Jews. But his stance has been concealed from us. This is the great sin of omission of all responsible national educators. For enlightenment about the true nature of the Jews is neither an act of hate or envy but a duty for self-preservation patriotism. We hope that this is the time when Luther will be shown as a warrior to the people. We also want to see the full picture of Luther's life in the church as the most proper place where truth must be honored.[82]

A number of anonymous anti-Semitic pieces appeared in *Der Stürmer* in the 1930s; some were attributed to Lutheran pastors. When Streicher was tried for war crimes in Nuremberg in 1946, he told the court that Luther would sit in his, Streicher's, place in the dock because of Luther's radical attacks in his treatise "On the Jews and Their Lies."[83]

Similar editorials appeared until the 1940s. Their content was repeated and enhanced in the Nazi paper *Völkischer Beobachter* ("National Observer"), edited by Alfred Rosenberg. In 1930, he elaborated his ideology in the book *The Myth of the Twentieth Century: An Evaluation of the Spiritual-Mental Struggles of Our Time (Der Mythos des 20. Jahrhunderts: Eine*

---

81. Quoted in Brosseder, *Luthers Stellung zu den Juden*, p. 178, from an editor of Luther's 1543 treatise, Walther Linden, a member of the "German Faith Movement."

82. Quoted in Brosseder, *Luthers Stellung zu den Juden*, p. 185.

83. See his statement quoted by Pinchas E. Lapide, "Stimmen jüdischer Zeitgenossen zu Martin Luther," in Kremers, ed., *Die Juden und Martin Luther*, p. 171.

Wertung der seelisch-geistigen Gestaltenkämpfe unserer Zeit). Luther is portrayed as the precursor of later German values as seen by the Nazis: the
struggle for freedom, national independence, and reliance on personal
conscience; but he stopped halfway by substituting the authority of Jerusalem, the Bible, for the authority of Rome.

Only very late did Luther free himself from "the Jews and their lies"
and declared that we no longer had anything to do with Moses. But
meanwhile the "Bible" had become a folk-book and Old Testament
"prophecy" had become religion. Thus the increasing influence of
Judaism and the numbness of our life took another step forward;
no wonder that from then on blond German children had to sing:
"To you, Jehovah, I will sing, for where is such a God as you."[84]

"The Covenant for a German Church" *(der Bund für Deutsche
Kirche)* and the Institute for Research of the Jewish Question, in Frankfurt am Main, continued the racist interpretation of Luther by praising
him for abandoning a conversion of Jews in 1543, a decision to make a
clear racial distinction between Germans and Jews.[85]

There were some critics of anti-Semitism such as the members of
the "Society for Resistance against Anti-Semitism" *(Verein zur Abwehr
des Anti-Semitismus).* Its most articulate voice was the Stuttgart pastor
Eduard Lamparter 1860-1945), who published a comprehensible booklet titled "The Evangelical Church and Judaism" *(Evangelische Kirche und
Judentum,* 1928). But he simply called for an appreciation of the younger
pro-Jewish Luther and expressed deep regret for the anti-Jewish attitude of the old Luther.[86] But the critics of anti-Semitism were heavily
outnumbered by their enemies. Some were influenced by the work of
Reinhold Lewin, who stressed the psychological change in Luther's attitude to the Jews without considering the theological issues.[87] Others
did pay attention to Luther's judgment that Jews, like "radicals"
(Schwärmer) and papists, represented the enduring temptation to use
the word of God as the basis for self-righteousness.[88]

Typical for the view of the Nazi movement is the extensive treat-

---

84. Quoted in Kremers, ed., *Die Juden und Martin Luther,* p. 197.
85. Kremers, ed., *Die Juden und Martin Luther,* p. 198.
86. Kremers, ed., *Die Juden und Martin Luther,* p. 215.
87. Kremers, ed., *Die Juden und Martin Luther,* pp. 112-13.
88. Kremers, ed., *Die Juden und Martin Luther,* p. 242.

ment of Luther's attitude to the Jews by Theodor Pauls, a professor at a German teachers' training college in Hirschberg/Riesengebirge.[89] His work was designed to instruct a "study group for 'positive Christianity'" (a Nazi definition) at the "Institute for the Examination and Elimination of the Jewish in German Church Life." It also was to be used by "all Christian construction efforts in the 'Third Reich.'" Pauls's intricate interpretation discloses his Nazi agenda: Luther used the gospel as a platform "to fight against any influence of Judaism in the church" and "to liberate Christians for the law of God in the German church"; this platform substitutes nationalism for Luther's Christ-centered Reformation.[90]

The Lutheran bishop Martin Sasse celebrated the burning of synagogues on November 10, 1938 (Luther's birthday), with a call for the liberation of Germany from Jewish economic oppression, praising Luther as "the greatest anti-Semite of his time."[91] Hitler's "final solution" of the Jewish problem through mass extermination met little, if any, resistance.[92]

Luther quotations were used in opposition to Nazi anti-Semitism by Dietrich Bonhoeffer, the martyr of the "Confessing Church" *(Bekennende Kirche)* movement in Germany. After the Nazi boycott of Jewish businesses and of legislation excluding Jews from government positions, Bonhoeffer published the text of a lecture on "the Jewish question" in 1933 in the context of the relationship between church and state. He introduced the lecture with two Luther quotations, one from his final "Exhortation against the Jews" (1546) and the other from his treatise "That Jesus Christ Was Born a Jew" (1523). Both quotations mention the possibility of a "brotherly" relationship.[93] But Bonhoeffer used Luther's words as a frame to talk about "the Jewish question" in the context of the issue of Christian resistance to the wheels of tyranny, which should cause the church "not just to bind up the victims be-

---

89. Theodor Pauls, *Luther und die Juden,* 3 vols. (Bonn, 1939).

90. Brosseder, *Luthers Stellung zu den Juden,* p. 137.

91. In a popular tract "Martin Luther über die Juden: Weg mit ihnen!" (1938), quoted in Ginzel, "Martin Luther: 'Chief Witness of Anti-Semitism,'" in Kremers, ed., *Die Juden und Martin Luther,* p. 207.

92. See Christopher R. Browning, *The Origins of the Final Solution: The Evolution of Nazi Jewish Policy 1939-1945* (London: Arrow Books, 2005).

93. Brosseder (*Luthers Stellung zu den Juden,* pp. 243-44) traced the texts. From 1546 in WA 51, 195:25-27; 39-41. From 1523 in WA 11, 315:19-24; 336:27-29. LW 45, 200-201, 229.

neath the wheel, but to halt the wheel itself."[94] His biographer, Eberhard Bethge, found a statement in Bonhoeffer's notes, denouncing the persecution of Jews.

The church confesses to have seen the arbitrary application of brutal force, the physical and spiritual suffering of innumerable innocent people, subjugation, hatred, and murder, without raising a voice for them, finding ways for them, and hurrying to help them. . . . It [the church] has become guilty of the lives of the weakest and most defenseless brothers of Jesus Christ.[95]

Other voices of the "Confessing Church" also dealt with Luther, but not in the context of resistance. Lutherans who supported Nazism, the "German Christians" *(deutsche Christen)*, did not mention Luther in their "Platform" of 1932, but adopted the anti-Semitic stance of the Hitler regime. In the early years of the "church struggle" *(Kirchenkampf)* in Germany, Luther's legacy, not his writings against the Jews, was the major issue.[96] In 1945, the "refugee service" of the World Council of Churches in Geneva commissioned a volume on the Jewish question and the Protestant Church in Germany.[97] The anonymous editor called Luther's treatise "On the Jews and Their Lies" (1543) the reason why he became famous "as a leading anti-Semite. It [the treatise] plainly can be called the arsenal from where anti-Semitism got its weapons."[98]

In 1945, a literary feud put the theme "Luther and the Jews" into the limelight. One year earlier, a British teacher of German and French, Peter F. Wiener, published a book contending that Luther was Hitler's spiritual ancestor.[99] It is sheer propaganda with the intention to show

94. Eberhard Bethge, *Dietrich Bonhoeffer: Theologian, Christian, Man for His Times. A Biography*, rev. ed. by Victoria J. Barnett (Minneapolis: Fortress Press, 2000), p. 275. See also Bethge, "Dietrich Bonhoeffer und die Juden," in Kremers, ed., *Die Juden und Martin Luther*, pp. 211-48.

95. Bethge, "Dietrich Bonhoeffer und die Juden," p. 240.

96. See Johann M. Schmidt, "Das Erbe Martin Luthers im Spiegel seiner Wirkungen auf die 'Judenfrage' zu Beginn des Kirchenkampfes," in Kremers, ed., *Die Juden und Martin Luther*, pp. 319-50.

97. *Die Evangelische Kirche und die Judenfrage. Ausgewählte Dokumente aus den Jahren des Kirchenkampfes 1933 bis 1943* (Geneva, 1945).

98. *Die Evangelische Kirche und die Judenfrage*, p. 18.

99. *Martin Luther — Hitler's Spiritual Ancestor*, Win the Peace Pamphlet 3 (London: Hutchinson, 1944).

that Luther's radical anti-Semitism made him "one of the darkest figures history has yet produced."[100] This is "proven" by a chain of historical distortions: Luther tolerated Jews in order to gain their support in
his struggle against the papal church, but turned against the Jews when
they did not join him; his demonic anti-Semitism was not grounded in
theology because his "religion" was a "Teutonic anti-Christian faith."
Wiener misquotes, misinterprets, and intentionally misunderstands.
His work "is nothing but a historical forgery based on ignorance or
malice."[101]

The British Luther scholar Ernest Gordon Rupp offered a devastating, yet elegantly executed critique.[102] One cannot win the peace,
Rupp observed, by reviving the propaganda of Joseph Goebbels, the
late but unlamented Minister of Nazi Propaganda. "The Nazi uniforms
which Mr. Wiener has put on Luther fit very oddly on the facts: they
were not made for him, nor he for them. Whatever be the truth about
Luther, it is not Mr. Wiener's caricature."[103]

Lutheran churches, many of them members of the Lutheran
World Federation since its foundation in 1947 (now called "Communion"), have held study conferences on Christian anti-Semitism and
issued resolutions since the 1960s. But Luther's views of the Jews are
not cited.[104] "The Logumkloster [in Denmark] Report" of 1964 is an
exception because it criticized the reformer for acting *against his better
judgment.*

> Luther opposed any kind of a "theology of glory," i.e., any attempt
> to see and proclaim God and his deeds and works (including the
> church) primarily in terms of might, of lordship, of victory and tri-
> umph. The theological paradox which confronted Luther in his
> historical situation, however, proved to be too much for him. This
> one can see from his later writings against the Jews. *In these polemic
> tracts a theology of glory does break in. Luther's anxiety about the church's*

100. *Martin Luther — Hitler's Spiritual Ancestor*, p. 65.
101. Brosseder, *Luthers Stellung zu den Juden*, p. 211.
102. *Martin Luther: Hitler's Cause — or Cure? In Reply to Peter F. Wiener* (London: Lutterworth Press, 1945).
103. *Martin Luther: Hitler's Cause — or Cure?* p. 82. See also Brosseder, *Luthers Stellung zu den Juden*, pp. 211-12.
104. See *From Federation to Communion: The History of the Lutheran World Federation*, ed. Jens H. Schjorring et al. (Minneapolis: Fortress Press, 1997). There are no entries on "Luther" and "Jews."

*existence became so strong that he found himself no longer able to let the fu-
ture rest in God's hands but, in anticipation of what he read to be God's future judgment, called upon the secular arm to effect that judgment in the
present. In doing so he overstepped the bounds of what he read to be God's
future judgment.*[105]

Stimulus for Critical Hindsight

After 1945, divergent scholarly assessments of Luther's attitude to the
Jews appeared. The most peculiar interpretation was offered in the doctoral dissertation of the Finnish-American Lutheran scholar Armas
Kristen Ejnar Holmio. It was published under the title *The Lutheran Reformation and the Jews: The Birth of the Protestant Jewish Mission.*[106] Holmio
contended that Luther's treatises of 1523, 1538, and 1546 were "mission
epistles." But this designation is a misreading of *senden* ("sending") and
Sendung ("mission"). In 1538, Luther wrote in "a letter to a good friend,"
with arguments "Against the Sabbatarians," that "the subject is far too
big to be disposed of in a letter *(Sendbrief).*"[107] Holmio's incorrect translation, "mission epistle," led him to assume that such an epistle was the
forthcoming treatise "On the Jews and Their Lies" (1543).[108] He also
might have used the translation "mission epistle" from the title page of
the Latin edition of the treatise, *dedicatoria epistola.*[109] Holmio's linguistic mistake makes his interpretation unacceptable.

There were two opposing views of Luther's attitude in the studies
by two German Lutheran scholars, Wilhelm Maurer and Martin Stöhr.
Both were concerned with reconcilable Christian-Jewish relations.
Maurer offered a substantial assessment in two parts: (1) the encounter
of church and synagogue in the course of history, and (2) Christians
and Jews in the Reformation.[110]

105. Harold H. Ditmanson, ed., *Stepping-Stones to Further Jewish-Lutheran Relationships,* Key Lutheran Statements (Minneapolis: Augsburg, 1990), p. 30. Italics added. This
report is not included in *From Federation to Communion: The History of the Lutheran World
Federation.*
106. Hancock, MI: Lutheran Book Concern, 1949.
107. WA 50, 337:8. LW 47, 98.
108. Holmio, *The Lutheran Reformation and the Jews,* p. 131.
109. Suggested by Brosseder, *Luthers Stellung zu den Juden,* p. 266.
110. (1) *Kirche und Synagoge. Motive und Formen der Auseinandersetzung der Kirche mit*

Maurer judged Luther's viewpoint on the basis of the reformer's theology — a necessary correction of the work of Reinhold Lewin. According to Maurer, Luther is consistent; there are no theological changes between his position of 1523 and 1543. The treatise "That Jesus Christ Was Born a Jew" is "a christological study about the human nature of Jesus with an apologetic-missionary tendency towards the Jews."[111] The tract "On the Jews and Their Lies" shows only "a change stressing the practical-legal attitude towards the Jews; it has nothing to do with a decline of a great hope or the conversion of the Jews, as was once assumed."[112] But Luther's outbursts have to be rejected as useless remnants of medieval traditions.[113]

Stöhr, the Director of the Evangelical Academy of Arnoldshain, offered a study of "Luther and the Jews" with the exact opposite of Maurer's position: there is a basic theological change in Luther's writings of 1523 and 1543.[114] They must be "sharply separated from each other in their spirit and consequences."[115] In 1523, Luther became convinced that the Reformation would break new ground for a rapprochement between a church, liberated from the papacy, and Jews, joining their covenant with the gospel.

> For Luther, the peculiarity of the Jews is not grounded in the future that Paul makes known as an apparent mystery in Rom. 11:25-26 [after a "hardening" of Israel and the entrance of the Gentiles, all Israel will be saved in the end], but in their glorious past, with the promises and the history of God as the Lord of this people. . . . This

---

dem Judentum im Laufe der Geschichte (Franz Delitzsch-Vorlesungen, 1951; Stuttgart: Kohlhammer, 1953). (2) "Die Zeit der Reformation," in *Kirche und Synagoge: Handbuch zur Geschichte von Christen und Juden,* ed. H. Rengstorf and S. von Kortzfleisch (Stuttgart: Klett, 1968).

111. Maurer, *Kirche und Synagoge,* vol. 2, pp. 338-39.

112. Maurer, *Kirche und Synagoge,* vol. 2, p. 403.

113. Maurer, *Kirche und Synagoge,* vol. 2, p. 421. But Maurer did not sufficiently treat Luther's doctrine of justification as a criterion of the Christian-Jewish encounter. See Brosseder, *Luthers Stellung zu den Juden,* p. 274.

114. Martin Stöhr, "Luther und die Juden," *Evangelische Theologie* 20 (1960): 157-82. "Martin Luther und die Juden," in W. D. Marsh and K. Thieme, eds., *Christen und Juden. Ihr Gegensatz vom Apostelkonzil bis heute* (Mainz and Göttingen, 1961), pp. 115-40. Reprinted in Kremers, ed., *Die Juden und Luther,* pp. 89-108.

115. Stöhr, "Martin Luther und die Juden," in Kremers, ed., *Die Juden und Luther,* p. 91.

glorious past is the eternal presence of Christ! . . . The universality of the offer of salvation corresponds to the need of *all* human beings who rely on this salvation. . . . Having received this message — and this was Luther's self-confidence based on his Reformation discovery — can never be a laurel to rest on, but is to be handed on as something one has received.[116]

Stöhr seemed to attribute to Luther an agreement with Paul (Rom. 11:25-26) that the old, divine covenant with the Jews will include the Gentiles, and both will be saved in the end — their common history as "people of God" is "eschatologically reserved." But Stöhr saw the Luther of 1543, twenty years later, drenched in frustration and despair over the lack of any positive Jewish response to the Reformation.

> The Jewish question is no longer a question for Luther. What remains is only the literary execution and communication of an already existing judgment about the Jews. He could no longer think of any possibility to change anything regarding the fate of the Jews. Only God could do that — so he returns fatalistically the mandate and responsibility for [missionary] proclamation to God; as if the Word of God could not be said in another, miraculous manner, through humans to humans! So Luther addresses, with a peculiar certainty, *only* Christians, among them only preachers and politicians. . . . The Jew has become the object of talk within the church rather than remaining a partner in dialogue.[117]

Stöhr concluded that Luther experienced anxieties about the strength of the Christian faith, about a solidarity of the faithful with the godless, and about the honor of God and Christ. These anxieties diminished his faith in his own faith, grounded in "the explosive power of the gospel" that has no limits — a judgment that needs to be better supported by a full consideration of Luther's theology.[118]

In 1968, the Leipzig church historian Kurt Meier offered a discerning study on the reception of Luther's anti-Jewish writings, based on the attitude of the Lutheran church in Germany during the regime

---

116. Kremers, ed., *Die Juden und Luther,* p. 98.

117. Kremers, ed., *Die Juden und Luther,* pp. 99, 100.

118. Kremers, ed., *Die Juden und Luther,* pp. 106-7. See the critique of Brosseder, *Luthers Stellung zu den Juden,* pp. 270-81.

of Hitler.[119] He rejected interpretations that concentrate only on Luther's writings of 1523 and 1543; his exegetical work, beginning in 1513, discloses the same attitude. Meier then showed how Luther failed in viewing the Jews from the perspective of the center of his theology, the doctrine of justification: the doctrine calls for a critical attitude to the Bible (Luther's rejection of the Letter of James) and for a universalistic view of salvation (that *in the end* all might be saved). Luther was too literalistic in his anti-Jewish exegesis, and he neglected the notion of toleration in Christian universalism. The American Lutheran theologian Aarne Siirala also called for an investigation of Luther's stance within the context of his theology.[120] But while he listed various tasks, such as the clarification of a Christian view of the Jewish heritage, he offered a psycho-historical thesis: "The stance of the older Luther is based on the inner conflicts of his [Luther's] evangelical breakthrough."[121]

Other studies — Jewish, Roman Catholic, and nonreligious — yield few, if any, new insights. Some make outrageous claims: "There is a direct path from Luther to Julius Streicher [the radical Nazi journal-ist]";[122] "What Hitler did, Luther advised, with the exception of murder through gas chambers."[123] There is even an attempt to show that Luther was not the author of his most offensive treatise in 1543. The best-selling biography of Luther by the American church historian Roland H. Bainton contains a pious desire: "One could wish that Luther had died before ever this tract ['On the Jews and Their Lies,' 1543] was written."[124] The Ger-

---

119. Kurt Meier, "Zur Interpretation von Luthers Judenschriften," in Meier, *Kirche und Judentum. Die Haltung der evangelischen Kirche zur Judenpolitik* (Göttingen: Vandenhoeck & Ruprecht, 1968). See also Brosseder, *Luthers Stellung zu den Juden,* pp. 285-90.

120. Aarne Siirala, "Luther und die Juden," *Lutherische Rundschau* 14 (1964): 427-52. Brosseder, *Luthers Stellung zu den Juden,* pp. 281-85.

121. Siirala, "Luther und die Juden," p. 438.

122. The "thesis" of the Roman Catholic "scholar" Friedrich Heer, quoted by Brosseder, *Luthers Stellung zu den Juden,* p. 309. He used the popular Freudian psycho-analytical study of the young Luther by the American psychiatrist Erik H. Erikson to show that Luther's anti-Semitism "is a reflex of his personal degeneration." Brosseder, *Luthers Stellung zu den Juden,* p. 309. Erikson, *Young Man Luther: A Study in Psychoanalysis and History* (New York: Norton, 1958). Critique in Eric W. Gritsch, *Martin — God's Court Jester: Luther in Retrospect,* 3rd ed. (Eugene, OR: Wipf & Stock, 2009), pp. 148-52.

123. The "judgment" of the agnostic philosopher Karl Jaspers, quoted in Brosseder, *Luthers Stellung zu den Juden,* p. 310.

124. Roland H. Bainton, *Here I Stand: A Life of Martin Luther* (Nashville and New York: Abingdon, 1950), p. 379.

man theologian Ernst Wolf criticized Luther for his distinction between "abiblical Israel" and "post-biblical Judaism."

> Because we are Christians we must again and again take seriously the promises of the blessing of Israel, and because we simultaneously know by faith and should confess by action the mystery of the church as the church consisting of Jews and Christians — not of "Jewish Christians" and "Gentile Christians." The unity of the church, in which we believe and which we confess, despite all disruption by the churches, rests on the mystery of the still valid divine promise for Israel, fulfilled in Christ.[125]

Significant insights were offered by the Berlin theologian Joachim Rogge.[126] He viewed Luther's anti-Jewish writings as centered in a Christ-centered biblical theology that did not change. Luther blamed the papacy for obscuring a clear Jewish view of the gospel, and, angered by rumors of Jewish missionary success, he slid back into the errors of medieval anti-Semitism. Thus he weakened his understanding of Scripture, ignoring Paul's proclamation (Rom. 11:32, "God has imprisoned all in disobedience so that he may be merciful to all") that Jews and Christians belong together.

> In the final analysis, we adhere not to Luther but to Holy Scripture — as he intended! — and be corrected by it, together with others. In this way, we will learn, after the experience of the unspeakable suffering of the Jews, to abandon any quick mission aiming at conversion.[127]

When the first English edition of "On the Jews and Their Lies" appeared in 1971 in the American edition of Luther's works (LW), the editor, Franklin Sherman, revised the introduction by the translator, Martin A. Bertram, alerting readers to Luther's offensive anti-Semitism and telling them that the edition "is in no way intended as an endorsement" of Luther's views.[128] Luther "shared to the full in the medieval

---

125. Ernst Wolf, quoted in Brosseder, *Luthers Stellung zu den Juden*, p. 320.

126. Joachim Rogge, "Luthers Stellung zu den Juden," *Luther — Zeitschrift der Luther-Gesellschaft* 40 (1969): 13-24. Text of a presentation at the 485th birthday of Luther and the 30th anniversary of the *Kristallnacht* on November 9, 1968, in the church of St. Peter and Paul in Eisleben where Luther had been baptized.

127. Rogge, "Luthers Stellung zu den Juden," p. 24.

128. LW 47, 123.

practices against the Jews," with a "temporary modification" in 1523.[129] Luther's radical anti-Semitism is medieval and linked to his view of the devil. "It appears that Luther accepted this aspect [anti-Semitic medieval superstitions] of popular culture at face value. Moreover, the intensity of his own sense of the demonic lent special vividness to these images in Luther's mind."[130]

In the extensive German biography of Luther by Martin Brecht, Luther's view of the Jews is treated in the context of his attitude to Turks and the pope as "enemies of Christ"; any link to a later racist anti-Semitism is denied.[131] But Brecht concluded that

> in advising the use of force, he [Luther] advocated means that were essentially incompatible with his faith in Christ. In addition, his criticism of the rabbinic interpretation of the Scriptures in part violated his own exegetical principles. Therefore, his attitude toward the Jews can be appropriately criticized both for his methods and also from the center of his theology.[132]

Again, Luther acted *against his own better judgment!*

The massive study of Luther's theology by the eminent German Luther scholar Bernhard Lohse treats Luther's attitude to the Jews only in a brief "excursus"; it was "exclusively religious."[133] The Marburg church historian Hans-Martin Barth offered a different opinion.

> He [Luther] is — in view of his attitude to Judaism — a miscarried professor of theology who overestimates his role and thus is a warning example for all those who are trying to present an appropriate evangelical theology . . . he himself needs the "justification of the ungodly" of which he so movingly spoke to and wrote for others.[134]

---

129. LW 47, 127.

130. LW 47, 131.

131. Martin Brecht, *Martin Luther*, 3 vols., trans. J. L. Schaaf (Minneapolis: Fortress Press, 1990-93; German ed. 1981-87), vol. 3, p. 351.

132. Brecht, *Martin Luther*, vol. 3, pp. 350-51.

133. Bernhard Lohse, *The Theology of Martin Luther: Its Historical and Systematic Development*, trans. and ed. Roy A. Harrisville (Minneapolis: Fortress Press, 1999), p. 339. The "excursus" consists of six pages (pp. 339-45) in a study of 393 pages.

134. Hans-Martin Barth, *Die Theologie Martin Luthers. Eine kritische Würdigung* (Gütersloh: Gütersloher Verlagshaus, 2009), p. 63.

The Roman Catholic theologian in Bonn, Johannes Brosseder, ended his detailed study of Luther's impact, especially in German-speaking areas, with a "critical appreciation of the center of Luther's argumentation" (*Luthers theologisches Argumentationszentrum in kritischer Würdigung*).[135] The center is the doctrine of justification, based on the young Luther's quest for a gracious God; and the doctrine of justification is elaborated in the context of a "gospel-law" dialectic. Brosseder viewed Luther's attitude to the Jews, especially his notion of a "sharp mercy" in "On the Jews and Their Lies" (1543), as part of the "second use of the law" (*usus theologicus*) — the "first" use is the maintaining of law and order by secular authority. This second use reveals human sin and drives sinners to the gospel, Christ. "Luther's 'sharp mercy' is in the service of the law; it is to reveal to the Jews their sins and drive them to the gospel."[136] The "strange work" of the "hidden God" is wrath against sin, but always related to the "proper work" of mercy and love. Christ appeased the divine wrath. Since Luther expected the Last Day to come soon, he increased his warnings to the Jews, hoping to save some from the full measure of God's wrath.[137]

In contrast to Brosseder, Bertold Klappert at the Lutheran seminary (*kirchliche Hochschule*) in Wuppertal viewed Luther in the context of a dialectic of "election and justification," as argued by Karl Barth.[138] He stressed "election" as the center of theological argumentation; it is anchored in the covenant with Abraham, according to Galatians 3:16-18 ("This covenant and its promise includes Christ as an offspring of Abraham; it cannot be nullified").

135. Brosseder, *Luthers Stellung zu den Juden*, pp. 381-92.

136. Brosseder, *Luthers Stellung zu den Juden*, p. 389. In his later summary of his work *Luthers Stellung zu den Juden*, Brosseder suggested that the Lutheran doctrine of justification should not be used to explain Luther's anti-Jewish stance. The historical weight of Christian-Jewish relations in the fifteenth and sixteenth centuries mandates a strictly theological Christian discussion of Judaism, focusing on the faith of Abraham, the eminent embodiment of the faith for Luther. "In this regard, did not Christians have a blindfold too long?" See Brosseder, "Luther und der Leidensweg der Juden," in Kremers, ed., *Die Juden und Martin Luther,* p. 135.

137. Brosseder, *Luthers Stellung zu den Juden*, p. 391. See also Brosseder, "Luther und der Leidensweg der Juden," p. 135.

138. Bertold Klappert, "Erwählung und Rechtfertigung," in Kremers, ed., *Die Juden und Martin Luther,* pp. 368-410.

Whoever wants to speak correctly about "law and gospel" must — according to Barth — *first* speak about the covenant and its promise. The "instruction" *(Torah)* would not be instruction if it were not sheltered in the reality of the covenant. And the gospel is only gospel if the instruction is sheltered and included in it.[139]

According to Klappert, Luther could not accept Romans 11:25-28. "That a rejection of the gospel of the justification of the ungodly does *not* cancel the election of Israel (Rom. 11:28) was for Luther an inconceivable idea."[140] He viewed "justification" as grounded in a "hidden divine election" or "predestination," making it a consolation for the troubled conscience. That is why Luther ignored, indeed rejected, Paul's teaching that Jews and Gentiles have an eschatological destiny that precludes any hostility, also during their earthly pilgrimage. *"By placing the election of Israel into the proclamation of justification, Luther had to dispute Paul's emphasis on the faithfulness of the people of Israel to the covenant and on the future of their election."*[141] The assumption of a double covenant led Luther to the historical conclusion that the old covenant had to be renewed, thus creating a biblical rationale for anti-Semitism.[142]

The American Luther scholar Mark U. Edwards investigated the possible impact of Luther's diseases on Luther's attitude and language, especially in his last fifteen years.[143] But he was criticized for buying into a misleading form of psycho-history regarding the "old" Luther. Luther used scatological language throughout his life. Moreover, monks were trained to use such language against the devil, who is always involved in "muck" *(Dreck).*[144]

---

139. Klappert, "Erwählung und Rechtfertigung," p. 392.
140. Klappert, "Erwählung und Rechtfertigung," p. 369.
141. Klappert, "Erwählung und Rechtfertigung," p. 399.
142. Klappert, "Erwählung und Rechtfertigung," p. 405.
143. Mark U. Edwards, *Luther's Last Battles: Politics and Polemics, 1531-1546* (Ithaca, NY: Cornell University Press, 1983), pp. 67-75.
144. See the critique of Heiko A. Oberman, *"Teufelsdreck:* Eschatology and Scatology in the 'Old' Luther," *Sixteenth Century Journal* 19 (1988): 435-50, esp. 444. On the balance of Luther's state of health and his accomplishments see the statistical survey in Gritsch, *Martin — God's Court Jester,* pp. 155-58.

Unbounded Hermeneutics

The topic "Luther and the Jews" is like a sea crowded with many vessels of various sizes, ranging from small boats to ocean liners — with an occasional warship! Some are steered well, others sail without reliable navigation, indeed, at times, colliding with each other, and a few land on a deserted island, sometimes damaged by warlike critique. Studies of the after-effects of Luther's anti-Semitism disclose a great variety. In the late nineteenth and early twentieth century, some studies become entangled with ideology, especially during the reign of German National Socialism ("Nazism"). They then perish like the *Titanic,* after boasting to be part of a "final solution."

I am selecting two studies that illustrate the vast differences of interpretations, disclosing an unlimited range of hermeneutics. Both studies have become popular and found strong support among those who would like to see Luther exonerated from the charge of "anti-Semitism." A parallel reading of the "Luther Evidence" (chapter 2) and the two samples of interpretation should alert readers to the hermeneutical dilemmas of this sensitive aspect of Luther research.

A. The selection and interpretation of texts by the German Luther scholar Walther Bienert (1909-1994), who experienced the Nazi era as a soldier, served as a pastor after World War II, and founded the Melanchthon Academy in 1962 in Cologne, directing it until he retired. He published his findings in 1982, one year before the quincentenary of Luther's birth with its wave of publications.[145]

B. The peculiarly creative and controversial view of the Dutch Reformed church historian Heiko A. Oberman (1930-2001), who taught in Germany (mainly at Tübingen University) and in the United States (Harvard University and the University of Arizona). He experienced the German occupation of his native country, The Netherlands, during World War II, and he published a Luther biography one year before the birthday celebrations for the Wittenberg reformer in 1983. His Luther biography, dedicated to the author of the international best-seller *Here I Stand,* Roland H. Bainton (1950), incorporates his controversial interpretation of "Luther and the Jews."[146]

---

145. Bienert, *Martin Luther und die Juden.*

146. Heiko Oberman, *Luther: Man Between God and the Devil,* trans. Eileen Walliser-Schwarzbart (New Haven: Yale University Press, 1989), pp. 292-97. Detail work in

A. *Walther Bienert*

He elaborated an apologetic point of view, summarized in ten "aspects," based on the thesis (expressed in a bombastic, indeed, convoluted way) that Luther pointed the way towards friendly Christian-Jewish relations through his rediscovery of the gospel and its Jewish roots, manifest in a common God, in common Hebrew Scriptures, and in the invitation of the Jews by Jesus and Paul.

> The man Martin Luther who, like no other theologian before him, changed world history, whose basic Reformation insights have become the common property of Protestantism and, in a world open to ecumenism, also in essential parts entered the Roman Catholic Church and many other churches — this Martin Luther, with his Reformation insights, despite being on an anti-Jewish church-political dogmatic wrong way *(antijüdisch kirchenpolitisch-dogmatischer Irrweg)*, pointed to a new way for understanding Jewish religion, to a friendly attitude of Christians to Jews, as well as to reaching for them with outstretched arms.[147]

But why was Luther anti-Jewish? Bienert answers the question by pointing to two "motives."

> But two un-Reformation *(unreformatorische)* motives seduced the later Luther into an anti-Jewish derailment: first, Luther's presumed *(vermeintlich)* responsibility as a guardian of dogma, then, the presumed governmental duty to protect the peaceful religious uniformity of the territorial church. *If the reputation spread, because of a false estimate of Luther based on the contemporary situation, that Luther was an enemy of the Jews in his faith and theology, the collected texts [in the study] can correct such a hasty judgment. It was not the reformer but the church politician Luther who showed himself as anti-Jewish in a specific historical situation. The reformer and the gospel he proclaimed are friendly to the Jews.*[148]

Oberman, *The Roots of Anti-Semitism in the Age of Renaissance and Reformation,* trans. James I. Porter (Philadelphia: Fortress Press, 1984; German edition 1981); and in "Die Juden in Luthers Sicht," in Kremers, ed., *Die Juden und Martin Luther,* pp. 136-62.

147. Bienert, *Martin Luther und die Juden,* p. 181. "Aspects," pp. 182-94.

148. Bienert, *Martin Luther und die Juden,* p. 181. Italics added.

The ten "aspects" are to consolidate this thesis.

1. From the beginning of the Reformation until his death, an enduring invitation to the Jews was the real motivating force of Luther's attitude to the Jews. He invited them to accept Christ as the Messiah, not through planned actions of conversion but by showing them what it means to be a Christian: to be a friend of all people, especially to Jews because of the injustice done to them in the Middle Ages and still at the beginning of the Reformation, which removed all obstacles for Jews to become Christians.

2. An evangelical-Reformation attitude to Jews is guided by the compassion with which Christ has accepted human beings. If one sets aside Luther's temporary derailments, his friendly attitude is not limited to a few years. He advocated equal human rights, an end to Jew-baiting, and instruction from the Bible about Jews as the elected people of God who, despite their dispersion after the destruction of Jerusalem in 70 C.E., still have an opportunity to be saved at the end of the world. Jews should be treated like everyone else in daily life, public or private. That is why Luther became known as a "protector of Jews" (*Juden-beschützer*) among Jews until 1540.

3. Luther did insist on showing the religious differences. But his harsh polemics, intolerable and incomprehensible today, is part of a late medieval tradition that he used, angered by Jewish views of Jesus as a magician, Mary as a whore, and salvation by the righteousness of good works. Both sides reflect the inability of an era to be tolerant. Both sides claimed to have absolute truths that could not be objectively communicated.

4. Jesus was the "cornerstone" (Luther) and "stumbling-block" (Jews). Luther made Jews responsible for the death of Jesus. But he rejected the notion that Christians have a right to seek revenge, since the Jews have been punished already through the destruction of Jerusalem. But Luther accused them of leaving the faith of their fathers by seeking salvation through the law, in opposition to "justification by faith alone."

5. The interpretation of Scripture also divided Luther and the Jews. Luther's Christ-centered view of the Old Testament and the Jewish rejection of the Messiah seemed to be irreconcilable.

6. Luther derailed into a hostility to the Jews because of his defense of responsibility for correct teaching and territorial religious politics.

The longstanding friendly disposition to the Jews, rooted in Reformation theology since 1514, snapped off into hostility through the course of history from 1538 to 1543; there is no explanation for it in Luther's theology. *The real reason for his anti-Judaism was the religious-political situation: Luther's concern for the truth of the gospel and of the church doctrines that had been contested by Jewish criticism. He tried to defend them in an intensifying polemics against the Jews.*[149]

Adhering to the late medieval view of a fusion of church and state *(corpus Christianum)*, Luther felt justified in calling on secular authorities to enforce peace and religious uniformity. Although his demands (the burning of synagogues, etc.) may have contemporary models, they are atrocious to us today and are not Christian. Such demands, including the expulsion of Jews, were part of imperial politics. But this does not justify Luther's doing the same.

7. Luther's derailment into a political hostility against the Jews is not rooted in his theology and contradicts his life's work. His radical recommendations between 1543 and 1546 constitute a foreign body. He adjusted to the climate of opinion *(Zeitgeist)* of the late Middle Ages.

The only suitable motive for Luther's hostility against the Jews would have been his polemics against the Jewish "righteousness through good works." *(Werkgerechtigkeit)*. But he never used it as a justification for anti-Jewish measures. *Luther never attempted to derive preventive measures against the Jews from his theology. They are based on church-political considerations, such as the defense of the ancient Christian dogmas. That is why we have no right to locate Luther's hostility against the Jews in his theology.*[150]

8. Luther lived with his own weaknesses and contradictions, illustrated by the difference between being a reformer and a church politician. His hostility against the Jews may be understandable in the light of history and psychology. "But it is neither evangelical *(reformatorisch)*, nor Christian, indeed, not even Lutheran. It is incompatible with Luther. . . . It is and should be an admonition and a warning not to break away from the Reformation faith."[151]

149. Bienert, *Martin Luther und die Juden*, p. 186. Italics added.
150. Bienert, *Martin Luther und die Juden*, p. 190. Italics added.
151. Bienert, *Martin Luther und die Juden*, pp. 190-91.

9. Luther did not attack the Jewish people but their religion. He consistently opposed any violence against Jewish life and limb. Compared to others, he showed restraint in the face of torture and death by fire as self-evident and uncontested punishment of the Jews.

10. The Jews are the chosen people of God, together with Christians. They will be fully united on the Last Day. There should be fraternal dialogue on the way.

In an epilogue Bienert regrets that the hopeful dialogue, begun by Luther, was strangled by dogmatics and church politics. Today, such a dialogue should be conducted on the basis of new insights: that "the doctrine of the deity of Jesus can no longer be viewed as an essential content of the ancient Christian proclamation but as an insertion of Hellenistic thought into the late portions of the New Testament and post-biblical literature";[152] that the traditional dogma of the Trinity "cannot be biblically proven" and needs to be reinterpreted as "a threefold activity of God as creator, redeemer, and as one who enables people to believe *(Gläubigmachender)*";[153] and that the doctrine of the Virgin Birth is only a late addition to the New Testament in Matthew and Luke as "an adjustment of the Christian proclamation to Hellenistic views with the help of false translation of Is. 7:14 ('young woman,' not 'virgin')."[154] If Luther were alive today, he would accept these new insights and would engage in a more constructive dialogue with Jews.

Bienert portrayed Luther's attitude to the Jews in stages: a call for penance to change their belief about becoming righteous through "good works" (1513-16); an invitation to join the reform movement (1517-21); a plea to become members of the new Reformation church and society (1522-30); a critical waiting (1531-38); the way to an "anti-Judaism" that was to preserve territorial Christian uniformity (1539-43); and finally, harsh polemics (1544-46).

Although Bienert's selection of texts is helpful, it is quite obvious that he offered an apologia to soften the critique of Luther's radical anti-Semitism. His work has been justly questioned regarding its scholarly quality "because in it Luther's theology is totally erroneously artic-

---

152. Bienert, *Martin Luther und die Juden*, p. 197. Bienert cites supporting evidence from New Testament scholars.

153. Bienert, *Martin Luther und die Juden*, p. 200.

154. Bienert, *Martin Luther und die Juden*, p. 201.

ulated *(völlig abwegig artikuliert)*, thus making judgments that again fall far back behind the already available insights."[155]

B. Heiko A. Oberman

He offered his views on Luther's attitude to the Jews in the context of anti-Semitism in the age of the Renaissance and Humanism; in an essay on Luther's views of the Jews as "ancestors" *(Ahnen)* who were punished *(Geahndete)*; and in a historical portrait of Luther.[156]

According to Oberman, Luther is not a traditional "reformer" but a prophet of the end-time. He proclaimed the final "longed-for Reformation" with his outcry against the devil's power as a call to survive the last day of history through a new appreciation of the original Christian message of the imminent kingdom of God.[157] Luther shared the Christian anxiety about Jewish legalistic piety that had attracted a large following in the papal church, in which "the righteousness of works" was offered through indulgences, an abuse of the Sacrament of Penance. He also felt the general desire for "peace and order" in the face of social and political upheavals: the peasant uprising of 1525, and the siege of Vienna by the Turks in 1529; the threat of religious radicals such as the Anabaptists; the superstitions about magic, witches, and other manifestations of evil; and, above all, popes, heretics, and Jews — all of them representing the fifth column of the devil in the last days.

Oberman's Luther is disappointed about the refusal of the Jews to convert. After all, Christians and Jews had common biblical roots and belonged together. But the last days left little, if any, time for an alliance. This is the context in which Oberman presents his revisionist thesis.

In the anguish of the Last Days the ever-existing alliance of God's enemies challenged Luther into radical opposition. But precisely

155. This is the convincing judgment of Brosseder, "Luther und der Leidensweg der Juden," p. 110.

156. Oberman, *The Roots of Anti-Semitism*, and "Die Juden in Luthers Sicht," in Kremers, ed., *Die Juden und Martin Luther*, pp. 136-62, and *Luther: Man between God and the Devil.* See my critical review in *Church History* 60 (1991): 383-85.

157. Oberman, *The Roots of Anti-Semitism*, pp. 79-81.

this view of history has a converse side, pointing to the future. *In the mirror of Jewish history Luther discovered "us wretched Christians" who are also links in the threatening chain of the devil. Through the Jews we found out who we actually are: by nature always heathens and enemies of God, hypocrites like the Jews when, before God, we rely on good pedigree, law, and works.* The revelations in the Jewish mirror were incredible: "Jews" — penetrating the Church, to make matters worse, having managed to get it firmly into their clutches. . . . *Through the Jews Martin Luther unmasked the capability of Christians to ally themselves with the primeval enemy of Heaven and Earth.*[158]

The thesis could be called a "boomerang effect": Christian hostility against the Jews is boomeranged back and subjects Christians to the same misery they try to inflict on the Jews. This is the vision of Oberman's Luther in the dialectic of the "history of disaster and salvation" *(Unheils-and Heilsgeschichte).* It makes Jews the "mirror" in which Christians see themselves punished for the same sin they attribute to the Jews: self-righteousness. Christian anti-Semitism is as "wretched" as Jewish ethnic pride and can only be truly reformed at the Last Day. That is why Oberman contended that the Jews are the "cornerstone" in Luther's theology.[159] They are the main part of the "exegetical key" or "canon" in Luther's vision of history, next to heretics, and "deserters" *(Abtrünnige),* revealing "the history of unbelief" — beginning with the Jews at the time of Christ, continuing in the heretics, and finally disclosing "us wretched Christians." All three groups deserted the covenant with God, the divine word and work, thus provoking the divine judgment. The Jews are the spiritual "measuring instrument" *(Messsonde)* of evil in the interim between Christ's first and second advent.

The Jews show that [1] clinging to one's own righteousness leads to contradiction, opposition, and finally to violence against God. [2] The Jews also bring to light the negative sequence of Luther's [dictum] "being simultaneously righteous and a sinner *(simul justus et peccator)*": not only to be a sinner but also to justify oneself, that is atheism, meaning a denial of God. [3] The Jews bring to light a

---

158. Oberman, *Luther: Man between God and the Devil,* p. 297. Italics added. The reference to "us wretched Christians" is found in Luther's "Lectures on the Psalms," 1513-15. WA 3, 564:31-32. LW 11, 44 ("we wretched, most evil Christians").

159. Oberman, "Die Juden in Luthers Sicht," p. 139.

third aspect: Turning away from Christ means to invoke the wrath of God, and to be driven back into, or remain, in the Babylonian captivity.[160]

Oberman viewed Luther in a missionary mode between 1519 and 1523, hoping that the rediscovery of the gospel would bring many back to the church. From 1523 to 1529, he supervised the formation of a territorial "Reformation" church in Saxony, based on liturgical, educational, and social reforms. But the pressure of Satan increased after the rejection of the Augsburg Confession in 1530, preceded by the Turkish siege of Vienna in 1529 and followed by imperial-papal military threats against the Reformation. In addition, radicals in his own camp attacked basic doctrines, such as the Lord's Supper (no "real presence") and the dogma of the Trinity (no divinity of Jesus). Between 1532 and 1539, Luther heard rumors that the Jews succeeded in converting Christians (in Bohemia, Moravia, and Poland), some of whom would become known as "Sabbatarians." Luther fumed against them in the treatise "Against the Sabbatarians" (1538), the beginning of his radical attacks against the Jews, now representing the growing intensity of evil, disclosing the imminent Last Day. In the end, so Oberman contended, Luther recommended the expulsion of Jews, but was still open to their conversion. The rest is history — with a twist.

> The solidarity in sin of us "wretched Christians" with the Jews loses its penitential and reforming power if one understands the Reformation as executed *(vollzogen)* exodus from the Babylonian Captivity. For such Reformation triumphalism also leaves the Jews behind as a dark past, together with heretics and papists. Then, the Jewish "measuring instrument," originating long ago in a categorically different, ancient Christian climate of opinion, is no longer immune to being used for a racist final solution. *Only if Luther's basic theological structure is suppressed, anti-Judaism, attributed to him as well as to the Christian faith as a whole, can become the plaything (Spielball) of modern anti-Semitism.*[161]

Oberman's fascinating and dramatically argued thesis that Luther saw himself and all Christians in an "eschatological mirror," as it

---

160. Oberman, "Die Juden in Luthers Sicht," pp. 146-47.
161. Oberman, "Die Juden in Luthers Sicht," pp. 161-62. Italics added.

were, in solidarity with self-righteous Judaism, has been and will continue to be taken to task. Leonore Siegele-Wenschkewitz at the Evangelical Academy in Arnoldshain has offered a lengthy critical review of Oberman's work.[162] She shows that Oberman's view of the Jews as the "cornerstone of Luther's theology" and as a "measuring instrument" is inconsistent, indeed wrong. For Luther also used popular medieval anti-Semitic stereotypes, "transforming theological anti-Judaism into merciless political hostility — hostility against the Jews in the sense that in Luther's late writings against the Jews there was de facto — despite verbal assertions — no longer any room for conversion; the final sentence had been passed."[163] In this sense, there is a change between the younger and older Luther, already embedded in his theology, which slides from a religious anti-Judaism into a political anti-Semitism.

The view of history, sketched by Oberman as derived from Luther's self-understanding, the solidarity of Jews and Christians in misery and exile, this view of history does not correspond with the historical reality in the Middle Ages and the Reformation and in Lutheran countries of subsequent centuries. Luther may have had an ideal vision of the church in misery, but in reality Lutheran and Roman Catholic Christians represented the positions of majority and might in the empire and the church, and Lutheran Christians claimed the right, fortified by Luther's political advice regarding the Jews, to bring to bear their positions of power in regard to the Jews.[164]

Oberman's thesis of Luther being a prophet of "a longed-for" but "unexpected Reformation" (the end-time)[165] must also be taken to task. Although Luther compared himself to Old Testament prophets like Jeremiah, he did not expect an apocalyptical reformation. He wanted a reform of abuses and return to the authority of the Word of God in Scripture as it was faithfully handed on in "tradition." Consequently, he appealed for a hearing in an ecumenical council to offer his

162. Leonore Siegele-Wenschkewitz, "Wurzeln des Antisemitismus in Luthers theologischen Antijudaismus," in Kremers, ed., *Die Juden und Martin Luther,* pp. 351-67.

163. Siegele-Wenschkewitz, "Wurzeln des Antisemitismus," pp. 361-62.

164. Siegele-Wenschkewitz, "Wurzeln des Antisemitismus," p. 359.

165. Oberman, *Luther: Man between God and the Devil,* pp. xxi and 111.

proposals for reform.[166] Through a reform of worship and education he demonstrated what a reformed church looks like in the territory of Electoral Saxony under the tutelage of Duke Frederick "the Wise," who supervised the reforms, just as Constantine I had done at the Council of Nicea in 325 C.E.[167]

Luther's early bouts with the devil stopped after a while. As he put it in his gallows humor,

> I resist the devil, and often it is with a fart that I chase him away. I remind myself of the forgiveness of sin and of Christ, and I remind Satan of the abomination of the pope. It is so great that I am of good cheer and rejoice, and I confess that the abomination of the pope after the time of Christ is a great consolation to me.[168]

Moreover, the massive Luther evidence on "Reformation" as a theological, political, and social movement simply does not reflect Oberman's view.

> For Luther reformation was the beginning not of modern times but of the Last Days. . . . *The only progress he expected from the reformation was the Devil's rage, provoked by the rediscovery of the Gospel.* The adversary would hurl himself at the Church with increased force, attacking from all sides and by all possible means. Before there could be consummation there would be intensified persecution, for a general reformation, as Luther had known since 1520, could not be expected from the pope, a council, or any "reformer." *God Himself would bring about reformation through consummation; it would be preceded by the Devil's counterreformation.*[169]

Oberman's thesis is fascinating, but his argumentation is a cut below the Luther evidence.

---

166. "Appeal for an Ecumenical Council" *(Appelatio F. Martini Lutheri ad concilium),* 1518. WA 2, 40:9-20.

167. See Gritsch, *Martin — God's Court Jester,* p. 65.

168. "Table Talk" No. 122, 1531. WA.TR 1, 48:9-13. LW 54, 16. See also Eric W. Gritsch, *The Wit of Martin Luther* (Minneapolis: Fortress Press, 2006).

169. Oberman, *Luther: Man between God and the Devil,* pp. 266, 267. Italics added.

Conclusion

Luther's anti-Semitism is an integral part of his life and work, clearly evidenced in his literary legacy. But his anti-Semitism is neither in harmony with the core of his theology nor with the stance of the Apostle Paul regarding the relationship between Jews and Christians. Consequently, Luther's attitude to the Jews is against his better judgment.[1]

1. Luther repeated traditional church teachings against the Jews, based on the view that the Old Testament is "Christian" because it contains the Christ-centered divine covenant between God and Israel, promising salvation from sin, evil, and death. It goes without saying that the "uniqueness of Luther's view of the Old Testament"[2] is unacceptable in any responsible biblical scholarship. Moses simply is not "a Christian"; and the dogma of the Trinity is not "prefigured" in the Old Testament, neither in a "literal" nor in a "spiritual sense" (as Luther, at times, described his exegetical work). On the other hand, his description of the

---

1. I have summarized my previous work on "Luther and the Jews" in 1983: (1) in my book *Martin — God's Court Jester: Martin Luther in Retrospect,* 3rd ed. (Eugene, OR: Wipf & Stock, 2009), ch. 7: "The Gospel and Israel"; (2) with modifications in "Luther and the Jews: Toward a Judgment in History," in Harold H. Ditmanson, ed., *Stepping-Stones to Further Jewish-Lutheran Relations: Key Lutheran Statements* (Minneapolis: Augsburg, 1990), pp. 104-19.
2. Heinrich Bornkamm, *Luther and the Old Testament,* trans. Eric W. and Ruth C. Gritsch (Philadelphia: Fortress Press, 1969), p. 247.

Old Testament as a "mirror of life"[3] in his lifelong exegetical exposition is a literary treasure. So are many of Luther's sermons on Old Testament texts.

2. Luther assumed the existence of a Judaism, begun with the rejection of Christ and based on the rabbinical teachings in the Talmud, that superseded the original covenant, thus denying the original promise.[4] Luther contended that Talmudic Judaism is segregated from the "pious Israel" defined by the divine promise of salvation. "Their [the rabbis'] decisive mistake is that they separate the formal commandments and signs of election of the Old Testament from the Word of God. . . . This is where their lies come from, as Luther listed them in his tract of 1543."[5] Luther saw in the complex, mysterious formulations of the Talmud, exemplified by the magical formula for the divine name, *Shem hamphoras,* the deliberate rabbinical distortion of the Old Testament. "The Israel of ancient times had the promise; the later Israel refused to believe in its fulfillment."[6] Luther concluded that the Jewish rejection of the Messiah, Christ, led them into a religion of self-righteous legalism that earned them the wrath of God.

3. Luther made a lifelong commitment to the conversion of the Jews. He used his vocation as a biblical scholar to "prove" to them that they had a future only in Christ. In his best moments, Luther rebuked the anti-Semitic intolerance embedded in society and especially in the papal church; he acted like a tolerant pastor looking for new members in the anti-papal reform movement ("That Jesus Christ Was Born a Jew," 1523). But when this friendly missionary approach failed, Luther concluded that the anti-Christian stance of the Jews made them the object of divine wrath, exemplified by the destruction of the temple in 70 C.E., followed by exile and suffering.

4. Frustrated, and perhaps motivated by his view of an imminent end of time, he added to his exegetical findings the historical judgment that fifteen hundred years of misery "prove" that God had forsaken the

---

3. Bornkamm, *Luther and the Old Testament,* p. 11.

4. The Talmud consists of oral rabbinical interpretations of Jewish laws and customs. They originated after the destruction of the temple in 70 C.E.; collections of teachings appeared after c. 200 C.E., and printed editions in 1520, tolerated by the medieval church. But Rome condemned the Talmud a few decades later. ET by Adin Steinsaltz, *The Essential Talmud,* 30th Anniversary Edition (New York: Random House, 2006).

5. Bornkamm, *Luther and the Old Testament,* p. 2.

6. Bornkamm, *Luther and the Old Testament,* p. 3.

Jews and justified the harsh environment of Christian anti-Semitism ("Against the Sabbatarians," 1538). In his attempts to change Jewish minds Luther came up against a brick wall, as it were. But instead of taking a deep vocational breath and pause for a dispassionate discernment (as he had done in the face of the Romanist walls),[7] Luther intensified his slanderous argumentation with a scatological rhetoric mirroring the worst of medieval anti-Semitism.

5. His talk about conversion changed into a warning against the deadly danger of Judaism. Moreover, he began to view the Jews as the new draftees in the devil's fifth column before the end-time, together with papists, radicals *(Schwärmer)*, and Turks. The Luther who pleaded for freedom of conscience at Worms in 1521 ("it is neither safe nor right to go against conscience")[8] became the anti-Semitic reformer who enforced religious uniformity in 1543, indeed the right to kill a Jew because he is a Jew.[9]

6. Although Luther was decisively influenced by Paul in his "theology of the cross" anchored in the doctrine of "justification by grace through faith rather than the works of law," he ignored, indeed rejected, Paul's "eschatological reservation" for Jewish Christian unity (Rom. 11:25-32). Luther succumbed to speculations about the fate of the Jews as victims of divine wrath for their refusal to convert: God canceled the old covenant with Abraham, prefiguring salvation in Christ, because the Jews transformed it into a Talmudic Judaism of self-righteousness based on laws without a Messiah. These speculations violated Luther's own theological judgment against any claims to know the will of the "hidden God" *(deus absconditus)* and be satisfied with the knowledge about the "revealed God" *(deus revelatus)* — as he argued against Erasmus in 1525.[10] The core of his theology, anchored in "the justification of the ungodly" through faith in Christ, agreed with Paul that God "will justify the circumcised on the ground of faith and the uncircumcised through the same faith" (Rom. 3:30). Such "good news," the gospel, is part of a dialectic with the "law." It leads to repentance, preceded by spiritual anxiety and suffering *(Anfechtung)*; the gospel leads to salvation fully realized after Christ's second coming. But Lu-

---

7. "To the Christian Nobility of the German Nation," 1520. WA 6, 405:21. LW 44, 126.

8. "Luther at the Diet of Worms," 1521. WA 7, 838:7-8. LW 32, 113.

9. See above, p. 94.

10. See above, pp. 73-74.

ther was sliding into a theological speculation about the Jews *against his better judgment grounded in Paul, namely, that faith in Christ can never "justify" the divine punishment of the Jews. They, together with the Christian Gentiles, share the interim leading to a full union when Christ will come again.*

7. Luther's neglect, indeed negation, of Paul's view derailed the "theology of the cross" into a "theology of glory." Although Luther saw such a theology dominate in the medieval papal church, he let it infiltrate into his own stance in the form of anti-Semitism, his own brand virtually outdoing that of the church he tried to reform. Moreover, had he listened to Paul, he would not have viewed the Jews as the new draftees of Satan's fifth column, together with papists, Turks, and radicals in his own camp *(Schwärmer);* they would have been tolerated victims of a society in need of justice and plain (not "sharp") mercy.

8. In the annals of post-Reformation history, Luther's anti-Semitism is not very prominent until the beginning of the twentieth century. Lutherans referred to his treatise "That Jesus Christ Was Born a Jew" (1523) in the context of a mission to the Jews; they ignored or criticized "On the Jews and Their Lies" (1543). But many, not all, Lutherans revived Luther's radical anti-Semitism when they marched to the tune of German nationalism and became bewitched by the National-Socialist siren song calling for a racially pure Germany led by Adolf Hitler.

9. Luther's anti-Semitism represents the dark underside of his life and work because it dimmed the light of the gospel he rediscovered as part and parcel of the ancient covenant between God and Abraham. The riddle of anti-Semitism seemed to overwhelm Luther. Although he struggled out of a slanderous medieval ecclesiastical system, he became the victim of a virulent anti-Semitism and manifested some of its worst features. He needed the patience of Job, as it were, to share the faith of Paul in the "unsearchable judgments and inscrutable ways" of God.

10. With Paul, and despite Luther, Christians and Jews must try again and again to be reconciled on the way towards the full realization of the one and only divine covenant. The Protestant German proponent for effective Christian-Jewish relations after the holocaust, Peter von der Osten-Sacken, pointed the way.

The apostle Paul closes his ode on love with the words, "And now faith, hope and love abide, these three" (1 Cor. 13:13). Perhaps none of us can compellingly say today *why* they abide. But that much is

clear: all three — under the pre-eminence of love — belong insepara-
bly together. . . . According to the Jewish as well as the Christian Bible, God needs the human being so that faith, hope, and love abide.
So the Jewish and Christian communities are called, each in their
own way, to mediate, in a trusting mutual encounter, a fore-taste of
their hope for the coming lordship of God. In the sign of the time,
identified with the name of "Auschwitz" or "Holocaust," this common hope can only have one mark, suitable since Abraham: it is
hope against hope even though much, if not everything, speaks
against such hope, and credibly so only insofar it is lived in the
present.[11]

11. Osten-Sacken, *Anstösse aus der Schrift* (1981), pp. 150-51. Quoted in Ernst L.
Ehrlich, "Luther und die Juden," in Heinz Kremers, ed., *Die Juden und Martin Luther. Mar-
tin Luther und die Juden. Geschichte, Wirkungsgeschichte, Herausforderung,* 2nd ed. (Neukirchen-
Vluyn: Neukirchener Verlag, 1987), p. 87.

Bibliography

Bainton, Roland H. *Here I Stand: A Life of Martin Luther.* Nashville and New York: Abingdon, 1950.

Baron, Salo W. *A Social and Religious History of the Jews.* 2nd rev. ed. 18 vols. New York: Columbia University Press, 1983.

Barr, James. *The Semantics of Biblical Language.* London: Oxford University Press, 1961.

Barth, Hans-Martin. *Die Theologie Martin Luthers. Eine kritische Würdigung.* Gütersloh: Gütersloher Verlagshaus, 2009.

Beck, Norman A. "The New Testament and the Teaching of Contempt." In Perry and Schweitzer, eds., *Jewish-Christian Encounters over the Centuries,* pp. 83-89.

Bein, Alex. *The Jewish Question: Biography of a World Problem.* Madison, NJ: Fairleigh Dickinson University Press, 1990.

Bethge, Eberhard. *Dietrich Bonhoeffer: Theologian, Christian, Man for His Times. A Biography.* 2nd ed. Edited and revised by Victoria J. Barnett. Minneapolis: Fortress Press, 2000.

———. "Dietrich Bonhoeffer und die Juden." In Kremers, ed., *Die Juden und Martin Luther,* pp. 211-48.

Bienert, Walter. *Martin Luther und die Juden.* Ein Quellenbuch mit zeitgenössischen Illustrationen, mit Einführungen und Erläuterungen. Frankfurt am Main: Evangelisches Verlagswerk, 1982.

"Biological Aspects of Race." In *American Journal of Physical Anthropologists* 101 (1996): 569-70.

The Book of Concord. In *The Confessions of the Evangelical Lutheran Church.* Edited by Robert Kolb and Timothy J. Wengert. Minneapolis: Fortress Press, 2000. ET of *Die Bekenntnisschriften der evangelisch-lutherischen Kirche.* 3rd ed. Göttingen: Vandenhoeck & Ruprecht, 1930.

Bornkamm, Heinrich. *Luther and the Old Testament.* Translated by Eric W. and Ruth C. Gritsch. Philadelphia: Fortress Press, 1969.

Brecht, Martin. *Martin Luther.* 3 vols. Translated by James L. Schaaf. Minneapolis: Fortress Press, 1999.

Brosseder, Johannes. "Die Juden im theologischen Werk von Johann Eck." In *Christen und Juden im Reformationszeitalter.* Veröffentlichungen des Instituts für Europäische Geschichte Mainz. Abt. für Abendländische Religionsgeschichte, Beiheft 72. Ed. Rolf Decot and Mathieu Arnold. Mainz: Philipp von Zabern, 2006, pp. 77-96.

————. *Luthers Stellung zu den Juden im Spiegel seiner Interpreten. Interpretation und Rezeption von Luthers Schriften und Äusserungen zum Judentum im 19. und 20. Jahrhundert vor allem im deutschsprachigen Raum.* Beiträge zur ökumenischen Theologie 8. München: Hueber, 1972.

Browning, Christopher R. *The Origins of the Final Solution: The Evolution of Nazi Jewish Policy 1929-1945.* London: Arrow Books, 2005.

Carroll, James. *Constantine's Sword: A Film.* Directed by Oren Jacobi. Vista, CA: Storyville Films, 2008.

————. *Constantine's Sword: The Church and the Jews — A History.* Boston: Houghton Mifflin, 2001.

Chamberlain, Houston Stewart. *The Foundations of the Nineteenth Century.* München, 1899.

Chesler, Phyllis. *The New Anti-Semitism: The Current Crisis and What We Must Do about It.* San Francisco: Jossey-Bass, 2003.

Cohen, Jeremy. *The Friars and the Jews: The Evolution of Medieval Anti-Semitism.* Ithaca, NY: Cornell University Press, 1982.

Cohn, Norman. *The Pursuit of the Millennium.* 3rd rev. ed. New York: Oxford University Press, 1970.

Daily Missal. Charlotte, NC: Catholic Co., 1962.

Daniels, J. L. "Anti-Semitism in the Hellenistic-Roman Period." *Journal of Biblical Literature* 98 (1979): 45-65.

Darwin, Charles. *The Descent of Man.* London: John Murray, 1871.

————. *On the Origin of Species by Means of Natural Selection.* London: John Murray, 1859.

Davidowicz, Lucy. *The War Against the Jews, 1933-1945.* New York: Bantam, 1986.

Degani, Ben-Zion. "Die Formulierung und Propagierung des jüdischen Sterotyps in der Zeit der Reformation und sein Einfluss auf den jungen Luther." In Kremers, ed., *Die Juden und Martin Luther,* pp. 4-44.

Denifle, Heinrich. *Luther und Luthertum in der ersten Entwicklung. Quellenmässig dargestellt.* 2nd rev. ed. Mainz: A. M. Weiss, 1906.

Denkwürdigkeiten der Glückel von Hameln. Aus dem Jüdisch-Deutschen übersetzt von Alfred Feilchenfeld. Darmstadt, 1979.

Dictionary of Anti-Semitism. Edited by Robert Michael and Philip Rosen. Lanham, MD: Scarecrow Press, 2006.

Die evangelische Kirche und die Judenfrage. Ausgewählte Dokumente aus den Jahren des Kirchenkampfes 1933 bis 1943. Geneva, Lanham, MD: Scarecrow Press, 1945.

Bibliography

Ditmanson, Harold H., ed. *Stepping-Stones to Further Jewish-Lutheran Relations: Key Lutheran Statements.* Minneapolis: Augsburg, 1990.

Döllinger, Johann Joseph Ignaz von. *Die Reformation.* 3 vols. Frankfurt am Main, 1848.

Ebeling, Gerhard. "Die Anfänge von Luthers Hermeneutik." In vol. 1 of *Lutherstudien.* Tübingen: Mohr, 1971.

Edwards, Mark U. *Luther's Last Battles: Politics and Polemics, 1531-1546.* Ithaca, NY: Cornell University Press, 1983.

Ehrlich, Ernst L. "Luther und die Juden." In Kremers, ed., *Die Juden und Marin Luther,* pp. 72-88.

Erasmus's Diatribe or Discourse Concerning Free Will. Edited by Gordon E. Rupp and Philip S. Watson. Library of Christian Classics 17. Philadelphia: Westminster Press, 1969.

Erikson, Erik H. *Young Man Luther: A Study in Psychoanalysis and History.* New York: Norton, 1958.

Eze, Emmanuel C. *Race and the Enlightenment: A Reader.* Somerset, NH: Wiley-Blackwell, 2008.

Field, Geoffrey G. *Evangelist of Race: The Germanic Vision of Houston Stewart Chamberlain.* New York: Columbia University Press, 1981.

Flannery, Edward H. *The Anguish of the Jews: Twenty-Three Centuries of Anti-Semitism.* Mahwah, NJ: Paulist Press, Stimulus Books, 2004.

Frankl, Viktor. *Man's Search for Meaning: An Introduction to Logotherapy.* Boston: Beacon Press, 2006.

————. *Trotzdem Ja zum Leben sagen. Ein Psychologe erlebt das Konzentrationslager.* München: Kösel-Verlag, 1946.

Fredrickson, George M. *Racism: A Short History.* Princeton: Princeton University Press, 2002.

Freund, Scarlett, and Teofilo F. Ruiz. "Jews, *Conversos,* and the Inquisition in Spain, 1391-1492: The Ambiguities of History." In Perry and Schweitzer, eds., *Jewish-Christian Encounters over the Centuries,* pp. 168-95.

Friedman, Jerome. "Sixteenth-Century Christian-Hebraica: Scripture and the Renaissance Myth of the Past." *Sixteenth Century Journal* 11 (1980): 67-85.

From Federation to Communion: The History of the Lutheran World Federation. Edited by H. Jens Schjorring et al. Minneapolis: Augsburg, 1997.

Geehr, Richard. *Karl Lueger: Mayor of Fin-de-Siècle Vienna.* Detroit: Wayne State University Press, 1989.

Geiger, Ludwig. "Die Juden und die deutsche Literatur." *Zeitschrift für die Geschichte der Juden in Deutschland* 2 (1888): 197-374.

Gilbert, Martin. *Kristallnacht: Prelude to Destruction.* New York: HarperCollins, 2006.

Ginzel, Günther B. "Martin Luther: 'Chief Witness of Anti-Semitism.'" In Kremers, ed., *Die Juden und Martin Luther,* pp. 189-210.

Gobineau, Arthur de. *The Inequality of the Human Races.* Translated by Adrian Collins. New York: Putman's Sons, 1915.

Gossett, Thomas F. *Race: The History of an Idea.* Oxford: Oxford University Press, 1997.

Grayzel, Solomon. *The Church and the Jews in the Thirteenth Century: A Study of Their Relations During the Years 1198-1254.* 2nd rev. ed. New York: Hermon Press, 1966.

Gritsch, Eric W. *The Boy from the Burgenland: From Hitler Youth to Seminary Professor.* West Conshohocken, PA: Infinity Publications, 2006.

————. *A History of Lutheranism.* 2nd rev. ed. Minneapolis: Fortress Press, 2010.

————. "The Jews in Reformation Theology." In Perry and Schweitzer, eds., *Jewish-Christian Encounters over the Centuries,* pp. 197-213.

————. "Luther and the Jews: Toward a Judgment in History." In Ditmanson, ed., *Stepping-Stones to Further Jewish-Lutheran Relations,* pp. 104-19.

————. "Luther as Bible Translator." In *The Cambridge Companion to Martin Luther.* Edited by Donald K. McKim, pp. 62-72. Cambridge: Cambridge University Press, 2003.

————. *Martin — God's Court Jester: Martin Luther in Retrospect.* 3rd ed. Eugene, OR: Wipf & Stock, 2009.

————. *"Professor Heussi? I Thought You Were a Book!" A Memoir of Memorable Theological Educators, 1950-2009.* Eugene, OR: Wipf & Stock, 2009.

————. *Thomas Müntzer: A Tragedy of Errors.* 2nd ed. Minneapolis: Fortress Press, 2006.

————. *Toxic Spirituality: Four Enduring Temptations of Christian Faith.* Minneapolis: Fortress Press, 2009.

————. *The Wit of Martin Luther.* Minneapolis: Fortress Press, 2006.

Harrington, Daniel J. *Paul on the Mystery of Israel.* Collegeville, MN: Liturgical Press, 1992.

Harkins, Paul, ed. *Saint John Chrysostom: Discourses Against Judaizing Christians.* Washington, DC: Catholic University Press, 1979.

Hitler, Adolf. *Mein Kampf.* 1924. 2 vols. München: Franz Eher Nachfolger, 1930. ET *My Struggle.* Translated by Ralph Mannheim. Boston: Houghton Mifflin, 1947.

Holmio, A. K. E. *The Lutheran Reformation and the Jews: The Birth of the Protestant Jewish Mission.* Hancock, MI: Lutheran Book Concern, 1949.

Hutten, Ulrich von, ed. *On the Eve of the Reformation: Letters of Obscure Men.* Translated by Francis C. Stokes. New York: Harper & Row, 1964.

Isaac, Jules. *The Teaching of Contempt: Christian Roots of Anti-Semitism.* Translated by Helen Weaver. New York: Rinehart & Winston, 1983.

Janz, Denis R. *Martin Luther.* The Westminster Handbook. Louisville: Westminster/John Knox Press, 2010.

Jenny, Markus, ed. *Luthers geistliche Lieder und Kirchengesänge.* Archiv zur Weimarer Ausgabe. Texte und Untersuchungen 4. Cologne and Vienna: Böhlau, 1985.

Johnson, Luke T. "Christians and Jews — Why the Real Dialogue Has Just Begun." *Commonweal* (January 11, 2003): 2.

Junghans, Helmar, ed. *Leben und Werk Martin Luthers von 1526-1546*. Festgabe zu seinem Geburtstag. 2 vols. Göttingen: Vandenhoeck & Ruprecht, 1983.

Kaufmann, Thomas. "Luther and the Jews." In *Jews, Judaism, and the Reformation in Sixteenth-Century Germany*. Ed. Dean Bell and Stephen Burnett. Studies in Central European History 37. Leiden: Brill, 2006, pp. 69-104.

_____. *Luthers "Judenschriften" in ihren historischen Kontexten*. Nachrichten der Akademie der Wissenschaften zu Göttingen 6. Göttingen: Vandenhoeck & Ruprecht, 2005, pp. 480-586.

Keck, Leander E. *The Letter of Paul to the Romans*. Abingdon New Testament Commentaries. Edited by Victor P. Furnish. Nashville: Abingdon, 2005.

Kisch, Guido. *Erasmus' Stellung zu Juden und Judentum*. Tübingen: Mohr-Siebeck, 1969.

———. *The Jews in Medieval Germany: A Study of Their Legal and Social Status*. Chicago: University of Chicago Press, 1949.

Klappert, Bertold. "Erwählung und Rechtfertigung." In Kremers, ed., *Die Juden und Martin Luther*, pp. 368-410.

Koester, Helmut. "Jesus the Victim." *Journal of Biblical Literature* III (1992): 3-15.

Köstlin, Julius, and Gustav Kawerau. *Martin Luther: Sein Leben und seine Schriften*. 2 vols. 3rd ed. Berlin, 1905.

Kolde, Theodor. *Martin Luther. Eine Biographie*. 2 vols. Gotha, 1899.

Kremers, Heinz, ed. *Die Juden und Martin Luther. Martin Luther und die Juden. Geschichte, Wirkungsgeschichte, Herausforderung*. 2nd ed. Neukirchen-Vluyn: Neukirchener Verlag, 1987.

Langmuir, Gavin I. *History, Religion, and Anti-Semitism*. Berkeley: University of California Press, 1990.

———. *Toward a Definition of Anti-Semitism*. Berkeley: University of California Press, 1990.

Lapide, Pinchas E. "Stimmen jüdischer Zeitgenossen zu Martin Luther." In Kremers, ed., *Die Juden und Martin Luther*, pp. 171-85.

Lewin, Reinhold. *Luthers Stellung zu den Juden. Ein Beitrag zur Geschichte der Juden wahrend des Reformationszeitalters*. Neue Studien zur Geschichte der Theologie und Kirche 10. Aalen: Scientia Verlag, 1973.

Lindemann, Albert S. *Anti-Semitism before the Holocaust*. Harlow, UK: Pearson Education, 2000.

Lowenthal, Marvin. *The Jews of Germany: A Story of Sixteen Centuries*. Philadelphia: Jewish Publication Society, 1936.

Lohse, Bernhard. *The Theology of Martin Luther: Its Historical and Systematic Development*. Translated and edited by Roy A. Harrisville. Minneapolis: Fortress Press, 1999.

Luther, Martin. *Dr. Martin Luthers sämmtliche Werke*. 65 vols. Erlangen: Heyder & Zimmer, 1857.

Lutheran Book of Worship. Minneapolis: Augsburg, 1978.

MacCulloch, Diarmaid. *The Reformation: Europe's House Divided, 1490-1700*. New York: Penguin, 2004.

Marr, Wilhelm. *Der Weg zum Sieg des Germanentums über das Judentum.* Bern, 1879.

Mathesius, Johannes. *D. Martin Luthers Leben. In siebzehn Predigten dargestellt.* In vol. 3 of *Ausgewählte Werke.* Edited by Georg Loesche. Prague, 1906.

Mau, Rudolf. "Luthers Stellung zu den Türken." In Junghans, ed., *Martin Luther von 1526 bis 1546,* vol. 1, pp. 647-62; vol. 2, pp. 956-66.

Maurer, Wilhelm. *Kirche und Synagoge. Motive und Formen der Auseinandersetzung der Kirche mit dem Judentum im Laufe der Geschichte.* Franz Delitzsch-Vorlesungen, 1951. Stuttgart: Kohlhammer, 1953.

―――. "Die Zeit der Reformation." In *Kirche und Synagoge. Handbuch zur Geschichte von Christen und Juden.* Edited by H. Rengstorf and S. von Kortzfleisch. Stuttgart: Klett, 1968.

Michael, Robert. "Anti-Semitism and the Church Fathers." In Perry and Schweitzer, eds., *Jewish-Christian Encounters over the Centuries,* pp. 101-30.

―――. "Luther, Luther Scholars, and the Jews." In *Encounter* 46, no. 4 (1985): 339-56.

Mundy, John. *Europe in the High Middle Ages, 1215-1309.* London: Longman, 1973.

Oberman, Heiko A. *Luther: Man Between God and the Devil.* Translated by Eileen Walliser-Schwarzbart. New Haven: Yale University Press, 1989.

―――. "Luthers Beziehungen zu den Juden. Ahnen und Geahndete." In Junghans, ed., *Leben und Werk Martin Luthers von 1526-1546,* vol. 1, pp. 519-30; vol. 2, pp. 894-904. Reprint in Kremers, ed., *Die Juden und Martin Luther,* pp. 136-62.

―――. *The Roots of Anti-Semitism in the Age of Renaissance and Reformation.* Translated by James I. Porter. Philadelphia: Fortress Press, 1984.

―――. "*Teufelsdreck:* Eschatology and Scatology in the 'Old? Luther." *Sixteenth Century Journal* 19 (1988): 435-50.

Osten-Sacken, Peter von. *Luther und die Juden — neu untersucht anhand von Anton Margarithas "Der gantz Jüdisch Glaub."* Stuttgart: Kohlhammer, 2002.

Pauls, Theodor. *Luther und die Juden.* 3 vols. Bonn, 1939.

Po-chia, Hsia R. *The Myth of Ritual Murder: Jews and Magic in Reformation Germany.* New Haven: Yale University Press, 1988.

Poliakow, Leon. *The History of Anti-Semitism.* 4 vols. Philadelphia: University of Pennsylvania Press, 2003.

Perry, Marvin. "Racial Nationalism and the Rise of Modern Anti-Semitism." In Perry and Schweitzer, eds., *Jewish-Christian Encounters over the Centuries,* pp. 241-76.

Perry, Marvin, and Frederick M. Schweitzer, eds. *Jewish-Christian Encounters over the Centuries: Symbiosis, Prejudice, Holocaust, Dialogue.* New York: Peter Lang, 1994.

Plitt, Gustav. *Kurze Geschichte der lutherischen Mission.* Erlangen, 1871.

Preus, James H. *From Shadow to Promise: Old Testament Interpretation from Augustine to Luther.* Cambridge, MA: Harvard University Press, 1974.

"Race." In *Online Etymological Dictionary.* Edited by Douglas Horton. 2001.

Race. United Nations International Convention on the Elimination of All Forms of Racial Discrimination. Part 1, Article 1. HR-NET: http:/hri.org/ ICERD66html.2001.

The Race Question. United Nations Educational Scientific, and Cultural Organization (UNESCO). Document 791. Par. 6. Paris, 1950.

Report on Global Anti-Semitism. U.S. State Department. January 5, 2005.

Rogge, Joachim. "Luthers Stellung zu den Juden." *Luther — Zeitschrift der Luther-gesellschaft* 40 (1969): 13-24.

Rose, Paul L. *Revolutionary Anti-Semitism from Kant to Wagner.* Princeton: Princeton University Press, 1990.

Rowan, Stephen. "Luther, Bucer, and Eck on the Jews." *Sixteenth Century Journal* 16 (1985): 79-90.

Roynesdal, Olaf. *Martin Luther and the Jews* (Bibliography). Sioux Falls, SD: published by author, 2009.

Ruether, Rosemary. *Faith and Fratricide.* New York: Seabury, 1974.

Rupp, Gordon E. *Martin Luther: Hitler's Cause — or Cure? In Reply to P. F. Wiener.* London: Lutterworth Press, 1945.

Schmidt, Johann M. "Das Erbe Martin Luthers im Spiegel seiner Wirkungen auf die 'Judenfrage' zu Beginn des Kirchenkampfes." In Kremers, ed., *Die Juden und Martin Luther,* pp. 319-48.

Schweitzer, Frederick M. "Medieval Perceptions of Jews and Judaism." In Perry and Schweitzer, eds., *Jewish-Christian Encounters over the Centuries,* pp. 131-68.

Shachar, Isaiah. *The Judensau: A Medieval Anti-Jewish Motif and Its History.* London: Wartburg Institute, 1974.

Shirer, William L. *The Rise and Fall of the Third Reich: A History of Nazi Germany.* New York: Simon & Schuster, 1960.

Siegele-Wenschkewitz, Leonore. "Wurzeln des Antisemitismus in Luthers theologischen Antijudaismus." In Kremers, ed., *Die Juden und Martin Luther,* pp. 351-67.

Siemon-Netto, Uwe. *The Fabricated Luther: The Rise and Fall of William Shirer's Myth.* St. Louis: Concordia, 1995.

Siirala, Arne. "Luther and the Jews." *Lutheran World* 11 (1964): 337-57.

Smith, Henry P., trans. *Luther's Correspondence and Other Contemporary Letters.* Philadelphia: Lutheran Publication Society, 1913.

Soulen, Kendall R. *The God of Israel and Christian Theology.* Minneapolis: Fortress Press, 1996.

Steinsaltz, Adin. *The Essential Talmud.* 30th Anniversary Edition. New York: Random House, 2006.

Stöhr, Martin. "Luther und die Juden." *Evangelische Theologie* 20 (1960): 157-82.

———. "Martin Luther und die Juden." In *Christen und Juden. Ihr Gegensatz vom Apostelkonzil bis heute.* Edited by W. D. Marsch and K. Thieme. Mainz and Göttingen, 1961. Reprinted in Kremers, ed., *Die Juden und Martin Luther,* pp. 89-108.

Sucher, Bernd, ed. *Luthers Stellung zu den Juden. Eine Interpretation aus germanistischer Sicht*. Bibliotheca Humanistica et Reformatoria 25. Nieuwkoop: De Graaf, 1977.

Suchy, Barbara. *Lexikographie und Juden im 18. Jahrhundert*. Cologne and Vienna, 1979.

Synan, Edward A. *The Popes and the Jews in the Middle Ages*. New York: Macmillan, 1965.

Trachtenberg, Joshua. *The Devil and the Jews: The Medieval Conception of the Jew and Its Relation to Modern Anti-Semitism*. New York: Oxford University Press, 1966.

Wallmann, Johannes. "The Reception of Luther's Writings on the Jews from the Reformation to the End of the 19th Century." In Ditmanson, ed., *Stepping-Stones to Further Jewish-Lutheran Relations*, pp. 120-36. Reprint in *The Lutheran Quarterly* 1 (Spring 1987): 72-97.

Wiener, P. F. *Martin Luther — Hitler's Spiritual Ancestor*. Win the Peace Pamphlet 3. London: Hutchinson, 1944.

Wilde, Robert. *The Treatment of the Jews in the Greek Christian Writers of the First Three Centuries*. Washington, DC: Catholic University Press, 1979.

Wilken, Robert. *Judaism and the Early Christian Mind: A Study of Cyril of Alexandria's Exegesis and Theology*. New Haven: Yale University Press, 1971.

Williams, George H. *The Radical Reformation*. 3rd rev. ed. Kirksville, MO: Sixteenth Century Journal Publishers, 1992.

Wistrich, Robert S. *Anti-Semitism: The Longest Hatred*. London: Methuen, 1991.

"Working Definition of Anti-Semitism." The European Monitoring Centre on Racism and Xenophobia. WebCite 5. 2005.

Zimmermann, Moshe. *Wilhelm Marr: The Patriarch of Anti-Semitism*. New York: Oxford University Press, 1986.

Index